The Coming Collecting Boom

The Coming Collecting Boom

By John Mebane

South Brunswick and New York: A.S. Barnes and Company
London: Thomas Yoseloff Ltd

© 1968 by A.S. Barnes and Co., Inc.
Library of Congress Catalogue Card Number: 67-17074

A.S. Barnes and Co., Inc.
Cranbury, New Jersey 08512

Thomas Yoseloff Ltd
108 New Bond Street
London W1Y OQX, England

SBN: 498 06536 7
Printed in the United States of America

This book is for Sister Mary William,
David and Barbara, and Jerry

For the Record

THE TROUBLE WITH IDEAS IS THAT SO MANY OF THEM SEEM DECEIVINGLY simple. When the idea for this book first occurred, I figured it would be a breeze to put together. It wasn't a breeze; it was a regular squall. I had to research everything from door hinges to the contents of a lady's boudoir; and —unless you're a lady—you'd be appalled at the things a lady's boudoir contains.

Nevertheless, boudoir research can be fun: I researched the boudoir and my wife researched my motives—and my findings. You'll discover the results of all this poking around in the chapters herein entitled "Milady's Boudoir" and "Dress Accessories and Baubles."

Naturally, I'm indebted to my wife, not only for keeping a watchful eye on me but also for some pertinent suggestions. I also am indebted to many other persons who helped by providing illustrations, editorial suggestions, and permissions. These include the following: For help in checking early business establishments: Carl Brown, Pittsburgh; R. Dunaway, St. Louis; and William Einspanier, St. Louis.

For permission to quote from books written or published by them: Bertha L. Betensley, Chicago, author of *Buttonhooks to Trade—to Treasure;* Eric E. Ericson, Denver, author of *A Guide to Colored Glass, 1903–1930, Book Two;* and the University of Oklahoma Press, Norman, Oklahoma, publisher of Henry D. and Frances T. McCallum's *The Wire that Fenced the West.*

For providing editorial help and illustrations: The Cleanliness Bureau, The Soap and Detergent Association, New York City; H. M. Cook, Whitney, Texas; Eaton Yale & Towne, Inc., New York City; Sally Erath, buyer for the Antique Toy Department, and F.A.O. Schwartz, New York City; Milton Klein, Atlanta; Wilbur G. Kurtz and The Coca-Cola Company, Atlanta; Ray Wentworth, San Leandro, California, and Paul C. Wilmot, Elkhart, Indiana.

For bibliographical and others suggestions: W. M. Morrison, Waco, Texas; Marcia Ray, former Managing Editor, and *The Spinning Wheel*, Hanover, Pennsylvania; and Pearl Ann Reeder, Editor, and *Hobbies*, Chicago.

I also am indebted to George Hatcher, Editor, *Atlanta Journal and Constitution Magazine*, for permission to quote from an article of mine first appearing in that publication; to Atlanta Newspapers, Inc., for permitting me to draw upon material first published in *The Atlanta Journal and Constitution's* Dixie Living section; and to all of those business firms—the majority of them no longer in existence—whose delightful catalogues I have drawn upon for many charming illustrations.

Contents

9

Coming Collecting Boom

1

Fashion Ever Is a Wayward Child

"EVERYONE AS HE LIKES," THE WOMAN SAID WHEN SHE KISSED HER COW. Rabelais, writing this, undoubtedly knew that nothing is so constant in the realms of taste and fashion as change; and in perhaps no area of fashion has change been so constant as in that of collecting. Nor is the pace of change in the field of antiques likely to lessen within the next few years; quite the contrary, in fact.

Until recent years, collectors by and large were a breed to themselves. They hobnobbed together, constituting a fraternity or a social order of sorts, even though many were strangers to the others. They amassed collections of distinguished furniture after the designs of Hepplewhite, Sheraton, Chippendale, and Shearer, faience from Nevers, porcelain treasures from China, and the manufactories at Meissen and Sevres, and paintings by the masters, ancient and modern.

By and large, too, they were individuals of some means, because antiques of the kind they pursued were costly. Some of these collectors—happily in the minority—even acquired treasures by the simple expedient of employing experts to direct their selections and handle their purchases.

Through their collective activities, they have helped to preserve thousands of significant vestiges of past times and cultures which otherwise—perish the thought!—might have been lost to posterity. Some of these accumulations they passed along to museums; some they bequeathed to their children, and some they preserved in their own establishments for their enlightenment and pleasure. This was all to the good.

13

A little over a quarter of a century ago, a new type of collector entered the fray. He was an individual of more modest means, but if this was a liability, it was more than offset by two major assets: a sense of keen discrimination, and a hungry curiosity about the more recent past. Historians have had a habit of waiting for the passage of centuries before they embark upon their frenetic investigations, clawing through crumbling tomes and papyrus, and pouring over artifacts of forgotten civilizations as if there were no tomorrow but only yesterday. But today, with the hydrogen bomb outmoding the atom bomb, the transcontinental flight paling before the interplanetary flight, and the human mind put to shame by the incredible computer, history has become not only an epoch ago or a century ago, but a generation ago and a year ago, and by tomorrow history may be yesterday—or the hour before.

This new tribe of collectors which has emerged in mid-twentieth century is determined, too, to do its share in preserving relics of the past, but of a more recent past than that which held its predecessors' interest—and more than that: to have a good time while doing so. The ranks of the new collectors swell daily as more persons discover that the quest of the collectible is an adventure in fascination, an excellent way in which to spend leisure time, and if the stars are auspicious perhaps a profitable way to boot.

Not too many years ago, these new collectors began salvaging such things as mechanical banks, spice cabinets, Rookwood pottery, Haviland china, fairy lamps, art glass, bisque figures, early maps, milk-white glass and a host of other relatively recent items, many of which are discussed in my previous books, *Treasure at Home* and *New Horizons in Collecting*.

But within the past year or two, the ranks of the collectors have swelled so rapidly and their demands have exerted such pressure against available supplies of collectibles that many prices—even those of choice nineteenth-century mementoes—are now soaring dizzily, and the supplies themselves are dwindling at an almost astonishing rate. Antiques dealers complain that the mounting scarcities are forcing them to turn to "junk." This would be a rash step and one that need not be taken. All the antiques dealer (and the collector, for that matter) needs to do is look around him with an extroverted eye that shuns the accustomed thoroughfare and peers beyond into those hedgerows and alleyways thus far unfamiliar with the relentless tread of the dedicated collector.

Then let his imagination take over. Right under his nose he will find scores of things produced in the late nineteenth and early twentieth centuries that were a delight to his forefathers or a boon to them and that now are a joy to behold and can provide the basis for a whole new realm of collectibles. Many of these things are not now being collected, apparently because no one has taken the time to examine them, with either a critical or uncritical eye.

Now that the widely recognized and avidly sought antiques are diminishing in quantity and increasing in price, a new opportunity presents itself to the imaginative: the opportunity to pioneer new and challenging areas of collecting—and the adventure will be worth it in knowledge gained and treasure acquired.

One purpose of this book is to suggest a variety of "new" items to collect. These are items worth preserving in the first place, because many of them are unlikely to be produced again, and they also are things which are of intrinsic merit or interest. Because many of the articles that we will discuss are not presently being collected or are just beginning to be preserved, it is difficult to establish values for them; but many of them can be acquired for quite low sums. Undoubtedly, this situation will not prevail for long, as more persons are becoming aware of their collectibility.

Some of the things we will talk about are being sought now by a few persons who are assuming—and probably correctly—that their values will soon be enhanced. The values listed in this book for these articles are based upon very recent quotations either by dealers or collectors and do not necessarily represent prices at which they can be bought generally.

A good many of the things we will talk about can probably be acquired in some areas of the country for the asking. Some of them will be found in salvage and junkyards whose operators do not yet consider them as collectibles; others will be found in old homes and outbuildings and in other deserted structures; still others will be found in old buildings about to be torn down. (Watch for them, then ask permission of the owners to search about the premises.)

Search the salvage yards, and you may come up with early towel racks or bars, a tin tub, oil cans, lithographed watering cans, refrigerator hinges, or cork pulls. In old homes destined to make way for "progress," you may perchance stumble across embossed letter drops, transom catches, stair buttons, or shelf brackets, all of which you can acquire for little or nothing. In old stores and mercantile establishments you may find such things as wrapping paper dispensers, cash registers, mechanical show window pieces, or placards and similar signs of bygone days. And in buildings that are to be torn down, you may chance across fascinating door knobs, latches, and escutcheons; or window catches, sash lifts, pull plates, and fasteners whose attractiveness will surprise you.

Do these things sound prosaic? Take a closer look at them in these pages. Builders' hardware was rarely so richly fascinating as it was in the last half of the nineteenth century. You will find door handles, screen door catches and shutter knobs that are works of art. You will come across drawer pulls and knobs, ring, drop, and lift handles, and wardrobe and cabinet locks that are delightful to behold.

Compare the starkly utilitarian paper clips of today with the decorated clips of 75 years ago. In what pasture now will you find a lithographed sheep bell?

The waning years of the nineteenth century and the opening years of the present one were years of fancy: one suspects that decoration was often preferred to ultilitarian value. Cases in point include watch fobs and charms, hairdo ornaments, and scarf, lace, and shawl pins, to mention only a few.

The kitchen of 1900 was a storehouse of gadgets that were both charming and mysterious: sieves and sifters, fruit seeders, stoners, parers and cutters, food grinders, cork pressers, and a host of other accessories to aid in the routine daily chores now obviated by such developments as frozen and dehydrated "convenience" foods and electrical accessories that operate with flawless perfection at the touch of a fingertip.

And have you ever really examined the artistic beauty of early undertakers' hardware?

The collectibles discussed in this book really represent only a starting point for an adventure into a world filled with treasures thus far largely unrecognized and not yet fully appreciated. They will suggest to you, we hope, many other mementoes of a century or a half-century ago, which possess intriguing merit and which should be preserved to enlighten our children and our children's children.

When you step into the path of hitherto unpursued collectibles, try taking the long way home. Tread the unfamiliar byways and become a pioneer and a discoverer. You may not thereby attain the fame of an Hernando De Soto or the riches of a Croesus—but you may have more fun than either. And life today without fun is a terrible bore.

Don't buy the items we discuss herein merely with the hope of being able to sell them for a profit before long. Of course, you may be able to do that; but the secret of successful and satisfying collecting lies in being able to appreciate, to understand, to learn from, and often, to use what you collect. As for some of the objects we talk about herein, you may have to remove the ravages of age, including rust, before you can truly appreciate their often remarkable beauty. And in many cases, you will find some charming contemporary uses to which you can put these things in your own home. Remember what others have done to create lamps and planters!

Some of the collectibles we discuss have been of interest for a few years to relatively small groups of collectors, and by talking about these and giving a bit of their history, we hope they may interest more persons. In this category are some of the articles dealt with in the chapters on "Bells: A Variety," "Milady's Boudoir: Accessories," "Dress Accessories and Baubles," "Speaking of Babies," and others.

We predict that should you embark along some of the paths suggested herein, the salvage yard soon will assume an air of greater respectability and roses may bloom in the nation's junkyards.

And what's wrong with that?

2

Bells: A Variety

BELLS HAVE BEEN COLLECTED FOR YEARS. THE AMERICAN BELL ASSOCIATION, an official organization for hobbyists in this field, boasts members throughout the nation, some of whom have assembled fabulous collections. Museums house many significant bells; books have been written about remarkable collections.

There are bells of brass, iron, pewter, glass, silver, and even marble and lava. Some date back to ancient civilizations: Lawrence Altman, of St. Louis, Missouri, a collector of and dealer in bells, has one of copper made in China about four centuries ago. It operates through the action of an inner gong. (Not all bells ring as a result of clapper action. Some utilize gongs and wind-up chimes.)

Among the favorites of collectors are those made in the shapes of figures and effigies. Other treasured bells in collections have historic associations.

There are, of course, dozens of collections featuring a miscellany of bell types, and there are collectors who specialize in altar bells, or tea bells, or elaborate Oriental bells, or sleigh bells, or town criers' bells. And there are specialized collections of temple bells, glass wedding bells, school bells, farm bells, ox bells, ships' bells, and prayer bells. There are collections of bells made exclusively of bronze, or featuring tonal scales, or designed for specific uses, and so on.

Many American bell collections have been brought together from all over the world. Another St. Louis collector, A. C. Meyer—and Mrs. Meyer—became interested in bells in 1928 and within 15 years had assembled a magnificent collection numbering more than 1,500, purchased or otherwise ac-

18

quired in their travels around this country and the world. Mr. Meyer wrote of his experiences in a book entitled *Travel Search for Bells* (Lightner Publishing Corporation, Chicago, 1944.)

Another distinguished collector, Mrs. Rebecca M. Mayer, of Atlanta, Georgia, served in 1964 as president of the American Bell Association and wrote *The Second Book of Bells of the American Bell Association*; it was so popular that it sold out completely within a very short time after publication. Still another noted bell collector was the late Martha Berry, who founded the famous Berry Schools, near Rome, Georgia.

If you're interested in bells generally, the books mentioned above and several other excellent ones are available for your perusal or study. The collector periodicals often carry articles about bells. However, there are some types of bells which thus far have not been sought with any great avidity and are, therefore, available in some abundance, compared to scarcer types—and they can form the basis of a fascinating collection. Let's take nineteenth- and early twentieth-century doorbells, pulls, and alarm bells as an example.

Not too many decades ago the majority of American city houses were equipped with rotary door bells, activated by the turning of a small metal lever, by pushing a button, or by turning or pulling a handle. Because 75 years ago or less almost every urban home was equipped with one, and because they served the rather prosaic purpose of letting the occupant know that someone awaited at the threshhold, these doorbells attracted virtually no attention or interest. Today, they cry out for a re-examination by collectors. Many of these doorbells featured extraordinary imaginative treatment. They were made of bronze, bell metal, copper, nickel-plate, iron, and other metals. Some were silver-plated.

The metal turn plates—usually oval or oblong in shape and equipped with a metal turn, a button, or pull—were attached to the exterior of the door. Many were embossed, engraved, or otherwise decorated in classic, ornate, rococo, or restrained designs. Fretwork and lacy embellishment characterized quite a number. Even the metal turns and pulls themselves were often elaborately ornamented.

A 1900 trade catalogue of John H. Graham & Co., hardware manufacturers of New York City, offered the following trimming finishes for rotary and push-button doorbells: light bronze in natural color, light bronze with sand blast finish, chocolate or statuary bronze, nickel-plated, brass in natural color, brass with sand blast finish, oxidized silver, antique brass, antique brass with sand blast finish, antique copper in medium, light, and sand blast finishes. The bells were available in either brass or iron.

Sargent & Company's patented door bells (top), door bell levers (center), and shield base and circular base door bell pulls of 1884, as pictured in the company's catalogue for that year. These once adorned many fine homes.

In 1884, Sargent & Co., hardware manufacturers of New York City and New Haven, Connecticut, issued an 882-page catalogue which illustrated and described the company's intriguing Sargent's Patent lever and pull door bells. The bells could be used with the company's patent bell lever or with a bell pull or a slide pull. Normally the bell was placed on the door or door jamb, but it was so versatile that it also could be carried, by the use of cranks, to any place it might be desired. These bells could be activated by a mortise crank, a pulley bell crank, a slide pull from the bell side; or from the outside with a direct wire and pull, or with the patent lever.

Pulls, attached to metal plates on the outside of the door, were of the same general shape as oval door knobs. They could be obtained in decorated bronze metal or in porcelain. When a lever instead of a pull was utilized, it was pulled forward and downward to work the bell. The lever knobs also were available in either metal or porcelain. Plain bells were offered as were also fancy (decorated) ones; and one had one's choice of bell metal, nickel-plate, or bronze. The lever and pull doorbells of this type sold in 1884 at prices ranging from $10 to $26 a dozen, depending on size. The levers (including some plated on brass) cost $3 to $18 a dozen wholesale, the price depending upon the material of which they were made and whether they were plain or fancy. Illustrations show that the levers and accompanying plates were adorned with geometric designs, flowers, scrolls, leaves, and birds. Also available were slide bell pulls which were operated by hooking a finger under a metal crook and then pulling to one side.

Widely used at the beginning of this century were rotary door bells, which were operated with a key-like turn in the outside plate. The New Departure Bell Company manufactured one well-known brand of these. You could obtain one of these bells finished in nickel-plate, copper, or bronze. The gongs were made of bell metal or iron. Quite similar were the push button door bells, activated by a push button in a case or plate on the exterior of the door.

The ordinary push button door bell was operated by touching the button, which released the bell mechanism; the bell sounded as long as the button was pressed. Some were made which operated on batteries or by the use of a mechanism that needed to be wound only once or twice a year.

Since the bells, the pulls, turns, and plates, or cases were so interestingly ornamented, they can provide a perfectly delightful collection. Many of them can still be found on older houses in towns and cities around the country, although some will have to be cleaned up a bit to restore their original sparkle and beauty.

Of course, they can still be used on outside doors to provide relief from the rather stark simplicity of so many modern door bells and chimes, but they also can be pressed into service for use in the home's bedrooms and studies, where privacy is often desired.

Door alarm bells also are highly collectible today. One type featured a small, oval bell, which could be attached to any door or to a wide sash. The mechanism was set by the act of closing the door, and the alarm would sound when the door was opened. They were equipped with stop mechanisms to silence them. John H. Graham & Co. offered this type in a 1905 catalogue at $9 a dozen wholesale. Both mechanical and electric alarm bells were produced.

Another type of alarm was a clapper bell mounted on a standard with a curved metal arm. Designed to be attached to the door, when the door was opened, the arm would vibrate, causing the clapper to strike the side of the bell. In its 1884 catalogue, Sargeant & Co. offered this type at prices ranging from $9.60 to $13.50 a dozen, wholesale, depending on the size of the bell.

Other alarm bells were housed in carriages. Clappers were suspended from a heavy brass loop cast into the bell. Because the bells emitted a jingling sound, they were often called jingle bells.

Numerous types of tap and hand bells were used inside the house and in offices and institutions for a variety of purposes. They also were used by milkmen and school teachers in years gone by. Some auctioneers and hotel desk clerks still use them. Made frequently of silver-plated bell metal, the hand bells ranged from about 2 inches in diameter to more than 7 inches. Some had handles of mahogany, rosewood, or other woods, often stained, and others were attached to handles of metal or imitation horn. Very small common hand bells wholesaled at the opening of this century for about $2 a dozen. Large (12-inch diameter) Swiss hand bells, nickel-plated, cost $55 to $60 a dozen at wholesale, and milkmen's and auctioneers' bells ranged from $15 to $25 a dozen, depending on size.

Tea bells, ranging from 1¾ to about 3 inches in diameter, were made in numerous shapes, and at the turn of the century bore a variety of trade names, including "Garland," "Corinthian," "Concave," and "Dome." The tea bells, of course, were used to summon members of the family or visitors to tea or to meals; some homes still use them for the same purpose. A 1905 manufacturers' catalogue pictures a set of dining room chimes consisting of four bells, accurately tuned, one atop the other. The set wholesaled for $6, complete with a rosewood mallet.

The most interesting tap or call bells were ornamented: some were made on marble, silver-plated, or bronzed bases or stands, many of which were richly decorated. A fascinating one had a metal donkey on the base. It was made by the Gong Bell Manufacturing Company and sold for $15 a dozen, whole-

862

Gong Bell Mfg. Co.'s Call Bells.

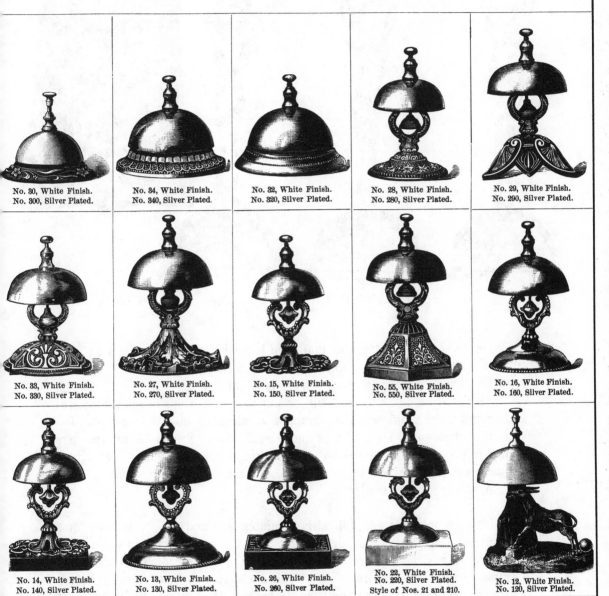

No. 30, White Finish.
No. 300, Silver Plated.

No. 34, White Finish.
No. 340, Silver Plated.

No. 32, White Finish.
No. 320, Silver Plated.

No. 28, White Finish.
No. 280, Silver Plated.

No. 29, White Finish.
No. 290, Silver Plated.

No. 33, White Finish.
No. 330, Silver Plated.

No. 27, White Finish.
No. 270, Silver Plated.

No. 15, White Finish.
No. 150, Silver Plated.

No. 55, White Finish.
No. 550, Silver Plated.

No. 16, White Finish.
No. 160, Silver Plated.

No. 14, White Finish.
No. 140, Silver Plated.

No. 13, White Finish.
No. 130, Silver Plated.

No. 26, White Finish.
No. 260, Silver Plated.

No. 22, White Finish.
No. 220, Silver Plated.
Style of Nos. 21 and 210.

No. 12, White Finish.
No. 120, Silver Plated.

A group of fancy call bells manufactured by the Gong Bell Manufacturing Company and offered for sale in 1884. From a catalogue of Sargent & Co.

Silver-mounted call bells and Kentucky cowbell of the late 1800's.

sale, in 1884. Similar types at that time had wholesale prices varying from $15 to $20 a dozen. The simpler bells wholesaled for as little as $6 a dozen up. The "Daisy" was one well-known brand of call bell.

The hand and call bells can still be put to effective use in such chores as summoning the children or hastening a recalcitrant husband to table. Because of their small size, a large and varied collection can be housed in a small display area. Arranged on shelves along a wall and effectively lighted from above or the sides, they can make an interesting contribution to décor in almost any room in the home.

Many animal bells are still fairly commonplace and can be bought for a dollar or so up. But the lithographed ones are more difficult to come by— and are usually more interesting and valuable. These customarily bore lithographed scenes of rural tranquility on their exterior surface. Made primarily for cows, in order to keep them from becoming lost or to help find them when they strayed from their accustomed pasture, they normally had a wrought iron loop at their tops, by which they could be attached to the cow's neck. The "Kentucky" lithographed cowbell was one favorite; the "Western" an-

A miscellany of animal and other bells. From left to right, top row: "Navajo" team bell, Swiss musical cow bell, and illustration showing size of the Swiss bell in relation to cow. Second row: three cab bells in different shapes fitted with malleable iron loops, and cast cow bell. Third row: two turkey bells, a sheep bell made of sheet steel, and a trip gong bell. Bottom row: bell metal "Daisy" call bells. All bells from the 1905 catalogue of John H. Graham & Co.

other. These ranged in height from 2¼ to 7 inches and wholesaled at $2.25 to $13 a dozen more than 80 years ago.

Sheep bells were somewhat similar in shape but smaller and lighter. Some came complete with straps that could be fastened to the sheep's neck. Turkey bells were usually oval and quite small. They enabled the flock to be located quickly and provided protection against hawks and predatory animals. These bells were fitted with leather straps.

Among the most melodious of the animal bells were the musical Swiss cow and team bells. These were beautifully ornamented and were celebrated for their distinct and musical tones. Often they were used in sets on herds of cows to produce melody galore. In diameter, they ranged from 3 to 6¼ inches, and the small ones could be bought for as little as 50 cents toward the close of last century. Some were sold in sets consisting of three to eight different sizes.

Before leaving the American animal bells, mention should be made of the sportsmen's bells, attached to hunting dogs when hunting in areas in which the dogs could not be easily seen; and of the tiny cab bells, which could be attached to a horse's harness and which emitted a silvery tinkle that could be heard for a quite a long distance. There also were much heavier team bells, attached by loops, shanks, or with threaded nuts. These were sold by the pound in rough polished, or polished-and-tinned finish.

Sleigh bells, of course, have long been highly collectible and were made in numerous shapes and sizes. Many were fastened in groups to shaft straps. There were musical chime sleigh bells with triple tongues; there also were saddle chime bells, which offer fine collecting possibilities. Some of the earlier sleigh bells, including those which could be bought singly, were gold- or silver-plated. These cost a dollar or more each in the last century and are worth substantially more today. We won't go into detail about the sleigh bells because other bell books discuss them, but they shouldn't be overlooked by collectors.

Late-nineteenth-century lodge bells, used by fraternal and other organizations, were usually half-oval in shape and were made in diameters ranging from 7 to 11 inches; they were struck with a mallet. There are not too many of these early ones around today.

Buggy and early automobile bells can still be found, but are getting scarce. They should be preserved along with the early bell signal devices of bicycles, fire engines, street cars, and locomotives.

Although a wide variety of horns, including the so-called "honk horns," were used on very early automobiles and some horse-drawn vehicles on occasion, a favorite signal for the horseless carriage was the New Departure auto-

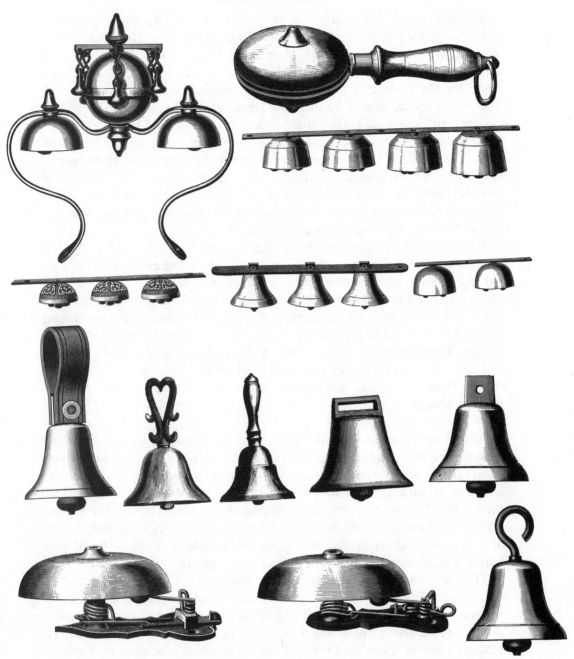

Top row: saddle chime bells; Cone's Patent Globe hand bell (above), and sleigh shaft strap musical chimes bells (below). Second row: triple tongue sleigh shaft bells, shaft strap White House wired-on bells, and cup chime bells. Third row: strapped team bell, white metal tea bell, bell metal hand tea bell, and two rough bell metal team bells. Bottom row: Abbe's Patent and Yankee gong door bells, and patent fastening team bell. From Sargent & Co's. 1884 catalogue.

mobile bell, which was attached to the foot board or bottom of the vehicle and was operated by stomping on a plunger with the foot. One New Departure bell consisted of two gongs of different tones. When the plunger was depressed, the hammer struck one gong; when it was released, it struck the other, thereby producing different tones. A single gong bell also was used. These were manufactured by the New Departure Bell Company, of Bristol, Connecticut. The cost ranged from about $5 to around $10 or $12 each.

The same company also made bicycle, fire chiefs' buggy, and fire alarm bells. The bells for chiefs' buggies were installed in much the same way as were those for the horseless carriage, and were made with two gongs and two hammers. The hammers continued to revolve while the foot plunger recovered for another push; a continuous alarm was thus possible. Needless to say, the alarm these bells emitted was loud and clear.

New Departure patented its rotary fire alarm bell on July 14, 1891. As was the case with the chiefs' buggy bell, the rotary fire alarm bells' striking hammers continued to revolve after the plunger was released; so a continuous alarm could be sounded with a frequent depression of the plunger. They gave from 12 to 15 strokes for each push. The bells were made in sizes ranging from 9 to 13 inches in diameter, and were finished in nickel plate or natural bronze. They originally sold for only $15 to $20 each, wholesale.

There were other types of nineteenth-century fire bells, including a rotary one operated with a pull, and another mechanism that was similar to that of the push alarms.

Bicycle bells came in when the traffic situation began to get bad. Our forefathers *thought* it was bad at the opening of this century; they should be living today! The Mead Cycle Company, of Chicago, was among the firms that sold a wide variety of them. Two separate gongs were also often used on bicycle bells to provide a continuous ringing chime. One type emitted a sound resembling a cuckoo's call. It was a real novelty, easily distinguishable from any other bell. Other bicycle bells were wound like watches; a touch of a button started them ringing. Still others were operated with a lever.

There was one type of bicycle bell that was operated by pressing a plunger that depressed the bell to the front tire, causing a siren-like alarm until the pressure was released and the bell rose again from the tire to an upright position on its standard, which was attached to the bicycle frame. You may remember some of these bells yourself, unless you're a schoolgirl or a schoolboy. And if you're as old as some of us, you may even have scared the daylights out of elderly ladies by riding up behind them on the sidewalk and suddenly sounding your bicycle bell.

You probably won't want to collect top-mounted locomotive bells, be-

SWEDISH SLEIGH BELLS.

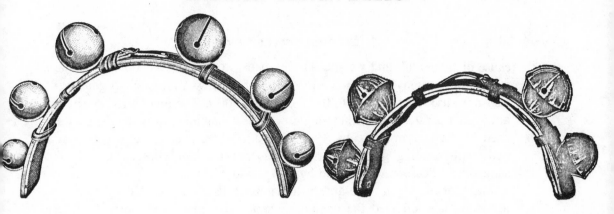

RUSSIAN SADDLE CHIMES.

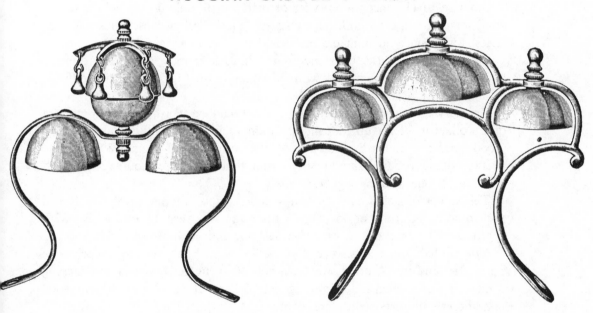

SHAFT CHIMES.

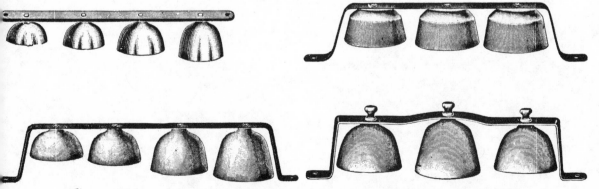

John H. Graham & Company offered these sleigh bells, saddle chimes, and shaft chimes in 1905.

cause of their bulk and weight. Trolley bells, however, were smaller and are more easily displayed. On some locomotives, however, fairly small gong bells also were used in the late 1800's and early 1900's. These were rotary-shaped and were operated with either single or double hammers of wood. They were used in the locomotive cabs. For cable and electric cars there were alarm bells with rotating gongs: the gong was never struck consecutively in the same place. These were operated by foot pressure.

Many of the locomotive and trolley gong bells were sounded by means of levers, which activated the hammers against the gong's exterior side. These trip gongs often had brass bases, and the bells themselves were made of bell metal. Since many of them were as small as 3 inches in diameter, their size should prove no deterrent to collecting them—but their scarcity may.

Other relatively uncommon types of bells worth looking for include patrol gongs made for use on children's wagons, those designed for ships and factories, fog signal and binnacle bells, and fire hose carriage bells.

Because some of the bells mentioned in this chapter are either difficult to locate or have been traded with infrequency thus far, values are difficult to suggest.

Ordinary cow, sheep, and turkey bells should be worth from a minimum of a dollar or $1.50 up, depending upon their age, condition and design. Good hand and call bells should start at a minimum of around $5, and the average ones probably should fetch from that figure to about $20 or $25 with scarcer ones coming higher.

The values of sleigh bells on straps depend upon the number of bells and their quality. A group of 35 on a 7-foot strap was recently offered for $20; a group of 49 on a 6-foot strap for $29.50; and 40 brass ones for $35.

You probably can find some door bells well worth acquiring at prices of $5 or $10 and up. A brass street-car bell 10 inches in diameter but lacking a clapper was tendered not long ago at $10; but bells of this type in good condition should bring considerably more.

All types of bells are fun to collect, but types discussed in this chapter may still be found at "bargain" prices, which may ascend more rapidly than those of types which have been collected for years.

3

Our Forefathers' Games

HAVE YOU EVER PLAYED "LOST HEIR" OR "THE LION'S PIC-NIC" OR "YANKEE Doodle"? Do the games "Halma" or "Anabasis" or "La Lutte" ring a bell somewhere in the recesses of your memory? These may be strange names to you unless you have left your tender years far behind or remember having seen one of them when you poked around as a child in your grandmother's storage trunk in the attic. Yet, these were the names of games which fascinated our ancestors and to which they devoted many a gaslit night in the years gone by.

In those days, just as is the case today, when games wore out from frequent handling and playing, they went into the discard and were replaced by new ones. Nevertheless, there are available for collectors today scores of game sets used 65 to 100 years ago, and a search for these can provide a hunt of challenging proportions. To seek them out, you first must know what they were, and to identify some of them is one of the purposes of this chapter.

Many of the games played yesterday closely resemble some which are popular today. In a few cases, little more has been changed than the name, perhaps some of the rules for playing, and the packaging. Others, however, bear little or no resemblance to those in current vogue. The best way to ascertain the most popular games of yesteryear is to search through the catalogues of the early manufacturers, distributors, and retailers of games and toys— but today, these have become exceedingly scarce, because trade catalogue collecting is now a widespread hobby itself.

Although an increasing amount of attention is being devoted by collectors to salvaging toys of past generations, little heed has been paid thus far to the

31

Games of yesteryear: left to right, the Monkey Donation Party, Redgrave's Bagatelle. Second row: Star Archarena Combination Board on which 16 to 26 games could be played, and Magnetic Jack Straws. Third row: Who Nose Me?, Bean Bag Game, and an exerciser, the Horsman Hydraulic Rowing Machine. Bottom: the Game of Negomi, and another exerciser, Byron's Hydraulic Rowing Machine.

games. Yet these, too, ought to be preserved, because they reflect an important part of the recreational activities of our fathers, our grandfathers and our great-grandfathers. These games—that is, the games played for relaxation rather than for exercise—were relatively simple, but many also were fascinating. Take the game of Halma, mentioned at the outset. This was a whiz of a game popular in the closing years of the nineteenth century. It was a contest of skill, played on a board similar to a chess or checker board; and its manufacturers claimed that it "combines in a happy manner the simplicity of checkers and the intricacy of chess." Each player played with one specific type of piece or "man," as it was called, and each "man" had only two kinds of moves.

"Halma is the most popular game in America, and it also is being played extensively throughout the civilized world," proclaimed its manufacturer in 1892. It obviously was a game that could be played in the most polite company, because tributes galore accrued to it—particularly from such a distinguished clergyman of that day as the Reverend Doctor Lyman Abbott, the Congregational minister, editor, and author; and the Reverend Charles Cuthbert Hall, of the First Presbyterian Church of Brooklyn, wrote of it in 1889:

"I have the pleasure to acknowledge your courtesy in presenting me with the very beautiful and interesting game 'Halma.' I have always felt deeply in sympathy with refined and pure games. Home amusement should be the most captivating and the most exhilarating of all amusements. You have conferred a favor upon many thousands of happy homes by inventing a game which is most amusing to young persons and most absorbing to the older ones. You have provided rational and restful entertainment for vast numbers of cosy winter evenings and breezy summer mornings in town or country."

Halma originally sold for $1 the set in the "popular edition" and $2 in the "fine edition." An edition utilizing men made of bone could be purchased for $3.50.

The game of "Progressive Angling" may be more familiar to some of you, though you may not recognize the name. It was introduced in 1888, and as many as 15 persons could participate in it. It was played with rods made of nickel to which lines and hooks were attached, 80 brass fish, and gold and silver markers. Also furnished with the game were invitation cards which the host or hostess could use for inviting friends to the "angling party," score cards, a "pool" for the "fish," and a bell for use on what was known as the "royal" or first table of players. Relatively speaking, "Progressive Angling" was an expensive game—costing $5—but then, it came in a handsome box covered with imitation alligator hide!

There is a fish pond game being played today; but it isn't spanking new: a game of Fish Pond was advertised in the 1889 catalogue of E. I. Horsman,

THE NEW GAME
CROKINOLE.

THE GAME OF MONETA
OR MONEY MAKES MONEY
BY THE AUTHOR OF LOGOMACHY
PUBLISHED BY F. A. WRIGHT CINCINNATI, O.

This new and remarkably interesting game, is by the same author as Logomachy, and bids fair to rival that celebrated game in popularity.

Per doz., $4.00

FISH POND GAME.

No. 46

The improved game of "Fish Pond" is a very popular amusement for the home circle. It is p'ayed on a table and the greater number of players the more exciting and interesting the game. It is about as difficult to catch a fish in this game as it is in the piscatorial pursuit. The game is gotten up in fine style. Sample by express on receipt of $1.00.   Per doz. $8.00

46½ Fish Pond Junior, Sample by express on receipt of 50c.   "   4 00

No. 100 ANGLING GAME,   "   8.00

"PARLOR QUOITS"
Can be Played on Any Table,

The game consists of a Printed Felt Mat, with Hub in centre, over which the player is to snap a bone ring, as in Tiddledy Winks.

"HALMA

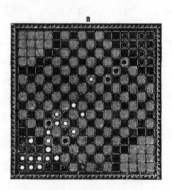

LOGOS.
A GAME OF WORDS
(NEW)

This highly interesting game can be played by three, four, five or six persons.   Per doz. net. $4.00

Sample by mail on receipt of 50 cents.

These games were popular in the late nineteenth and early twentieth centuries. How many can you remember?

of New York City, manufacturer of games, toys, and amateur photographic outfits. These retailed for $1 a set or could be purchased wholesale for $8 a dozen sets.

Scrabble has become one of today's most popular games for teen-agers and "thinking" adults. Its counterpart late in the nineteenth century was another word game called "Logos." This could be played by as many as six persons. It retailed for only 50 cents and cost $4 a dozen wholesale. Variations of it have been popular through the years.

Games utilizing play money have also enjoyed years of popularity. One of these, made in 1889 by F. A. Wright, of Cincinnati, Ohio, was called "Moneta." It was devised, the manufacturers reported at that time, by the inventor or "author" of "Logomarchy" and "bids fair to rival that celebrated game in popularity." Its wholesale price was $4 a dozen sets.

"Crokinole" has about passed from the scene today, but it too was extremely popular earlier in this century, although it originated in the nineteenth century. It was played on a special board with flat checker-like disks that were pushed or shot across the board by a snap of the finger and thumb. The object was to force as many pieces (or "men") of your opponent's color into a depressed portion of the board as possible while leaving your shooting piece or disk, often called a "carom," within the board's inner circle. The price of this game depended upon the wood from which the set was made. It could be purchased in ash for $4, but cherry cost $2 more.

Somewhat similar was the game of "Disco," the object of which was to flip rubber-edge steel disks with a short cue stick into the pocket that belonged to one's opponent. The player who first flipped a total of nine disks into his opponent's pocket was the winner. The playing boards were manufactured in various sizes, the size governing the price of the set. In 1892, the prices ranged from $3 to $5 a set.

Numerous other types of boards and simple parlor games were popular in the 1890's; among them: "Pockets," "Bagatelle," "Ring Toss," "Ten Pins," "Ring-a-Peg," "Lo Lo," "Carroms" (whose popularity continued well into the twentieth century), "La Lutte," and "Wikette."

Nineteenth century games which continued to be played in this century, and some of which are still being played, include "backgammon," "cribbage," "jack straws," "dominoes," "fish pond," and "Faba Baga." The last-named was better known later on as the bean bag game.

A wide variety of card games was available in the last quarter of the nineteenth century. Some of these, too, are still being played and others were popular until relatively recent years. These included "Hidden Book Titles," "Celebrated Poets," "Artists of the 19th Century," "Who Can Tell," "Peerless Authors," "The Aviary," "Fortunatus," "Old Maid," "The Great Mogul," "Longfellow Authors," "Whist," "Din," "Pinochle," "Flinch," and "Bridge Whist."

Games calling for physical exercise also included a number that still are being played. Among these were croquet, lawn tennis, and "Spoons." The last of these was played on the lawn with long-handled "spoons," colored balls, and a large bowl.

For the very young there were many party games, including several variations of "pin the donkey." These variations bore such names as "Who Nose Me?", "A Watermelon Frolic," "Dressing the New Woman," and "The Monkey Donation." There also were several magnetic and electric games for the young, and these were primarily educational in nature.

Here are some other nineteenth-century games to search for in your collecting peregrinations: "Putting the Girl on Bicycle," "Parlor Quoits," "Pouch Ball," "Bino," "Negomi," "Magnetic Jack Straws," "Klein's Man Targets," "Panic in Wall Street," "Pit," "Lost Heir," "Royalty," "The Game of Life," "Golden Game of Letters," "Stars and Stripes," "Syllabus," "Tally Ho," "Education," "Logomachist," and "Snap."

All types of puzzles were of interest to the younger folk years ago just as they are today. Popular late-nineteenth-century puzzles included those known as "Combination Horses," "Subway Puzzle," and "Sphinx." Cardboard puzzles of several types were given away as premiums by a number of manufacturers of nineteenth-century merchandise and foods.

Baseball, of course, was a highly popular spectator sport in the preceding century, and various nineteenth-century baseball accessories are well worth collecting—if you can find them. These include such things as uniforms, balls, bats, mitts and gloves, masks, caps, safety shoe plates, belts, body protectors, bat bags, and bases. In much the same category and worth preserving are relics of early football, tennis, basketball, and a whole host of century-old exercising devices.

Men and women watched their figures during the last century just about as carefully as they watch them today, so exercise apparatus was manufactured by many firms. Early examples of these to watch for include pulley exercises, hydraulic rowing machines, wooden and nickel-plated dumb bells, Indian clubs, striking bags, portable home gymnasiums, vaulting horses, and jump ropes.

Some rather fascinating rowing machines, in particular, were available for those who needed to watch their figures in the late 1800's. An 1885 catalogue of E. I. Horsman listed a "Pneumatic Parlor Rowing Machine," which it described as follows:

"A cylinder made of brass, having a closed end and a highly polished interior, is placed in front of the oarsman. The piston rod of the cylinder is connected with the short oars by means of a whiffletree and connecting rods. The act of taking a stroke draws the piston away from the closed end of the cylinder, produces a vacuum, and the pressure of the atmosphere upon the piston simulates the resistance that is afforded by the water in rowing a boat. The cylinder is provided with a series of small holes commencing about half way from [the] closed end, which allows the atmosphere to enter, and as the piston is drawn past them gradually relieve the vacuum. Hence, the stroke is hard at the beginning, when the vacuum is perfect, and gradually becomes easier as these holes are passed. The air thus accumulated in the cylinder finds free exit through a large opening in the closed end as it is pushed before the piston in the 'recovery.' This opening is closed by a valve automatically upon the commencement of a new stroke. There is, therefore, neither assistance nor resistance to recovery. The oars turn so as to allow of feathering."

This particular rowing machine sold for $20, and reportedly was endorsed by Columbia College and others. A similar device, the "Eureka Parlor Rowing Machine," could be purchased for only $10.

Because so few early games and exercising devices are handled by dealers in collectible items, no fixed values for most of these have as yet been established. Consequently, the pioneer has an opportunity to pick many of them up now for a very small amount. Their values in the years ahead could go the way that those of early toys have gone—well up. The most likely places to look for them include trunks and boxes long stored in attics and basements. It might pay you also to shop the Good Will stores and the Salvation Army occasionally in case some of these games turn up in contributions of toys made to them to be reconditioned for Christmas giving.

There were many nineteenth-century manufacturers of games, including a few major ones; among them McLoughlin Brothers, established shortly after the turn of the nineteenth century. This company eventually was sold to another noted producer of games, Milton Bradley Company, of which much is still heard.

Other game makers included Parker Brothers, which has turned out some of the best-known games in this century; E. I. Horsman Company, which produced all types of toys, novelties, and allied items and was a major distributor for games; and John W. Iliff & Company.

You will find games advertised in the collector periodicals, and to give you a very rough idea of some present values, here are prices recently asked for certain of them:

"Parcheesi," dated 1918, $2.50; "Mah-Jong" in leather carrying case with five drawers, $15; a less elaborate "Mah-Jong" set, $10; a "Mah-Jong" set in ivory, $50; "The Game of Colors," copyrighted 1888 by McLaughlin Bros., $4.50; "Whirl It," a Parker Bros. game dated 1907, $3.50; "The Peanut Race," $2.50; "The Merry Game of Old Maid," in original colored pictorial box, about 1870, $15; "Swing a Peg," a Milton Bradley game similar to "Quoits," $3.75; "Story of Sewing Cards," a needlework game, $3; "Nerve Croquet," $4.50.

Also, "Funny Little Brownies," around 1900, $2.50; "Dissected Map of the United States," an early jigsaw puzzle, $4.50; "India Bombay," manufactured by Butler & Soleeby, Inc., $4.75; "Backgammon," dated 1930, $3.75; "Captain Kidd Junior," 1926, $4.75; "Dominoes," with 1884 as the last patent date, $4.50; "The Game of Letters," an anagram game, $4.50; "Kit-Cat," a card game dated 1907, $4.50; and "Peter Coddle's Trip to New York," another word game, $4.50.

Early still banks. Top row: two bronze Life Insurance Savings Banks and an Electric Savings Bank. Below: State Bank, Trunk Bank, Iron Safe Bank with combination lock, and handled bank of bronze.

Although mechanical banks—the type activated by the deposit of a coin —have been collected for a good many years and have risen substantially in value in recent years, the collection of "still" banks is just getting under way in earnest. By a stretch of the imagination, these may be considered in the category of educational games, since they encouraged children to save money.

Still banks. From left: two Surplus Banks (one for nickels, one for dimes) which registered deposits and unlocked when full; the Home Savings Bank; the Electric Savings Bank, with a turn of the combination throwing the coin in the bank; and the Book Bank, entitled on the back "The Road to Wealth."

Mechanical banks were discussed in my earlier book, *Treasure at Home* (A. S. Barnes and Company, Inc., Cranbury, New Jersey), and there also is a chapter on them in Louis H. Hertz's *The Handbook of Old American Toys* (Mark Haber & Co., Wethersfield, Connecticut). An excellent book about them is *Old Mechanical Banks* by Ina Hayward Bellows (Lightner Publishing Corporation, Chicago).

Still banks, generally available at much more modest prices than the more intricate mechanical banks, were made of a wide variety of materials, including cast iron, glass, tin, steel, die-cast metal, pottery, wood, "white metal," and composition materials. They were fashioned in many shapes: some simple, some intricate. Produced in abundance years ago were still banks in the shape of houses or other buildings, miniature safes, and vaults. A large percentage of these were equipped with combination locks. We will not include the so-called registering banks, which automatically totaled up the coins deposited in them, in the category of still banks here.

Scores of the early still banks are pictured in old manufacturers' catalogues at prices so low that they will astonish those now shelling out more per bank than they sold for per dozen 65 or more years ago. A fancy bronze "Life Insurance Savings Bank" was offered in 1903 at $9 a dozen wholesale, complete with lock and key. In the same year, a square bronze "Life Insurance Savings Bank" with lock and key sold for $6 a dozen. An E. I. Horsman Company 1906 catalogue has a series of iron house-shaped banks wholesaling from only 40 cents to $2 a dozen! The same company offered iron banks with combination locks at 75 cents to $9 a dozen. A year later this company advertised the "Electric Savings Bank," opened by means of a magnet intended to be kept safely by the parents of the young saver, at $8 a dozen,

A small but representative group of antique cast iron penny banks of the late nineteenth and early twentieth centuries. Top row, left to right: English tower, Jewel Safe, Deer, Kenton combination safe, Bear Robbing Beehive, and Mutt and Jeff. Bottom: Bulldog, Pass the Hat, Gargoyle, a metal mesh register, Heathen Chinese, and Lion. (Photo courtesy of Sally Erath, Antique Toy Department, F. A. O. Schwartz, New York City.)

and a "Trunk Bank," so named because of its resemblance in shape to a trunk, at $2 to $6 a dozen.

The values of still banks today depend upon their age, condition, and design. Many desirable ones are still available at prices of $10 and under, although the more intricately-designed ones are higher.

A bank in the shape of a Victorian house is advertised at $6 and a bronze lion's head bank with a marble base at $14. Here are some recently advertised prices of still banks of iron which will give both an indication of values and of types available:

Sitting puppy, a ribbon with bee on its back, $6; bust of General Pershing, $20; dog on pillow, $16; standing dog, 5 inches high, $6; sitting bear, $9; standing pig, $6; buffalo, $13.50; standing bear, $12; dog with pack, $12; prancing horse, $9; reindeer, $8.50; Weatherbird, $8.50; bank building, 3 inches high, $3.50; U.S. mail box, post type, $5.50; treasure chest with handle, $6; standing policeman (crack on ear), $9; Empire State Building, large, $12; same, small, $7.50; Security Safe Deposit bank, $10; large four-turret bank buildings, $7; and "Good Luck Billiken," $8.75.

Bear in mind, of course, that still banks continue to be made. Also, several of the older types of mechanical banks are being reproduced today.

And have you thought about the intriguing possibilities of having a party at your house utilizing games 75 or 100 years old?

4

The General Store

FEW MEMORIES SUMMON SUCH DELIGHTFUL IMAGERY AS DO THOSE OF THE old-time general store whose shelves were stocked with everything from animal crackers to zwieback. The general store existed in communities all over America a century ago, but as the towns grew into cities and the general store gave way to specialized establishments, the "old time store," as many fondly recall it today, became relegated largely to rural areas whose sparse populations could not support more than one or two mercantile establishments.

But today, thousands of one-time rural hamlets have become the suburbs of cities, and the general store has largely, though not yet entirely, disappeared from the merchandising scene. Its fascination, however, may be viewed in the replicas of the old-time country stores that have begun to spring up here and there around the countryside.

These old stores once housed, either among their stock or their fixtures, scores of things which can provide the basis for a collection that will be treasured greatly in the years to come. The items with which we will deal in this chapter are the store accessories which once were part and parcel of merchandising and which should, for that very reason, be salvaged and preserved. A good many of them can serve useful purposes in homes today; and the values of these in particular should increase in the years ahead. Others can be utilized to provide novelty in the decor of the home, or to generate nostalgic memories among one's older guests, and marvel among the younger ones.

Some of the old string holders, twine boxes, and wrapping paper dispensers —once necessities in every well-regulated mercantile establishment—were

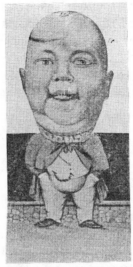

Mechanical store window display or show pieces in use at the turn of this century. These operated for five-hour periods. The heads swung on a pendulum operated by clock work, and the eyes of all these except the crying boy moved. These mechanical pieces, which were real attention-getters, were manufactured by E. I. Horsman Company, New York City.

charmingly ornamented pieces indeed. A collection of the smaller string holders or dispensers can be arrayed to advantage along a relatively narrow shelf.

Twine holders, often called "boxes," were made of copper—sometimes "bronzed"—or iron in the nineteenth century. They consisted of two sections, which could be opened so a ball of string could be inserted inside. The holders were oval or round in shape, and had a hole in one end so that the string could be pulled through and could be broken with the fingers—or snipped in two with shears—when a sufficient amount to tie up the parcel had been dispensed.

Some of these holders were designed to sit on a counter top and frequently had elaborate scrolled legs. The hole was in the top of the counter-type. Others had a ring attached at the top so they could be hung up, and the dispensing hole was in the bottom of these. One very popular type of string holder was the "Bee Hive," so named because in shape it perfectly resembled its namesake.

The prices of these twine holders were based upon their size and the ornateness of their design, but a japanned Bee Hive dispenser with a twine chamber measuring 4 x 4¼ inches sold for only $7 a dozen wholesale in 1884, and similar ones with twine chambers measuring 5 x 5½ inches cost about $11 a dozen. The highest-priced dispensers of this type were gold bronzed ones, which in the larger size cost $15 a dozen, wholesale.

The hanging types were usually cheaper, ranging from $2.60 to $3.75 a dozen in the same year. An open-work counter type with an open-work metal oval base cost $6.75 a dozen japanned and $7.50 a dozen copper bronzed.

Earlier in this century, the Chicago firm of Thayer & Chandler offered a group of inexpensive holders for twine at only 40 cents each. The twine was placed behind decorated fronts, including fronts shaped, for example, as peacocks, ballet dancers, Dutch girls, parrots, or love birds. You could color the fronts yourself.

Try using a good metal polish on those whose brightness has been dulled by the passage of the years and the accumulation of grime.

Bee Hive metal holders should be worth $7.50 to $15 now. Other ornate footed counter-top holders should bring about $7.50 to as high as perhaps $20, depending upon their decoration and age. The hanging type should sell for a little less.

There also were twine holders made of glass; and not long ago one in camphor glass was offered at $12.

Wrapping paper dispensers—one type of which consisted of two metal supports, each with a hole to receive the ends of the core around which the paper was wrapped—were normally fastened to counters. They are not so interesting as twine boxes, but some were made of decorated metal and a set should be included in any general collection of country-store collectibles. They are worth $5 to $10.

The small wall or tabletop coffee grinders or mills, which were found in most homes years ago, have been collected for some time; but the larger floor-type (and also counter-type) coffee and spice mills used to grind coffee beans and spices in grocery stores and general stores in the late nineteenth and early twentieth centuries have thus far attracted few collectors, primarily because of their size. Nevertheless, they are fascinating contrivances; and, of course, every modern replica of the old-time store should have at least one. And if you have a large enough den or playroom at home, one of the store counter-type mills will certainly provide a conversation piece.

The "Enterprise" was a popular brand of coffee, spice, and drug mill in the latter part of last century and early in this one. Another was the "Swift." These mills were made of fancy iron, and sometimes had an ornamented dome atop the hopper. Grinding was accomplished by means of two metal wheels attached to, and on the outside of, the hopper. They had various capacities for grinding, ranging from six ounces per minute to about three pounds a minute.

The counter mills offered in an 1884 catalogue of Sargent & Co. ranged in wholesale price from as little as $2 for the smallest size to $37 for the largest. The big floor mills came a good bit higher, ranging up to $100 in price. The Sargent catalogue pictures one of the counter type with an eagle on top of a nickeled dome.

In the early 1900's the Coles Manufacturing Company made a line of coffee, drug, and spice mills for stores, hotels, and restaurants on which it had obtained some patents for special features. These ranged in price from $6 to $100. The largest ones were designed for power use rather than manual operation.

Incidentally, Coles also manufactured a wheel-turned iron shaker for milk shakes and mixed drinks. The company said each turn of the crank wheel "gives ten distinct shocks to the liquid." These stood 2 feet tall on a base measuring 7 x 12 inches and cost $8 in 1900.

The store-counter coffee, drug, and spice mills are worth from $25 to around $50; and the floor models will bring more—though not too much more because their use is limited by their cumbersomeness.

One of the best places to get an ice-cold drink of water on a hot summer day early in this century was in the general store, most of which had 10- or 12-gallon water coolers somewhere around the place, with a tin dipper or a glass nearby. At home, you may have had your own water cooler, but primarily they were found in business houses, manufacturing plants, hotels and restaurants, and large offices. They ranged in size from a capacity of 2 gallons to 12.

Many of the early-twentieth-century water coolers were japanned in color and decorated—usually with flowers or cool green vines, but sometimes with full-blown scenes as well. Most coolers had galvanized steel reservoirs and

Late-Nineteenth-Century twine boxes. Both counter-top and hanging types are shown.

nickel-plated lever faucets. Some were made of enameled sheet steel; but there also were coolers of stoneware, on the outside of which cool moisture accumulated so that they looked particularly tempting on a sweltering day.

One type of cooler had a galvanized cylinder which was suspended from the cooler cover and inside of which small pieces of ice were placed so that the ice did not come in direct contact with the water and thus lasted longer.

At the turn of this century, you could buy a 2-gallon decorated metal water cooler for as little as $2 or $2.50 and a 12-gallon cooler for $10 or so—although the type with the suspended galvanized ice cylinder was more expensive. A 5-gallon decorated stone cooler would have cost you $3.50 or $4. Of course, stands—usually of metal—were available on which to place the coolers, and these often cost a little more than the coolers themselves.

Also in use earlier in this century were water filters designed to filter out impurities, including dregs. A good many of these were the kind that attached to water faucets; but others were rather large cylindrical affairs, made either of sheet metal or stone, which could be placed on a stand, counter, or table top. In some of these the water was filtered through porous stone fitted into the bottom of an upper container or jar.

A 1906 catalogue of Belknap Hardware and Manufacturing Company, of St. Louis, Missouri, featured a "Flemish Stone" filter, which was charmingly decorated in color on the outside. These could filter from 3 to 12 gallons of water daily, depending on their size.

Remove the top from these decorated water coolers and filters and you can use them for plants. You also can use them as storage space for miscellaneous articles.

The most collectible of these coolers and filters are those which have their original decorations in good condition; but there is no rule preventing you from exercising your own artistic talents on them if the decorations have worn off.

We haven't seen any of these advertised for sale recently, but you probably can buy one—if you can locate it—for very little indeed. You can use them for their original purpose, or even for holding beverages other than water at patio and garden parties.

Most general stores of earlier days sold, among a host of other things, needles, screws, and bolts. These were frequently displayed in fairly good-sized cases. Spool or thread cases have been selling for the past few years at what their original owners surely would consider fabulous prices, and one day—perhaps before too long—the values of the needle, screw, and bolt cases will reach those of the thread cases.

Both types were made of wood, most often oak or walnut. The needle cabinets were made in two-, three- and four-drawer sizes, each drawer being equipped with a set of tills or partitions. The tills were sometimes concave. One standard size for needle cabinets was 17 or 17½ inches long by 11½ inches deep. Height, of course, varied with the number of drawers. The cabinets were often lettered with the name of the manufacturer of the needles they displayed.

Needle cases can be used in the modern home for storage of a variety of very small objects, not excluding, naturally, needles and pins, which are so

Country store collectibles. Top row: water cooler, decorated stone water filter, screw case, needle dispensing case and (below) tea scales. Second row: two mills for grinding coffee, spice and drugs, and a counter scales. Below: a cigar case with a till at the rear, a 1900 cash register and (at bottom left) automatic scales and confectionery scales.

frequently exceedingly difficult to find around the house when one most needs them. The cases are worth $5 and up—larger sizes well up.

The screw and bolt cases were larger, some containing well over 100 drawers. These drawers, too, were compartmentalized, and some cases contained more than 500 compartments or spaces. They originally held just what their name indicates—screws, bolts, and other small types of hardware goods. Some cases were square, some were taller than they were wide, and others were octagonal-shaped. A revolving octagonal case was made for use on counter tops. The drawers had small metal pulls by which they could be pulled out from the case so that one might view their contents.

These cases also can be used for the storage of a host of small articles.

If the cases are in fairly good condition with original lettering on them, it is best to clean them with soapy water, wiping dry quickly, but you can refinish them if you'd rather, and you can even decorate their tops if you have a violent urge to do so.

A variety of small display cases of other types once used in general stores and specialty establishments can be collected and used to advantage to display other treasures. This is particularly true of those with glass fronts or tops, or both. Cigar cases with glass fronts and tops are an excellent example. These were made in various sizes, including one designed to be used on top of a counter. Some of these cigar cases came with attached automatic-locking money drawers in the back. The glass was framed in a durable wood, such as oak. The wooden backs of the cases were opened to remove the cigars.

The smaller sizes of these cigar cases can be used to display collections of coins, daguerreotypes, food molds, small toys, banks, dolls, mustard jars, and a great variety of other collectors' items.

Pencil display cabinets with numerous small drawers will vie for favor one of these days with the spool cabinets, too.

Larger glass display cases can be used for collections of glass or china, pewter, figures or figurines, and so on. Other types of show cases can be used for the same purpose, but unless you have a large home or a large collection (or both), you'll probably want to seek the smaller ones. Some were built with mirror-lined doors, which will be an advantage in displaying certain types of collectibles. You can line the bottoms with colored cloth in order to give your display added zip.

If one has sufficient room, he can assemble a most interesting collection of early store alarm tills and cash registers, numerous types of which were in use during the latter part of the nineteenth century and early in this one.

About 1885, a very small and simple alarm till-lock and drawer was in use. It was made of wood and contained compartments for coins and bills. Oak, walnut, and cherry were the most frequently used woods. The coin trays and compartments were varnished and polished. Normally, the coin trays (which were removable) were made of a solid block of wood. These slid from front to back in the tills to disclose spaces for bills and bank notes. Sometimes the tills contained special bowls for gold and odd coins.

The alarm tills were equipped with gongs, most of which sounded every time the tills were opened. Tills were usually kept under a counter, though occasionally on top. One type was made with an alarm that could be specially set to sound only when tampered with by an unauthorized person. This was done by throwing a set of levers, which operated bolts or tumblers.

At the century's turn, alarm tills sold for prices ranging from about $15 to more than $20 a dozen at wholesale, but a 1905 catalogue shows prices of from $22 to $96 a dozen.

The very small alarm tills would make an excellent substitute for today's "piggy banks" or the old sugar bowl in which to keep change.

Early ornate metal cash registers also are collectible though they are considerably bulkier than the small tills. They were originally comparatively more expensive. Catalogues of 1900 feature them at prices of $350 to $400 each for the more intricate types, which performed such extra chores as adding up the total cash receipts for the day. However, because the early cash registers are outmoded, and bulky, you can pick some of them up today for a fraction of their original selling cost. About the middle of last century an Ohio company made a register that operated when clay marbles were placed in slots at the top. Each marble bore a numeral. After being placed in the appropriate slots, they dropped through into compartments inside, so that to total the day's receipts, the merchant added up the numerals on the marbles. This contrivance was a forerunner of the register which operated by means of gears. Such a machine in the possession of Jack Murdock, Detroit, Michigan, is described by Helen Langworthy in a brief article in the March, 1966, issue of *The Antiques Journal.*

Scales and balances were essential for the general store in weighing out portions of everything from cheese to sugar and meats. Hanging and counter scales were used for various purposes. Those used on the counter usually featured a sizable metal scoop or a flat platform for holding produce, meats, or other items to be weighed; and a set of weights of graduated sizes. The scoop and a smaller platform for holding the weights were balanced on a metal arm, usually suspended above a metal base. Some scoops were of tin, others of brass, and the weights were normally of iron. Metal parts were japanned and often decorated.

Store scales and balances could weigh produce, tea, coffee, and other foods totaling anywhere from about half an ounce to 9 pounds. An early-twentieth-century catalogue shows a group of these at wholesale prices of from $15 to $42 a dozen. Those with brass scoops cost more than the ones with scoops of heavy tin.

Then there were the so-called "automatic" counter-top scales, also used for weighing vegetables, hardware items, and the like. Some had a simple platform on top and others had the scoop. One group was made with small scoops and was designed especially for weighing confectionery. These usually had a capacity of 4 or 5 pounds, while the larger ones for hardware and heavier items could handle weights up to 60 pounds. Weight was computed on a dial on the front of these scales. Most of them sold in those days for only a few dollars each.

There also were hanging spring balances equipped with a hook at the end, though some had weight pans of metal. These had calibrated plates on the front and a pointer which indicated weight instantly. They could be attached to the ceiling or other overhead surface by means of a metal ring. One type was made for weighing as much as 400 pounds of ice.

Numerous other types of scales and balances also are available for the collector and for museums. These include postal and apothecary scales, as well as platform scales for weighing bulky items. In addition, one may find scale beams or balances, which utilized metal weights called "poises." These could either be suspended or came with frames so they could be placed on the floor. They were made for weighing such commodities as cotton. There were also roving scales designed to weigh yarn and similar materials in the textile industry, cloth computing scales that determined the weight per running yard of cloth by weighing a small sample, laboratory scales for weighing chemicals, bottle testing scales used in glass blowing to ascertain whether the bottles were up to standard, and moisture percentage scales that made sure the correct percentage of moisture in ores was present.

In fact, you probably will be surprised at just how many different types of scales and balances were manufactured and the purposes to which they were put. There was a special ratio scale which gave the weight of a dozen articles simply by weighing one. There were platform scales for weighing heavy commodities. There were, of course, weight scales for the use of physicians, insurance examiners, and others. Special scales were made to weigh such dairy products as milk, cream, and cheese. There were rolling mill scales used in steel mills and warehouses to weigh metal bars and plates. There were abattoir scales for use in abattoirs, packing plants, and cold storage houses. And there were big scales for weighing trucks and their contents—coal, stock and so on—most of which are of such size as to be of little interest to the average collector.

The small scales and balances can come in handy around the home for weighing such things as small packages before mailing them. Scales and balances also can be put to use as interesting planters for vines or can be transformed into novel table centerpieces by utilizing fruits or vegetables.

Because few persons thus far have started collecting them, you can often pick up desirable scales for a trifle. An old Texas cotton scale, made partly of brass, was recently offered for only $10. On the other hand, a fine apothecary scale with a marble top and a glass-enclosed balancing scale was advertised not long ago for $42, complete with a box of tiny brass weights. A hanging balance with a brass front, dated 1892, was available not long ago for $3.50. A general store counter-top scale with a scoop, brass dial, and hand was offered at $5.

Fairbanks has been a famous name in the scales industry for many years; this company had more than 300 scales, balances, and weighing devices on exhibit in Machinery Hall at the Centennial Exposition in Philadelphia in 1876. Many of the devices on view were graduated for use in countries abroad, since Fairbanks exported large quantities of them. Other exhibitors of scales at the Exposition included Brandon Manufacturing Company, of Vermont, the Philadelphia Scale and Testing Machine Works, and the noted Howe firm. Another famous name is the Strait Scales Company.

Store tobacco cutter known as the "Imp."

Among other interesting general store items which lend themselves to a colorful display are the plug tobacco cutters, which were made in a number of shapes and designs. One of the favorites was called the "Imp," or the "Image." This bore a metal likeness of a man impudently thumbing his nose while perched on top of the cutting blade lever. During the final quarter of

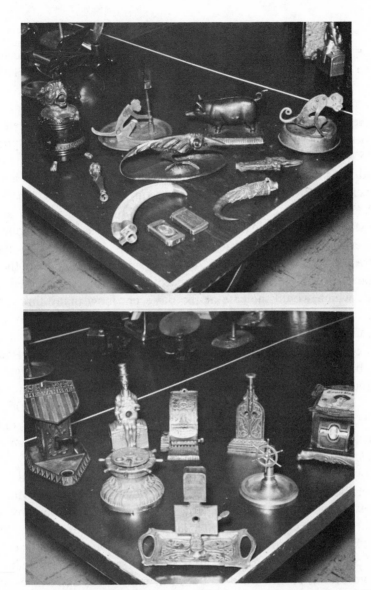

A few of the "old-time" cigar and tobacco cutters in the extensive collection of Milton Klein, of Atlanta, Georgia.

the nineteenth century these sold for $10 to $14 a *dozen,* and some have been offered for sale of late at that much, and more, *each.*

Other cutters of this type, designed for counter use to cut a "chaw" of tobacco from a large plug, bore such names as "Little Giant," "Peter Schuyler," "Improved Champion," "Clipper," "Daisy," and "Jumbo." These cutters were equipped with long handles, often decorated, which were used to raise and lower the steel cutting blades, housed in an iron frame. Usually, the blade was operated by means of a ratchet. There also were tobacco shaves, which were used for shaving plug tobacco for smoking in pipes. They could be adjusted to yield fine or coarse pipe tobacco.

Also collectible are cigar cutters, used to trim the ends of cigars. Some of these were elaborately fashioned. One of them, the "King Alfred" cutter, measured about 13 inches tall and held a Waterbury clock. This type should bring $35 or more. There also were small scissors-type cutters, some of which were gold- or silver-plated. These are worth $5 or more. A little later, cigar cutters were combined with lighters for use on store counters. One of these, dated 1889 and bearing the name "Austin Nichols," was recently advertised at $10. Milton Klein, of Atlanta, has assembled a fascinating collection of cigar cutters over a period of more than ten years, including store types that later were banned as "unsanitary," because smokers would lick the end of their cigars before cutting the tips. Some of these cutters contained a counting device which would indicate at the day's end how many times they had been used. Many of the small cutters were so interesting that they could be used as charms for bracelets.

Mr. Klein calls some of the mechanical cigar cutters the "poor man's mechanical banks." In the late 1800's and early 1900's counter cigar cutters were found in all tobacco stores and in most establishments selling tobacco products. The last patent was taken out on a cigar cutter about 1906, according to Mr. Klein. Since that time most of the older and heavier ones have found their way to the scrap pile, and many were melted down for use during World War I.

Probably the two major manufacturers of cigar cutters (since their names appear on most of the advertising cutters) were the Brunhoff Manufacturing Company, of Cincinnati, Ohio, and the Erie Specialty Company, of Erie, Pennsylvania. Cigars once advertised widely on the store counter cutters included Aleppo, Paul Kauvar, Beacon, Court Royal, Queen's Necklace, Modoc —and a couple which are still around, Roi-tan and Flor de Melba.

The commercial cutters were produced in many sizes and shapes and with various types of cuttting mechanisms. Most had two or three holes for different sizes of cigars, with a blade that crossed over all holes at the same time, making a straight cut of the tip. However, there were some with a straight cut on one blade and a V-shaped cut on the other.

Mr. Klein, who provided the author with much background on these devices, says that the smallest type of cigar cutter for counter use (or at least the smallest which remained on the counters for any length of time!) had a base measuring 3 by 4¼ inches with the cutter rising to 3⅛ inches from the counter. It had two holes in the top with a small thumb lever which was pressed to move the blade across them.

A larger type had a bar at the front with three holes and a glass plate above. Bases of the cutters were usually embossed with scroll-like designs. One type had "arms," which when pressed down forced a blade across a single hole to cut the tip of the cigar. Although the bases of these cutters frequently varied, many used the same type of Brunhoff cutting arm.

Of much interest are the mechanical types operated by a mainspring and with blades that "snapped" around swiftly to cut the tips of cigars inserted in the holes. Many of these had glass domes and were painted inside and "adorned" with an advertisement. To find these with the paint still in good condition is a stroke of fortune. They had a hole in the top of the dome with a lettered warning reading "Be careful of fingers."

Metal wind-up types also are available, and they may still be found in much better condition than those with the glass domes. Probably the tallest (and perhaps the most expensive) of the metal types, according to Mr. Klein, is one which advertised "Artie, the best Cigar of the Year." It stands 10 inches high with a small man made of metal perched on top. The little man "bites the tip" from his metal cigar when a real cigar is inserted in the cutting hole. This action certainly resembles that of a mechanical bank.

Other types dispense matches when a cigar is cut. One called "The Yankee" feeds a match from the top (after having walked it up a series of steps with each cutting), turning it stem up; upon being pulled out, the match is struck. Another advertising Royal Court Cigars feeds a match to the front by means of a spring turning a drum and picking up the match when a cigar is cut. This one, along with a good many others, has a striking surface on the side.

There also are flat types of cigar cutters for use on desks, match safes with cutters on one end designed to be carried in one's pocket, and small watch fob types.

In addition, counter types of cigar cutters were made for gambling use, and some of these are described later in Chapter 31.

Before leaving the category of store tobacco collectibles, cigar box openers should be mentioned. These were, in effect, knives made of solid forged steel and were used, as their name indicates, to open boxes of cigars. At the beginning of this century good ones could be bought for as little as $3 a dozen, wholesale, while simpler types were available for $1.75 to $2 a dozen.

The collectibles mentioned thus far constitute just a beginning for those interested in the intriguing relics of the old general store days. Containers of various types constitute a big category in themselves. These include candy jars, pickle jars, cheese boxes, and lithographed coffee and tea cannisters; also boxes, biscuit tins, numerous types of lithographed wooden boxes, and even wooden kegs and barrels with advertising or other lettering on them.

Here are some recently advertised prices for containers, but these will vary widely all around the country: glass cheese case, $20; cheese box made with wrought copper nails and containing a high, shaped handle attached with pegs, $22.50; Sunshine Biscuit store tin with glass top and metal rim, $5; coffee and tea cannisters, $7.50 to $12.50; wooden tea box with original paper labels, $7.50; and wooden barrel with original lettering advertising coffee, $18. The candy jars, however, can often be found for 50 cents to a couple of dollars, depending on age and size. And other smaller boxes and similar containers can probably be found for prices less than those listed above if you search ardently enough for them.

Listed below are just a few of the many other general store articles worth preserving. Where prices are listed in parentheses, they represent those asked in recent advertisements:

Diamond Match dispenser of tin with penny slot and company name stencilled on front ($12.50); barrel bung starters ($3); cheese cutters ($8); small supply bins ($5–$7.50); scoops of various types (ice cream, $3.75); popcorn dispensers ($9); meat slicers; hanging lamps; advertising signs, placards, and mechanical show window pieces. The last-named, incidentally, can provide an amazingly interesting collection. The mechanical show pieces were designed for use in windows to catch the attention of passersby. Often in the form of figures, some had eyes and heads that moved and were operated by a clockwork mechanism. Made in various sizes and frequently of cardboard embossed in colors, they would operate for several hours on a single winding. One of the manufacturers of these mechanical pieces, E. I. Horsman Company, offered them in 1903 at prices ranging from $18 to $24 a dozen. They are worth a great deal more than that today.

Of course, there are modern automated window attention-getters which shouldn't be confused with the early cruder and more whimsical ones.

5

Our Forefathers' Office

THE ACCOUTERMENTS THAT ADORNED THE WELL-OPERATED OFFICE OF SOME
decades ago consisted of a variety of small and not-so-small objects, which have
their more efficient counterparts in the well-run office of today. These ranged
from paper clips to pencil sharpeners, from envelope moisteners to duplicating
machines.

But if the young executive or young secretary of today were able to walk
into an office of 1890, he would find himself discovering a strange new world.
The implements, devices, and accessories of yesteryear's business or personal
office may be less efficient than those of the late 1960's, but in the main they
are far more fascinating—and far more attractive.

Take the paper clip for example. The small, almost antiseptic bit of bent
wire that, for a Lilliputian, performs such a Gargantuan service, pales in comparison with the strikingly handsome embossed metal clips of 70 or 100 years
ago. Some of those early clips measured nearly 4 inches in length. They
clamped paper tightly between two metal sides with the aid of a relatively
heavy wire spring. Those decorated with replicas of animal heads, hands,
horseshoes, and other objects certainly must have brightened the beholders'
day.

Exterior metal surfaces of these early clips were frequently embossed with
geometric designs, scrolls, and curlicues. In the latter part of the nineteenth
century, you could purchase Tuscan Bronzed paper clips for $1.38 a dozen
at wholesale prices, Berlin Bronzed ones at $1.50 a dozen, and Bronze Metal
ones for $6 a dozen. One type was equipped with spikes or pins for holding
the paper quite securely. This type in Berlin Bronze cost $2 a dozen.

Office accessories: Left to right, top: two pen wipers and a fancy embossed rolling blotter. Second row: metal paperweight, pen cleaner, and paper hook. Third row: embossed metal paperweights, and pencil pointers. Fourth row: fancy paper clips. Bottom: glass paperweight, desk file hook with embossed base, and harp file hook.

Special paper clips were made for some of the fraternal organizations and were adorned with their special emblems or insignia. By the turn of the century the wholesale prices of this type had dropped. Tower Manufacturing & Novelty Company, of New York City, advertised "Good Luck" clips in the shape of a horseshoe at 70 cents a dozen for the small size in brass. It also offered 5½-inch clips in the shape of a pair of hands made of heavy sheet stamped brass at $2.50 a dozen.

Today, one of the brass fraternal clips is likely to bring $7.50 or a bit more. A clip with a duck's head with glass eyes was advertised within the past year at $8.

Early spike-type paper files also are of interest. Some of these were designed to be placed atop the desk and were made with either square, round, or octagonal decorated bases. Others were intended to be attached to a wall or other vertical surface, and had curved hooks or spikes for this purpose. Their bases were fashioned in numerous intricate designs. One attractive base was in the shape of a harp.

About 1885, the wall-type hooks, at wholesale, were priced from $1 to $1.45 a dozen; and prices of the desk types ranged from $1.75 to $2 a dozen. Some desk types had hooks ending in a spear-shaped point. In 1908, the harp-back files with japanned finish wholesaled for $8.50 a gross. Files in the shape of an anchor with a rope twined around it cost $9.60 a gross in enameled finish. Similar to the files were steel message hooks, consisting of a simple curved hook which fastened to the wall.

A good many of these paper files and message hooks are still around and probably can be acquired from their owners for small sums—but watch the prices rise as the supply shrinks.

These hooks can be pressed into service around the home of today for such useful purposes as holding messages for various members of the family or the maid, for recipes, or as a temporary residing place for addresses or names that may or may not have to be filed away permanently at some time later.

Handsome glass paperweights of the millefiori (or candy cane), and other blown types have been collected for years, and the prices of some of these approach the fantastic; but a large group of novelty-type and metal weights used 50 to 100 years ago still awaits the serious collector. Naturally, these will not approach the monetary values of the blown glass weights made last century in the glasshouses at Clichy, Baccarat, Millville (New Jersey), and elsewhere; but they do hold an interest of their own, and a sizeable collection can be made of them for a fraction of the outlay that would be required for the blown weights.

In 1915, Keuffel & Esser Company, manufacturers and importers, of New

York City, offered a paperweight consisting of shot in a lined chamois bag. One of these, weighing 2 pounds, could be bought for $1. A similar 3-pound weight cost $1.50.

The same company advertised a combination ink bottle holder and paper-weight made of bronzed iron or enameled iron. The ink bottle was inserted from the bottom of the holder and was secured by a bayonet flange. One of these weighing 8 ounces cost 30 cents, and one weighing 2 pounds cost 75 cents.

Other types of weights popular in offices of years ago were made of lead or iron in fancy shapes. An octagonal one with embossed sides and an octagonal finial could be had in Tuscan Bronzed metal in 1885 for $2.50 a dozen! The same weight in nickel-plate cost $4 a dozen.

Simple flat lead paperweights covered with leather were in use during the first quarter of this century. Their prices ranged from about 80 cents to a dollar each. Iron weights with knobs were slightly cheaper.

One interesting type was an octagonal weight made of glass with a clamp for holding paper attached to the top. This bears a patent date of December 5, 1893, and was made by the P. N. Mfg. Company.

Round and square glass paperweights with flat tops and pictures inserted in the crystal were popular around the turn of the century. These included illustrations of humans, animals, and classical portraits as well as occasional outdoor scenes. In the first decade of this century this type wholesaled for $2.50 to $3.50 a dozen, less than what you could expect to pay for *one* today.

Among other popular designs were glass cubes in color—most frequently blue—some having a mirror in one side, others featuring tinsel scenes. Oblong glass paperweights were made, inside of which photographs could be inserted; one of these, with a photo of his wife or children, was often found on the boss's desk. There also was a dice paperweight made of a hollow globe of glass, containing sevral small dice and with a picture background on the bottom. If the office of 1910 had a coffee break, you can guess to what use these dice paperweights were put in addition to holding down papers.

A good many of the old weights, both round and oblong, were covered with cloth or leather and had knobs or handles by which they were lifted. There were numerous combination paperweights and pen racks. A bit later the advertising paperweights of glass were made in profusion. Souvenir weights of this type also were produced in abundance and are still fairly plentiful.

Those who like paperweights but can't afford the costly ones from the famous glasshouses can build a nice collection of these metal and novelty weights. One of these days, the values of these, too, will surely be on the ascendancy.

Who collects early pencil sharpeners? Perhaps no one yet—but they can be collected and could form an enlightening display of devices used to "point" pencils in days gone by. The aforementioned Keuffel & Esser Company sold an interesting combination "Useful Pencil Pointer and Paper Weight." The device was made of enameled iron, and the sharpener consisted of a roller covered with flint paper and mounted in a heavy metal box with a cloth-lined bottom. The box was designed for catching the pencil's shavings and also was heavy enough to serve as a paperweight. The roller, incidentally, had six "faces" so that it would last a long time, and two extra sandpaper coverings for the roller were provided with each pencil pointer. The pointers were made in two sizes, the smaller selling for 40 cents and the larger for a dollar.

The "Jupiter Pencil Pointer" was a rather cumbersome contrivance, which came equipped with a compensatory weight, an extra cutting wheel, an oil can, and—happily—directions for operating it. The compensatory weight was for holding the sharpener during use, provided it was not bolted down. The sharpener was operated with a crank handle. The cutting wheel could not be re-sharpened when it wore dull, but new wheels were available at 50 cents. The sharpener itself cost $6 and was made of metal throughout.

A rather crude forerunner of today's efficient sharpeners was the "Planetary Pencil Sharpener," which also operated by means of a handle crank and a cutting blade. It had two uprights and could be fastened to the wall or a table. It cost $4.50, and extra knives were available at 65 cents each.

An early A. W. Faber Company sharpener of a type which continued in use for many years was pictured in a catalogue of artists' materials issued about 1894. It was a small tubelike iron device with a blade inside. The pencil was inserted in one end of the tube and turned against the blade. These cost only $1.25 a dozen.

Many types of early letter openers, of course, are highly desirable. Some of these were extremely handsome instruments, and a large collection of them may be assembled—and rather inexpensively, if one has the patience and a good eye to look for them in out-of-the-way places.

Some letter openers fabricated around the latter part of last century were a part of "writing sets." These sets usually consisted of a paper knife (or letter opener), a pen holder, and a metal eraser. The implements in the sets often had silver handles, while a good many letter opener blades were of pearl. Other sets had pearl handles. There were also many other types of ornately decorated or embossed handles.

A 1900 wholesale catalogue offered these sets, with sterling silver handles, for as little as 79 cents. Better sets cost up to $4. In some sets a seal was substituted for the pen holder.

A good many jewelry establishments sold writing sets—or the openers, pen holders, seals, and erasers separately. You can therefore collect letter openers or paper cutters by themselves or entire desk or writing sets. Although the terms "letter opener" and "paper cutter" are frequently used interchangeably, the paper cutter usually had a wider blade. The seals were actually holders for wax seals used for fastening envelopes. The metal ink erasers featured a small metal blade which tapered on each side from the center to sharp cutting edges.

One combination was a knife and paper cutter, the blade of the knife being concealed in the handle.

Inkwells and ink stands really constitute a category in themselves and many collectors are busy in this field. If you're interested, you'll find a discussion of these, together with lap desks, in this writer's book *Treasure at Home*.

The individual items in desk sets of bygone days are valued according to their quality. Pen and quill holders may be found for as little as a couple of dollars up. One in glass was advertised recently for $3.50. Letter openers can be found from a dollar up, but chiefly up. Good metal ink erasers and blotters come a bit higher, and stamp boxes will probably be found in a wide range of prices, those of sterling silver sometimes priced fairly high. Very few persons seem to have started collecting early fountain pens, and you can pick some of these up right now for little or nothing.

In addition to inkwells, early ink bottles are worth collecting. Some of these have been offered in the recent past for a very few dollars each, but they probably will soon go higher in view of the momentum in bottle collecting of all types. And don't forget early mucilage bottles. Those with lettering in the glass are preferable to those with paper labels, but those with paper labels still attached are preferable to those whose labels are missing. Almost no one seems to be collecting mucilage bottles yet, so you should be able to buy them for very little.

Not usually a part of the customary accessories of the average office, but used by draftsmen, artists, and others were special paper cutters. One type was a very small implement, consisting of a cutting blade housed in a decorated metal case. The blade was adjustable to cut any thickness of paper or Bristol-type board without sinking into the cutting surface itself. The little blade could be removed for sharpening. If you come across any of these, which were in use early in this century, grab them—if you can acquire them for a small sum. They are most attractive.

Pencil holders—decorated metal rings that fitted around the pencils—also are worth collecting. You can amass a horde of these and display them all in a space only a foot or two square.

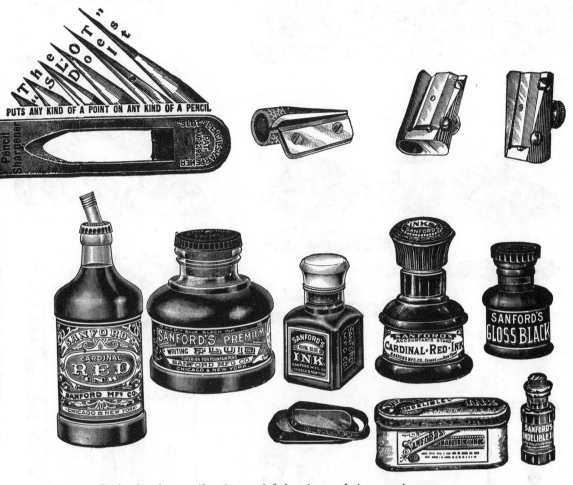

Early simple pencil pointers, ink bottles, and tin containers.

Early penholders should be saved; but did you ever think of the possibilities of collecting early pen points? These were made in numerous shapes by many companies, and most of them bore the names of their manufacturers or a trade name. Why not try to see how many trade names you can assemble? To name just a few of them, there were "Wallace's Falcon," "Wallace's Vertical Writer," "Tower Carbon," "Ball-Pointed," "Lyceum," "Manhattan Stub," "Coloriscript," "Eagle Pencil Company Magistrate," "Eagle Pencil Company Extra Elastic," "Perfection Falcon," "Cosmograph," "Esterbrook & Company Fine Business," "Spencerian Mercantile Pen," "Platinum," and "Joseph Gillatt's Principality." There were scores of others.

The penholders bore as many manufacturers' and trade names as did the pen points. Penholders were made of wood, cork, celluloid, rubber, and other

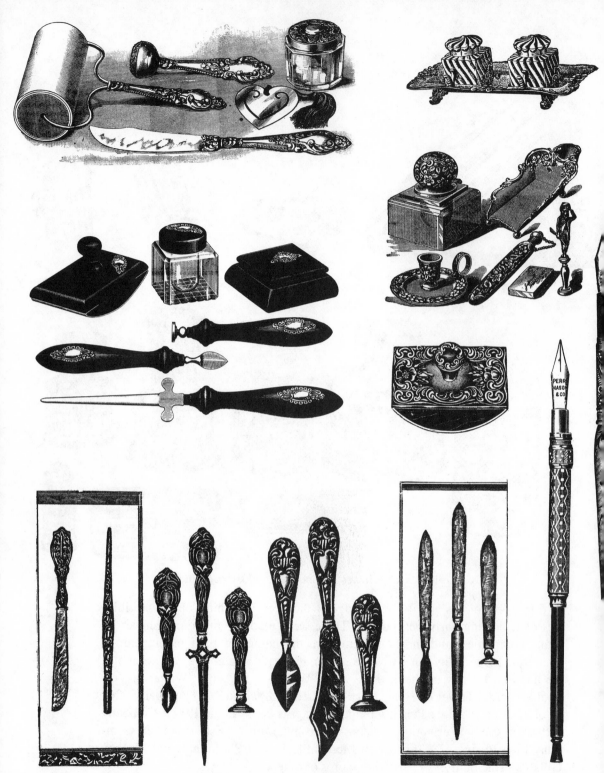

Office and writing accessories of earlier days, including a variety of letter openers and seals.

substances. Some had decorated tips of nickel, and one type of these bore a depiction of an eagle. It was made by Eagle Pencil Company. Eberhard Faber made fine penholders with enameled taper handles.

Some delightful pen wipers were made. One type, the "Teddy Bear," was made of chamois with a metal teddy bear in the center. Others boasted colored pictures in their centers. These types were customarily fabricated of two or three pieces of chamois joined together. There also were pen cleaners with bases of cut glass and chamois or sponge tops. And don't forget the silver and silver-plated pen point boxes for holding extra points.

Another office accessory was (and still is) the stamp and envelope moistener. Various types of these were produced, primarily of glass or metal. Some had rollers covered with sponge that revolved in their water-filled containers; others had gummed surface tops. Sponge cups were made in a great variety of shapes and of pressed and cut glass as well as fancy crystal.

Most offices had cups or holders for straight pins. In 1908, you could buy a beautiful fancy crystal pin cup for a dime. Pin holders of wood with cushion tops came complete with 360 pins each. Lithographed boxes holding several sizes of pins are well worth collecting—if you can find them.

Metal desk blotter holders constitute another type of office accessory. Many of these were curved in much the same manner as a chair rocker, but others were flat. Blotters were held by clamps. Some of the holders had small metal knobs, while others had handles. Those with silver handles or knobs are very desirable.

Various types of boxes were used to hold stamps in the office of bygone days. There were nickled stamp boxes with hinged lids and others which were closed by snap devices. Most of these were similar to match safes in shape.

Metal racks for holding rubber stamps are collectible. A well-known type in the early part of this century was the "Universal Castor Rack," with a metal rod holding a series of revolving wheels to which the little racks for the stamps were attached. These were made with from one to four wheels finished in black enamel with silver stripes. The rods usually had a handle at the top end, but an accessory was a pad attachment which could be substituted for the handle and used to hold the ink pad. There also were spring rubber stamp racks which could be attached to a wall or some other flat surface.

Other early office accessories you may want to look out for include staple fasteners of decorated metal, check protectors which came in many novel shapes, and duplicating machines, which were quite crude in comparison with today's streamlined models.

6

The Kitchen

YESTERYEAR'S KITCHENS WERE VERITABLE STOREHOUSES OF WONDROUS gadgets, implements, and devices; and from the old-time kitchen come perhaps more of today's collectibles than from any other room in these homes of earlier decades. Some are not so valuable as many of the objects found in other rooms, but many are more intriguing.

Kitchen collectibles range from can openers to sausage stuffers, from apple parers to sieves, and from fruit jar wrenches to cork pressers. A good many kitchen wares are now being collected, and other items from the kitchens of the early 1900's are going to be collected soon. The purpose of this chapter is to review and identify certain objects now being collected, and certain others likely to be; so that if you wish, you can join the search with at least a modicum of knowledge.

For those interested in kitchen wares of the very early homes in this country, one of the finest references available is Mary Earle Gould's *The Early American House* (Charles E. Tuttle Company, Rutland, Vermont).

Can openers, corkscrews, cork pulls and pressers, and fruit jar wrenches compose a category in which kinships exist. Various kinds of corkscrews or pullers have been manufactured through the years. Probably the simplest type was a steel wire spiral screw which was attached to a small oblong wooden handle. In 1909, one popular type was called "Walker's Universal Self-Puller." This had a nickel-plated steel wire spiral screw, with a crown, seal and aluminum stopper opener, and wire cutter. These were attached to a small, round metal bar which fitted into a wooden handle. They sold for $4.50 a dozen. Simple pullers of this type are in use today.

Much more handsome and ornate types also were in service at the opening of the century. Some had fine pearl handles mounted on sterling silver with the metal screw attached. Others boasted embossed sterling silver handles. These were fairly expensive, wholesaling from $21 to $39 a dozen. There was a popular miniature corkscrew in which the screw was rivited to an oval chased sterling silver handle, the screw folding inside the handle when not in use. These were $12 a dozen. An extremely handsome one came attached to a silver-mounted stag horn handle and sold for $2. The "Magic Pocket Cork Screw" featured a screw concealed inside a sterling silver cover. The House of Quality in Chicago offered a cork puller with a chased silver handle in 1907 at $7.20, wholesale. One interesting type housed a screw within a silver case in the shape of a bottle just 3 inches long. It sold for $5 in 1908.

Bottle openers also were manufactured in a variety of shapes and sizes, but their appearance on the market came later than that of corkscrews. The more expensive types of these also had silver handles, and some were sold in jewelry stores. Earlier in this century they were referred to primarily as "cap removers," and one type of fine steel cap remover with a sterling chased silver handle was offered in 1907 at $1.60, wholesale. There were, of course, a great many less expensive ones made entirely of steel.

Can openers were in almost universal use well before the advent of the cap remover. One early type was manufactured by Sargeant & Co., of New York City and New Haven, and was called the "Sargent-Sprague" opener. These had steel cutting blades housed in narrow metal slots and attached to either steel or wooden handles. They wholesaled from $2 to $2.25 a dozen with $2.50 being asked for a type with a handle of imitation ebony wood. A cheaper two-piece type had a cutting blade attached by a screw to a metal handle.

The "Star" opener was an adjustable device and cost $7.25 a dozen, wholesale, about the turn of the century. Popular types in 1905 included the "Delmonico," the "Boston," and the "Peerless." The "Boston" could cut two different size openings without any adjustment, turning the edge of the tin outward.

You should be able to find a great many can openers at very low prices, but corkscrews and bottle openers with fancy handles in silver, brass, pearl, or stag will come higher. Bottle openers featuring figures on their handles are worth from $4 up, and figure-type corkscrews may cost you more than some really unusual ones.

Ice shavers, chippers, and breakers were in use many years before the advent of the electric refrigrator. So, too, were ice awls or picks. The simplest ice awls for cutting block ice had rather thick blades and pointed picks attached to either iron or wooden handles and retailed for about a quarter

Kitchen implements of 1900. At the top are a bottle opener, a champagne tap, a cork presser, and assorted corkscrews. Below, center, is a fruit jar wrench and to its right, a lemon squeezer. Along the third row are a flour sifter, soap holder, and two egg beaters. On the next-to-bottom row from left to right are a wooden rim sieve, a flour sifter, a meat press, and a flour bin with a built-in sifter. Bottom row: coffee and tea strainers, an extension strainer, and a fruit-jelly-soup strainer.

each in the latter part of last century. By the end of the century the steel blades had become much thinner, and they could be bought with enameled handles.

Chippers were used to chip ice quickly to the necessary fineness for cooling or freezing purposes. One type made by the American Machine Company, of Philadelphia, around 1885 had four heavy metal pointed tines attached to a thick metal back. It was held by a wooden handle. The ice chisel was simpler, consisting of a tang, or metal prong, with four pointed tines attached by a brass ferrule to a wooden handle. You broke the ice with it by using a stabbing motion.

In 1900, the "Gem" ice shave was in use. Made by North Bros. Manufacturing Company, Philadelphia, it consisted of an oblong metal case resembling an iron plane in shape, with a cutting blade. The shaved ice was scooped up inside the metal case. When it was filled, the lid was raised and the contents emptied. The shave was especially useful for shaving ice from blocks without removing the latter from the ice box or refrigerator.

The ice breaker was used for breaking off large pieces of ice. One type had two points which were held in contact with the ice until the piece was separated by the blows of a hammer, leaving a clean break. There also was a big, wheel-operated ice breaker for use in hotels, restaurants, and institutions. The machines were equipped with two combs through which metal teeth passed. One comb was designed for yielding coarse pieces of ice and the other for finer pieces.

Ice picks, chips, shavers, and the small breakers should be worth from a dollar or two to several dollars each, depending on their age and intricacy. Picks with spring-action handles are worth about $2.50 to $3. Ice tongs for use in the home also are collectible. Those that were hand-forged are worth more than the factory-produced ones, but they also are scarcer.

There are numerous types of fruit juice squeezers and juice extractors which were widely used before the electric juicers came on the market. Those most frequently encountered are the simple metal or wooden lemon squeezers. The lemon was sliced in two pieces. One half at a time was placed inside a concave chamber, and the juice was forced out through holes in the bottom of this chamber when one pressed together the device's handles to force the convex top half of the squeezer (or a ball) down on the lemon. In 1885, the "Star" lemon squeezers manufactured by Jennings & Company sold for $5 a dozen, wholesale. They were made of tinned malleable iron. In 1900, simple wooden squeezers were selling by the thousands. Those with a bowl and ball of aluminum and handles of cherry wood cost $48 a gross. Those with porcelain balls and bowls and maple handles were $3 a gross cheaper. Some with wooden bowls and balls cost only $9 or $10 a gross. Other lemon squeez-

Left to right, top row: two fruit and vegetable slicers and a one-knife vegetable cutter. Second row: Tucker & Dorsey Manufacturing Company slaw cutters. Third row: lemon squeezers. Fourth row: lemon squeezer, ice tongs, ice cream disher, and glass lemon juice extractor. Fifth row: Enterprise lard press, cedar wash tub, tin strainer pail, and mincing knife. Bottom: bread and meat slicer with a 17-inch knife, and an apple-paring machine invented by Charles P. Carter, of New York City, and patented in 1849.

ers made of malleable iron, triple tinned, cost from $14 to $18 a gross.

There also were presses for mashing berries, small fruits, and lard. These usually were made of iron and steel, being operated by means of a crank handle. They also were called jelly presses, because the juice extracted from the fruit was so often used for making jelly and marmalade. In a similar category was the sausage stuffer, which was utilized to press sausage meat into casings. Often the fruit, lard, and jelly presses, and the sausage stuffers, were manufactured as a single unit; one of the best-known makes of these in the late 1900's was produced by the Enterprise Manufacturing Company. These wholesaled from $2.50 to $9 each, depending upon their capacity and whether they were made of galvanized iron or were japanned.

There were dozens of types of meat choppers, most of which clamped to a table top and were operated by a crank-type handle. This type was used well into the 1900's. They cost only a few dollars each for the smaller sizes.

Many similar articles for preparing food in the kitchen ought to be preserved for the edification of today's young housewives. These include slaw and kraut cutters (wooden frames with blades in the bottom); many types of cleavers, choppers, and mincing knives for cutting or mincing meats and vegetables; meat pounders; the "Steakgreith," a device with metal blades for tenderizing beef steaks; cake and bread makers (some types of which are still in use today); potato slicers and mashers; egg beaters and cream whippers; graters and shredders for such things as nutmeg, vegetables, and cheese; and measures of various types.

In another group were the fabulous cherry and raisin seeders, apple corers, parers and cutters, and peach stoners—few of which the young homemaker of today has ever seen. The "Rollman" cherry seeder was heralded in a 1909 catalogue of Norvell-Shapleigh Hardware Company, of St. Louis, Missouri, as a device which would seed 20 quarts of cherries an hour, leaving the cherries whole. It was equipped with a seed-extracting knife, which drove the seeds into one dish and threw the cherries into another. Other popular cherry seeders included the "Enterprise" and the "Goodell."

One type of peach stoner was designed to be used in the hand. The peach was placed inside an iron holder with a hole in the bottom. A metal rod was thrust through the center of the peach, pushing the stone through the hole. Stoners also could be clamped to a table top.

A simple type of apple cutter was a tool with cutting edges that was placed over an apple and then pressed down upon it, cutting it into eighths or twelfths, depending upon the number of cutting edges. It dug out the apple core while cutting the fruit and also could be used for cutting potatoes for making French fries.

Apple parers and corers were far more intricate: usually made of cast iron with steel knives, they were designed to be clamped to a table top. Some were equipped with a "push off," which pushed the apple off the machine after it had been pared and cored. These were operated by means of a crank handle attached to a flywheel.

Peach parers and corers were similar. Raisin seeders extracted the seeds from raisins and from fresh grapes.

Some of these devices should be included in any collection of nineteenth- or early-twentieth-century kitchen utensils.

Another collectible category embraces sieves, sifters, strainers, riddles, and funnels. The bulk of these were made of tin and were used to do such things as sift flour for bread, strain gravy, milk, jelly, and other liquids. The riddle actually is more often associated with sifting sand and gravel than foods. The colander is one type of strainer used for draining off liquids.

Milk skimmers usually had a deep perforated bowl attached to a handle, but some types had flat metal perforated disks attached to a handle.

Wall or table-top coffee mills, of course, were accessories in the majority of kitchens last century and early in this one for grinding the coffee beans. Numerous types were made. Some were entirely of iron; while others were made of iron with wooden backs; there were types that had iron hoppers and cranks but wooden box-like cases, and another kind had hoppers of Britannia metal; still others were made of a combination of metal and glass. Some mills had metal-lined drawers of wood to catch the pulverized coffee; others utilized tin cups for this purpose.

They came in so many sizes and shapes and are still so relatively plentiful that a most interesting collection of them can be assembled. Those with decorated cases which bear the manufacturers' labels are most desirable. They may be found today at prices of from about $9 to $25. They frequently come up for sale at country auctions or may be found in many small antique shops.

Not primarily for use in the kitchen, but associated with foods prepared there, were a variety of triers and testers for sampling foods and food commodities. You could operate them by inserting them into a quantity of the commodity to be tested and extracting a small sample. These include cheese, butter, flour, tallow, grain, ham, seed, coffee, and wheat triers. There also are sugar and flour augurs and samplers and flour testers. Most of the triers were scoop-like devices made of cast steel with handles. The grain, coffee, and seed triers, however, were hollow metal tubes with an opening about a third of the way from the bottom. The triers and testers were made in various lengths because of the varying sizes of the containers to be sampled.

Dippers, which were so common in kitchens until well into this century,

ENTERPRISE

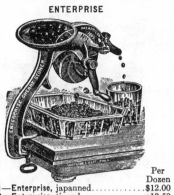

Per Dozen
—Enterprise, japanned...........$12.00
2—Enterprise, tinned...............13.50
dozen in a case; weight per case 125 lbs.

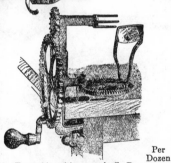

No. 90—New Lightning, the most rapid hand-paring machine. One forward movement of the handle pares an apple from stem to blossom. A return of the handle pushes the apple off the fork.
Per Dozen..$14.00

One dozen in a case.

Weight 42 lbs.

Per Dozen
72—Turntable, without pushoff. Does ood work and gives satisfaction......$7.00
One dozen in a case. Weight 40 lbs.

CHERRY SEEDERS
GOODELL

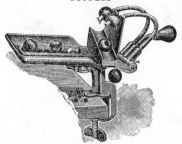

Per Dozen
No. 10—Goodell, family size, japanned.. $9.00
One dozen in a case; weight 20 lbs.

APPLE PARERS

Per Dozen
No. 98—Improved Turn Table, weight per dozen, 35 lbs..........................$14.00

Per Dozen
No. 15—Bay State, family size, weight per dozen, 40 lbs. $28.00
No. 35—Bay State, large size, with push-off, weight per dozen, 156 lbs........ 66.00

FLY TRAPS

Per Dozen
No. 3B—Balloon, plated wire gauze..$2.30
One dozen in a case; weight 8 lbs.

ROLLMAN

Seeds 20 quarts in an hour and leaves the cherry whole. Per Dozen
No. 5—Rollman, tinned, weight per dozen, 42 lbs.................................$12.50
One dozen in a case.

Per Dozen
No. 78—Reading, automatic push-off, improved curved knife, weight per dozen, 55 lbs...............................$14.00

PARERS, CORERS AND SLICERS, WITH PUSH-OFF.
Per Dozen
No. 55—Daisy...........................$ 8.50
No. 50—White Mountain.............. 10.50

FLY KILLERS

Per Dozen
No. 2—Bigelow, wire broom blade, well secured to neat wood handle, entire length 18 inches.. $1.70

Per Dozen
2P—Paragon, green wire, tin top.... $2.50
One dozen in a case; weight 10 lbs.

A page from the 1909 catalogue of Norvell-Shapleigh Hardware Company, St. Louis, showing a fine group of cherry seeders, apple parers and corers, and fly traps with their wholesale prices for that year.

Kitchenwares of years ago. Reading left to right, top row: japanned bread box, coffee cannister and tea cannister, box grater, dredge box, food chopper, and vegetable slicer. Second row: sausage stuffer, family grist mill, fruit and jelly press and milk kettle with bail. Third row: apple parer, peach parer, and a pair of Britannia dippers. Fourth row: granite ware coffee boiler, De Muth's biscuit beater, and Eclipse bread maker. Bottom row: four graters, a sorghum skimmer, and a biscuit cutter, and doughnut cutter.

are rarely used today except in rural homes; but they once were turned out in so many shapes and sizes and of so many different materials that they virtually challenge the adventurous to make a collection of them. Hundreds of thousands of dippers were made of stamped tinware, some with steel and some with wooden handles. Many were oval in shape, some round. Some had flat bottoms and flared tops. Dippers also were made of glass and of gourds, and some were made of Britannia metal. Because they were so abundant not too long ago, they can be bought quite inexpensively now, and thousands of them are still around somewhere in the older homes, likely out of sight.

Biscuit beaters, once clamped to numerous kitchen tables, should not be overlooked. These consisted of round steel rollers in a frame and were operated with a crank handle. The dough for bread was fed through the rollers and came out just right for cutting out biscuits. Some biscuit beaters were made complete with their own tables with a slab of marble on top, though some tables were made with wooden tops. Around 1900, the combination tables and beaters sold from about $13 to $20 each, and the beaters alone were several dollars cheaper.

An entire book could be written about the other kitchen collectibles, but, here's a brief listing of some of them to watch out for:

Biscuit, doughnut, and cookie cutters; food molds of all types; rolling pins of wood and glass; blue-and-white and other types of enameled or granite ware coffee pots, and boilers; tea kettles, milk, or rice boilers, measures, and other enameled ware items; flour boxes; nickel-plated coffee pots; bread mixers; flour scoops and other scoops; early wooden chopping bowls; butter paddles; pastry crimpers; noodle cutters; early wooden spoons and forks; salt boxes of wood or stoneware; butter molds, stamps, and boxes; churns; cheese ladders, (used to hold the drainer when making cheese); spice boxes and cabinets; iron pots, kettles, and pans; long-handled frying pans; trivets of all types, particularly the triangular ones used for sad irons and the round ones for coffee pots; early tin, glass, and earthenware pitchers; toasters; waffle and wafer irons; skewers; sardine shears or scissors; pot hooks; fish scalers; and canning jars.

Canning jars, in fact, are just beginning to be widely collected as a phase in the bottle craze which has now been in progress for several years. These jars, chiefly in pint and quart sizes, were produced by the hundreds of thousands and are still abundant, but their values are going up nevertheless. They may now be found in a price range of 50 or 75 cents to several dollars each with very scarce types bringing $15 to $40. The trick is to distinguish between relatively modern jars and the old ones. Mason fruit jars, for example, have varied little in their basic design for more than a century. The very early ones have pontil marks and sheared lips, and also a "keystone" design in the glass. The Mason glass jar was patented November 30, 1858. In an article in the February, 1956, issue of *The Antiques Journal,* Katharine Morrison McClinton says the first Mason jars were blown by Samuel Crowley in southern New Jersey.

Among the names found on other collectible canning jars of glass are: Acme, Atlas, Ball, Climax, Consolidated, Dandy, Drey, Globe, Knox, Lightning, Quick Seal, Sealfast, Victory, Whiteman.

Don't just rush out and buy any canning jars you come across. Learn something about the collectible types first. To help you in this respect, Ronald B. Burris—of 2941 Campus Drive, Visalia, California 93277—has written *An Illustrated Guide for Collecting Fruit Jars.* This contains a price guide and is available direct from the author at $1.75 a copy, plus a small postage and handling charge when ordered by mail.

Here are some recently-advertised prices of kitchen collectibles (though in your area values may vary somewhat from these):

White House bread mixer, tin, $10; iron lemon squeezer, handled, $5; wooden squeezer, $4.75; wooden-handled potato mashers, $2; wooden butter paddles, $2; wooden spoons, 75 cents and $1; rolling pins, $1 to $10; meat press, $12.50; brass pie crimper, $4; wooden pastry crimper, $3.75; round bread board, undercut for fingers, $5; Crown noodle cutter, $3.50; iron chopper with wooden shaft, $3.50; doughnut cutter with handle, $4; and handmade wooden flour scoop, $12.

Values of numerous types of kitchen wares have been compiled by Louise K. Lantz, who has written a book about them entitled *Price Guide to Old Kitchenware,* which is available from the author at Box 155A, Williams Road, Hydes, Maryland 21082, at $2 a copy.

Of course, kitchen wares larger than those mentioned in this chapter (such as ice cream freezers and boilers) may also be collected; but many are so bulky that they are difficult to either display or use. Of course, too, some of the items listed above—including items of so-called granite ware, wooden chopping bowls and ladles, and so on—were still being produced not many years ago and are pictured in catalogues of the 1930's.

Very early kitchen wares are discussed with great authority by Mary Earle Gould in two of her other books, *Early American Wooden Ware* and *Antique Tin & Tole Ware,* published by Charles E. Tuttle Company, Rutland, Vermont.

7

Serving Trays, Baskets, and Bowls

PAINTED TIN AND TOLE ARTICLES OF VARIOUS TYPES—PARTICULARLY THOSE associated with the Pennsylvania Dutch country—have been eagerly sought by collectors for some time. There are some beautiful trays in this category, but the early ones are scarce and are becoming scarcer.

On the other hand, there are available today thousands of late-nineteenth- and early-twentieth-century trays of tin and other materials which not only are worth collecting but which can be used advantageously in the home for such purposes as serving coffee, tea, or other beverages; snacks, fruit, cake, and so on.

These collectible trays were designed for many items—from beer to bread, to bon bon—and many are available right now at prices anyone can afford. They were made in numerous sizes and shapes, ornamented and unornamented, and of such materials—in addition to tin—as papier-mâché, silverplate, nickel, copper, and glass.

Beer and soft-drink trays compose a category in themselves. Many of these were made in the past (and, of course, many are still being made) by breweries and soft drink companies to advertise their products. They were often lettered with the name of the company or of the product, in addition to being otherwise decorated or embellished. Such trays with attractive scenes lithographed in colors are particularly desirable; and some of these, it should be noted, were lithographed in 8 to 12 colors.

In addition to the various trays issued on behalf of beer companies, early ones advertising such soft drinks as Coca-Cola, Moxie, Dr. Swett's Root Beer, and Pepsi Cola are going to be increasingly sought.

Inexpensive lithographed steel trays, circa 1910.

Stencil design beer trays were issued bearing such names as Budweiser, Knickerbocker, Bohemian, Schaefer, Pabst, Rheingold, Ballantine, Ruppert, Narragansett, Krug and others. A good many drink trays are decorated with depictions of attractive young women, scenery, flowers, convivial men, dogs and other animals, fruits, and sometimes of breweries.

During the first quarter of this century, drink trays of various sizes with scenery and people lithographed in colors were quite popular and sold for as little as $1.95 a dozen. Soft drink trays and beer trays can be picked up now in some antiques shops and second-hand establishments at prices of from $1.50 to $5. Not long ago one individual advertised a lot of 25 early tin trays advertising Coca-Cola for $12.50, but it is doubtful that you will find many at a price this low now.

So many of these advertising trays of tin were issued that you can specialize in types, such as those with likenesses of theatrical stars, or girls in bathing suits, or flowers. You might want to try decorating a wall of your den or playroom with trays lithographed in colors.

Coffee, tea, and chocolate trays were frequently produced as part of a set that consisted of a tray, a coffee, tea, or chocolate pot, a creamer, and a sugar

These lithographed steel trays were advertised in 1915 at $1.95 a dozen, whole-sale. They were lithographed in eight to twelve colors.

bowl. A great many of these were made in plated silver late last century. Although the phrase "silver-plate" is frequently used now to denote plated silver, it should be borne in mind that plated silver is not solid silver but is silver applied to a base of other metal—copper, German or nickel silver (an alloy of nickel, copper, and zinc), or white metal—usually by the electroplating method. The method was patented by an English firm in 1840 and came into general use shortly thereafter. In this method, an electric current is used to lay a coating of silver on the base metal.

Since these electroplated wares could be turned out by mass-production factory methods, these pieces were far less expensive than genuine silver plate. Electroplated wares were made by dozens of companies in this country and elsewhere, including most of the older established silver firms. Largely for economic reasons, electroplate replaced Sheffield plate in the latter part of last century.

Much electroplated ware is being ignored now because the silver has worn off and the articles thus have a dull appearance. But this ware can be easily stripped and replated with silver—a procedure about which there is absolutely nothing immoral, even for the fastidious collector. Moreover, some of these wares need nothing more than the application of a good silver polish to bring back the luster.

Plated silver articles should be judged primarily by form, shape, and decoration. Some are quite attractive; some are mediocre; and some are rather atrocious. Designs on the articles we shall discuss range from rococo through baroque. Scores of classic designs were copied in late-nineteenth-century American electroplated wares. Mechanical mass-production methods were used to cast or mold the design, while chasing was used to complete the design or touch it up a bit. There was some hand engraving but most of this type of work was done by an impressing process.

The Rogers brothers in the United States made the electroplating process

The two large serving trays on this page are beautifully decorated and were electroplated on nickel silver by John Round & Son, Ltd., of Sheffield, England. At the right top is a crumb scraper and below is a novel plated card receiver. Bottom, left to right: a cigar tray and accessories, a 7-inch diameter waiter tray, and a handled card receiver.

truly practical just before the turn of the century, and in the ensuing years designers almost literally ran rampant. At first, they copied classic designs, but later they turned to countries in Europe and the Orient for their decorative ideas. The designs of one manufacturer frequently were copied by others in their search for something that would appeal to the masses of buyers of electroplate, so producers began patenting their designs; but even this did not prevent the "borrowing" of basic ideas which then were utilized with a few alterations, additions, or subtractions.

As a result, one will encounter today a great deal of electroplated ware that appears to be in poor taste; but it must be remembered that the ware was designed for the masses, that it had to be relatively low priced, and that creative geniuses do not come at a dime a dozen. And the manufacturers did make available for lower-income families wares of a type better than that to which they had been accustomed, so the level of appreciation of somewhat better artistry was raised throughout the country.

The tendency toward over-ornamentation and utilization of the high rococo have subsided today, and we have trended to much greater simplicity. This is all to the good, but it certainly does not necessarily follow that the gaudiness of an earlier period was all to the bad.

Incidentally, there are some differences among types of the decoration of silver-plate and other metals. *Engraving* is done by cutting lines into the metal. *Repoussé* work is done by raising a design in relief by hammering on the metal. When we refer to *embossing,* we generally mean work of this type achieved by hammering from the back of the article, while *chasing* is done by hammering from the front. (Unfortunately, chasing has also commonly come to mean ornamentation done by either engraving or embossing. But don't concern yourself too much with the terms.)

Quadruple-plate refers to plated ware with a relatively heavy coating of silver. *Triple-plate* has a bit less. Quadruple- and triple-plated trays—once a part of coffee, tea, and chocolate sets—can sometimes be found in quite good condition, but if they appear dull, try a little silver polish and elbow grease. It is often worth the effort.

A 1900 Otto Young & Company catalogue offered an attractive quadruple-plated five-piece coffee set, including tray, for $16.25. The pieces were hand-engraved, and had a beaded trimming; the creamer and spooner were gold-lined. The same company offered individual pieces of these beverage sets, for sale with trays, priced at $3 to $6.25. Most trays were either round or oblong.

Bread, cake, and fruit trays made of plated silver were used by thousands of families early in this century, while only the wealthier could afford those of sterling silver. Otto Young featured a sterling bread tray, hand burnished,

Top to bottom from left: Crumb tray and scraper, handsomely decorated cake tray, and satin-finished waiter tray. With the exception of the crumb set at the top right and the sandwich tray next to the bottom, the other trays on this page are for bread.

with an attractive chased border for $28. It was 13 inches long and 6 inches wide. Quadruple-plated bread trays, on the other hand, were advertised at prices of from $2.10 to $6. Rococo borders were popular and are livelier than the rather plain beaded borders. Some of these trays had the word "Bread" engraved in the center; others bore the phrase "Give us this day our daily bread."

Quite a number of attractive bread trays were offered in 1907 by A. L. Jordan Cutlery Company, of St. Louis, Missouri. Those in quadruple-silver-plate ranged in price from $2.75 to $11.75. Bread trays of nickel ware, engraved, were made early in this century by the W. H. Sweeney Manufacturing Company, of Brooklyn, and by other firms. Prices of these inexpensive wares ranged from $3 to $5 a dozen! One popular Sweeney design was given the trade name "Carpathian."

Handled cake and fruit baskets were made earlier in a great variety of designs and shapes. As this century opened, you could find quadruple-plated baskets with either flat, round bases or with feet—or with a combination of both. You could buy a variety of them with interestingly embossed or chased borders and handles, while others were lined with gold. It's fun to make a study of the handles. There was one type of handle embossed with a trimming of grapes; others featured floral or geometrical designs. Floral and rococo-type decorations also often adorned the centers of the basket trays. A great many baskets were lacquered so they wouldn't tarnish. You can do the same thing with plated silver today if you wish.

Plated fruit and nut containers were fashioned as relatively shallow bowls or in footed compote shapes. One company—I. De Keyser & Company, of New York City, an importer and jobber—offered porcelain cake trays housed in zinc and brass frames. Its Deft decorated trays in brass frames were quite attractive. These sold for only $45 a dozen, wholesale, early in this century.

The late-nineteenth- and early-twentieth-century bread-and-cake trays and baskets today make fine containers for sandwiches and other snacks. Incidentally, Marshall Field & Company, of Chicago, offered a group of special sandwich and snack trays silver-plated on nickel at prices of $13 to $16.50 each in 1919.

Fairly large general-purpose serving trays offer a wide field to the collector. These trays—either round or oblong and with engraved centers and rococo borders—were popular early in the 1900's. W. H. Sweeney issued a catalogue in 1906 that illustrated a tremendous variety of nickel (and other) plated metal trays with elaborately-engraved centers. You are likely to find some of these around today. They bore such trade names as "Windsor," "Oxford," "Brighton," "Newport," "Corinthian," "Royal," "Manhattan," and "Richmond."

Nickel-plated serving and crumb trays and brushes of the early 1900's.

The Rochester Stamping Company, of New York City, made a line of nickel-plated trays (some of nickel-plated brass), including bread, cake, and fruit trays; some with pierced handles and openwork borders. Oriental-type designs were featured on the centers of some of these.

Do you remember the heyday of the crumb tray? Sets consisting of a metal tray and metal scraper or brush were used as late as the years immediately following World War I but are not too frequently encountered today. Thousands of silver-plated sets of this type—for use in scraping crumbs from the tablecloth after a meal—were sold early in this century. Less expensive were nickel-plated sets. Some of these trays also had openwork handles, while others had handles of wood, frequently imitating ebony.

Ornamentation of the crumb sets was closely akin to that of serving trays, including the rococo borders. Quadruple-plated scrapers sold for as little as $1.06 and matching trays for $1.44 as the century opened. But a bit of inflation set in soon, because similar sets in 1907 were selling at prices of from $4.10 to $15. The nickel-plated brass sets cost $10 to $33 a dozen sets at wholesale. If you wanted to get into the really inexpensive type, you bought those of nickel-plated block tin, which cost only $3 to $9 a dozen.

W. H. Sweeney offered a "hand" set, which was appealing. The tray's shape resembled that of a pair of hands and the scraper was in the shape of a single hand. You could buy a set of this type in nickel-plated brass at retail for around $2. The crumb brushes, which sometimes were used instead of metal scrapers, customarily had backs or handles of metal.

The quaintest trays were made for children, the better ones having been made of quadruple-silver-plate and the less expensive ones of tin. Adorned with scenes of child life, they were designed for use either on high chairs or the table itself. Some ingenious inventor devised a type with wire springs, which permitted it to be clamped to the table top so it could not be easily overturned. This feature undoubtedly was a great comfort to mothers and maids. Among the popular scenes on children's trays were those illustrating fairy tales. At least one company produced trays with Oriental decor. Alphabet plates and other articles designed for the use or amusement of babies and small children are discussed later in this book in chapter 22.

Celery, asparagus, and lettuce trays were oblong and frequently footed, sometimes with a glass liner fitted inside. Oblong spoon trays were sometimes used for sweetmeats.

In another category are fancy metal trays and bowls for bon bons and other candies, salted nuts, and fruit and berries. There were some extremely interesting glass berry bowls in metal frames. Bohemian and other colored glass bowls of this kind are prized items today. The glass was made in colors of rose, heliotrope, pink, green, and ivory. Shaded glass bowls were not uncommon; and of course, some were made of fine crystal and of cut glass. Your mouth probably will water at some of the berry bowls of cut glass in quadruple-silver-plated frames which were advertised in 1900 at prices starting at $1.88. Those made of Bohemian glass ranged from $2.20 to $7, and shaded glass could be purchased for only a dollar or two more. Today, many of these will fetch $35 to $75 each.

Card trays (or "card receivers," as they once were termed) were in widespread use earlier in this century: some of them shallow and flat, others footed. These were used, as their name implies, to receive the calling cards of one's visitors in the days when it was the fashion for men as well as ladies to carry personal engraved name cards when calling on newcomers to the neighborhood or when visiting individuals or families for the first time. Round card receivers normally measured about 3 or 4 inches in diameter; other trays were oblong. It is the richly-embossed tray of this type that will attract the collector's attention.

We mustn't forget that many of our ancestors smoked, perhaps not having heard about lung cancer and that sort of thing; and there are thousands of collectible ash trays around today. These were fashioned of many materials and in a great diversity of shapes.

Since ash trays can still be used around most homes, you may find that some of the early ones will lend interest to your rooms. Intriguing novelties in plated silver and other metals were produced in abundance early in this century. A few of these may surprise you, revealing that some of our ancestors were not particularly prudish, regardless of what we may have heard about them. We are speaking now of the types which featured scantily-clad (and even unclad) young ladies as decorations. You could buy simple ones of this risqué type at the turn of this century at prices of from 80 cents to about $2. Our ancestors loved color and articles that had a lavish or rich appearance, so it is not surprising to find gold-lined ash trays in some of the early catalogues.

Combination ash trays and match stands were fabricated of tin, bronze, cast iron, and other substances. One tray rather widely in evidence early in the century was of cast bronze in an ornamented antique finish with a safety match box holder attached. These had leather or cloth padded bases so they wouldn't mar the furniture.

Much costlier ash trays of heavily-plated silver in reproductions of antique Dutch were in use during World War I. These were made in various shapes and sizes and were decorated with embossed Dutch scenes. Depending on size and shape, they retailed from around $1.50 to $11 each. One type had a partially-covered top and was box-shaped with tiny feet. It had two metal cigar or cigarette holders and a match box holder attached. Others were made with the match containers atop the handles.

Also available were smoking sets in metal, glass, or china, housed on a tray. These usually included a cigar holder, ash receiver, and match safe. A few sets were housed in metal boxes, richly embellished with scrolls and other designs.

Early pottery and porcelain ash receivers and trays are of great interest, but apparently not too many survive. Just as was the case with glass, they were easily broken when knocked off on the floor, or dropped or mishandled in cleaning.

Match safes have been collected for years—but they are in another category and have been written about rather exhaustively. Match cases are discussed later in this book in Chapter 10.

If you have any artistic talent, don't shy away from trays with interesting shapes but whose decorations have worn off. If you can find them for a dollar or two, decorate them yourself. You may thus create a handsome piece for use in your home. If you don't know how to go about this, there's a book available for your guidance. It's Maria D. Murray's *Art of Tray Painting*

Trays of the nineteenth century. Reading left to right, top row: card tray, waiter, and crumb tray. Second row: pin or trinket tray, crumb scraper, and ash tray. Third row: group of card receivers. Bottom: ash trays.

(Studio Publications, distributed by the Viking Press, New York City).

Incidentally, a perfectly fabulous series of serving trays was produced in the latter part of the nineteenth century by John Round & Sons, Ltd., of Sheffield, England, and some found their way into this country. These were large hand-engraved trays electroplated on nickel silver. Those depicting birds and dogs were done with remarkable artistry.

8

Hook Your Wagon to a Hook

A ROSE MAY BE ONLY A ROSE; BUT A HOOK IS A COAT HANGER, A SUPPORTER OF bird cages, a stalwart in the picture gallery, an essential of the chandelier, an ally of the hammock, and more.

A hook, says the *American College Dictionary,* is "a curved or angular piece of metal or other firm substance catching, pulling, or sustaining something." And who wants to collect curved or angular pieces of metal? Perhaps you may after investigating what wondrous chores the lowly hook has performed and what a truly splendid appearance it actually has made in hundreds of thousands of homes and buildings over the land.

Unquestionably, the fellow who devised the first hook dreamed neither of the uses for which it would be subsequently employed nor the deviating forms it would assume in the hands of men of talent and imagination.

We shall deal in this chapter with collectible hooks of the nineteenth and early twentieth centuries and discuss some of the uses to which they were put. We hope the accompanying illustrations will convince you that many of them were attractive and intriguing as well as utilitarian, and that as a result you may wish to set out on your own to discover some of the other uses to which the hook has been put through the years.

One of the most commonplace uses of hooks a century ago and less was as a support for coats and hats. In the hallways of homes of the 1880's, the hook did valiant duty as a temporary resting place for milady's bonnet, the gentleman's bowler, topcoats, raincoats, shawls, umbrellas, and other assorted articles of apparel. Iron hooks, often japanned and coppered, were entranceway or hallway essentials in late Victorian homes. They were attached to the wall by a metal support, which often was an integral part of the hook itself. One might characterize one type of these as three-part hooks consisting of a support, an upper hook for hats, and a lower hook for coats.

This type of hat-and-coat hook was shipped out by manufacturers in barrels and sold by the pound. The upper and lower branches of the hook frequently had finial-type attachments or knobs, so that hats and coats could be hung easily and without damage.

Some of these hooks were attached to the wall by the use of screws—holes having been bored in the supports—while other types had screw ends, and were simply screwed into the wall by turning the hook itself. There was still another type with wrought nails which flanged out when driven into the wall.

Hooks were made with single, double, and triple prongs, and there also were some ornate types with as many as five prongs. Hat-and-coat hooks made of embossed or otherwise decorated metal will be of chief interest to today's collector. Many of these were designed by creative artists who realized that the lowly hat and coat hook could, if treated with something akin to loving care, make its own aesthetic contribution to décor.

Berlin bronzed hooks with geometrical and leaf designs gave a little zip to otherwise drab hallways—and sometimes to school and hotel corridors and "cloak closets" in offices and mercantile establishments. Berlin bronzed metal showed a contrast between a dark background and a much brighter exterior surface, which was ground to give it a sheen. There also were Tuscan bronzed hooks, which were similar, except that they did not have the ground surfaces.

Of special interest are hooks with openwork designs, metal knobs imitating acorns, porcelain knobs, or decorated cast brass; and those with faces or figures as an integral part of the hook.

One interesting hook of the 1880's had the appearance of a curved tree limb with sawed-off branches and leaf, and with porcelain knobs decorated with rosettes. They wholesaled at $72 a gross in cast brass, polished and lacquered; and $87 a gross in bronze metal.

A type made of japanned iron and with openwork leaves and vines and porcelain knobs sold at wholesale for $24 a gross. This same type in cast brass was $84 a gross and in bronze, $108 a gross.

Somewhat later, hooks attached to wooden backs came into popularity. The hooks were usually finished in either nickel or brass plate. Some of these hat-and-coat racks had either metal or wooden hooks with fancy brass balls on their tips. Others were made with small mirrors in the center of the wooden backs.

Another type in use in 1900 had simple nickel or brass-plated hooks attached to two parallel oblong pieces of oak molding. They came with two to six hooks. Some had hooks which could be turned flat against the wall when

An "art" hat-and-coat hook made in the latter part of last century, of cast bronze with a hand-chased figure. It measures 16 by 13 inches at its greatest width.

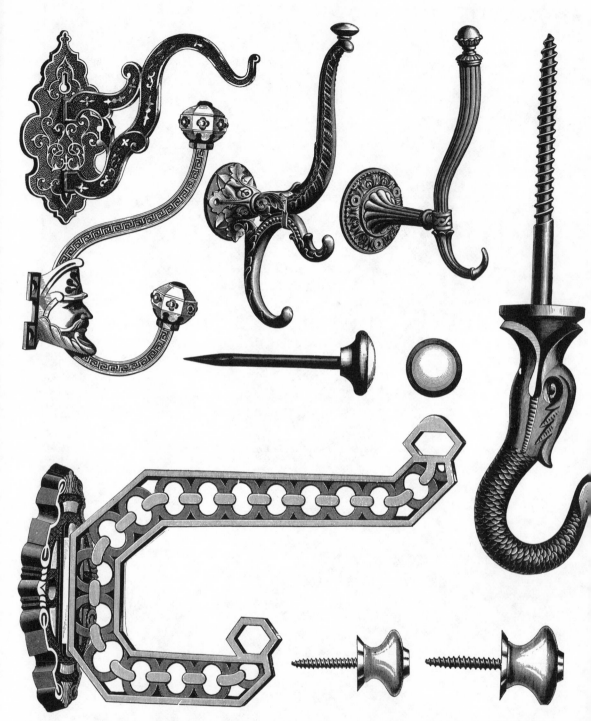

Bird cage hook (top left) with a hat-and-coat hook just below, and to the right, two hall-stand hooks and a Dolphin chandelier hook. In the center below, the hallstand hooks are a picture nail with a porcelain head and a picture nail head. Bottom, left, is another hat-and-coat hook, and at right are two porcelain picture knobs.

not in use. One type called the "Phoenix" consisted of a series of malleable, tinned detachable hooks with parallel rods across their tops attached to a narrow wooden panel of oak.

Sales have been reported recently of the bulky, awkward-looking hall coat-and-hat stands that had hooks attached and long mirrors in the center. Well, everyone to his own taste.

Accordion-type wooden racks with wooden knobs are not nearly so interesting as the decorated metal hooks. Neither are the simple hat pins of wood.

Bird-cage hooks are of great interest and date back to antiquity, but many delightful ones are now available from the middle and late nineteenth century. (Bird-cage collecting is a field in itself, and we shall deal here only with the hooks designed to hold these cages either vertically or horizontally.) Dozens of bird cage hooks were delightfully adorned, and some were extremely elaborate, reflecting the rococo in taste at its ornate extreme. These hooks were made of cast iron, brass, bronze, and bronzed wire. Some were designed to be attached to the wall or ceiling with screws; others had screw ends as a part of the hook itself. Openwork arms with hook ends or with swinging hooks attached to an open end can provide an interesting collection in themselves. Some hooks had oval arms, while others had flat arms gaudily embossed. There also were swinging hooks, which could be placed at any angle or turned back against the wall when not in use. There were small wire hooks attached to bronze and other metal bases for hanging light-weight cages, which could be bought painted green, red or blue.

Despite the intricacy of their designs, these bird-cage hooks were quite inexpensive, selling at wholesale for as little as $1 to $5.75 a dozen in 1885.

Spring cage hooks could be purchased in 1900 for as little as $4.50 a gross, and those of steel wire sold for $9.50 to $15 a gross. While these are not of nearly so much interest as the more ornate ones, an example or two should be included in any bird-cage-hook collection.

Bird cage hooks can be used in the home for hanging flower arrangements in baskets, or for hanging similar small types of flower containers and other objects.

Back in the days when chandeliers were in vogue, quite heavy hooks were used for suspending them from the tall ceilings. These were produced in various designs and patterns. (You'll have a real treasure if you can find one in the Dolphin pattern, complete with imitation fish scales.) The chandelier hooks were made with long screws so that the heavy chandeliers could be held securely close to the ceiling. These hooks were made of japanned iron, bronze, and cast brass. One type was decorated with a Grecian pattern.

Lamp hooks were also manufactured, and were much lighter and usually less ornate. Both the old chandelier and lamp hooks can be used today for hanging lamps, which are coming back into vogue.

Decorated solid brass molding hooks about 65 years old.

Largely neglected thus far, but not at all deserving of this fate, are picture and molding hooks used by our grandfathers and great-grandfathers for suspending paintings, prints, and other framed pictorials from the ceiling moldings and walls.

Thousands of these were once made in fancy-stamped brass, steel, nickel, and even silver. The molding hooks were fashioned in the shape of an "S" curve, a rolled-back edge fitting over the molding and the other edge turned up so that the wire attached to the picture frame could be hung over it. Other picture hooks had a flat metal back surface so they could be nailed or attached by screws to the wall in a position lower than the moldings.

The plain hooks are of little interest, but those stamped with floral, geometrical and other designs should be preserved.

Now while the hook collector may be content to limit herself to the picture hooks, the picture accessory collector will insist, happily, upon extending her collection to picture nails and picture knobs. Of interest here are the porcelain and glass knobs and the picture nails with porcelain and glass heads. Ruby, green, and blue glass heads were most popular early in this century. They were made of pressed, blown and molded glass; some were cut. Wholesale prices for the picture nails with plain porcelain heads were around $2.40 to $2.80 a gross, but those with colored glass heads cost a little more.

The picture nails to search for most avidly are those with decorated colored glass heads and silver-plated burnished rims. Some glass centers were even decorated with gold, and of course these were the highest priced of all —as much as $6 a gross! *Be certain not to hammer on the glass heads, which were not permanently attached to the nails.*

Some of the picture knobs (which were screwed into the wall) had fancy glass centers made of ruby, green, or blue glass. The best of them had silver-plated rims and bases.

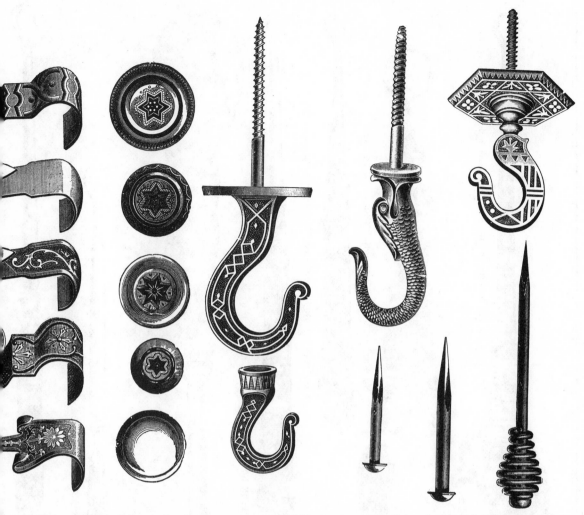

Left to right: Picture hooks for use over molding, picture nail heads, chandelier hooks, and (below) two picture nails of coppered steel wire and a picture nail of crown steel wire with a coiled wire spring.

Wardrobe hooks—which were similar to hat and coat hooks but usually much plainer and hardly ever decorated—are of some minor interest, and those desiring to assemble an exhaustive collection of hooks should include one or two of them.

Cup hooks of the late nineteenth century are worth seeking. Designed to hang cups in cabinets or on cup racks, they all had the same basic form with only slight differences. Most were of japanned iron, brass wire, or cast brass. They ranged in length from three-fourths of an inch to 2 inches. Cup hooks

QUADRUPLE PLATE SILVERWARE.

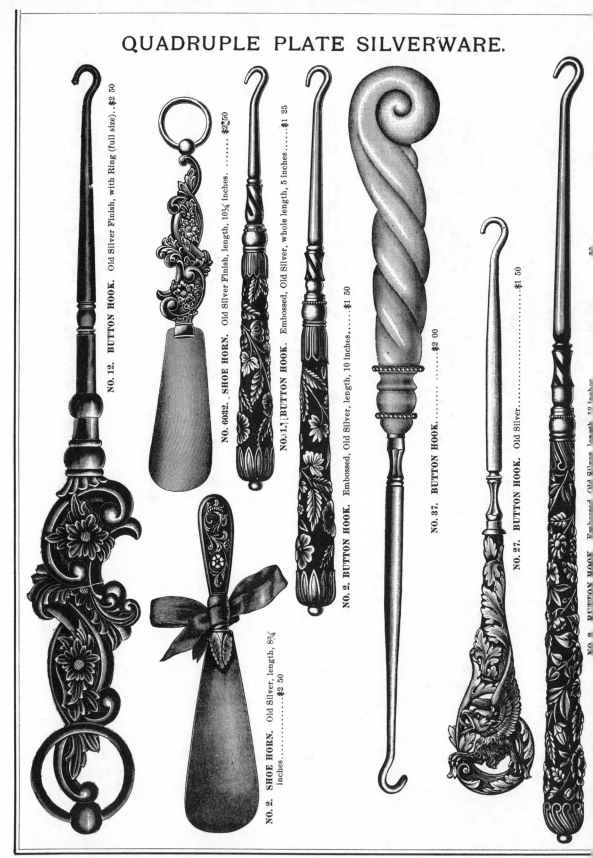

NO. 12. BUTTON HOOK. Old Silver Finish, with Ring (full size)..$2 50

NO. 6082. SHOE HORN. Old Silver Finish, length, 10¼ inches........$2 50

NO. 11. BUTTON HOOK. Embossed, Old Silver, whole length, 5 inches.....$1 25

NO. 2. SHOE HORN. Old Silver, length, 8¾ inches.................$2 50

NO. 2. BUTTON HOOK. Embossed, Old Silver, length, 10 inches.....$1 50

NO. 37. BUTTON HOOK.........$2 00

NO. 27. BUTTON HOOK. Old Silver...........$1 50

These delightful button hooks and shoe horns were sold by B. F. Norris, Alister & Co. in 1892.

of the same general type as those used 75 years ago are still being made, but the cup collector will be interested in trying to locate the older one for use in displaying her collection.

Lacquered and polished brass tassel hooks, which can be used for holding a variety of objects from towels to wash cloths, were made in several shapes and designs.

Nor, in the field of hooks, should we ignore those little devices which once rendered such yeoman service in the boudoir—button and glove hooks. Milady's dress today isn't adorned with as many buttons as once was the case, but in the days of high-button shoes the female of the species would have had a difficult time completing her dressing without the aid of those simple but versatile hooks. In its heyday the button hook's use was by no means limited to shoes: it often was pressed into service to fasten buttons on the male's heavily-starched shirt, and while a special glove hook was made (differing only in dimensions from button hooks), it frequently doubled as a glove hook as well.

Many shoe emporia in days gone by, and a few other mercantile establishments as well, gave button hooks to their customers; but these were quite simple and inexpensive devices which today are worth little. It is the ornate button hook which the collector will seek. These came with handles of silver, ivory, horn, wood, plastic, and even gold. Some hooks were combined with knives or other devices, and sometimes folded into a neat case.

A check of catalogues issued early in this century shows that button hooks with sterling silver handles were available then at prices of from 75 cents to $1.50. A silver-plated hook in a satin-lined case was advertised in 1886 for $3.80, which was quite a large sum then.

You can find desirable button hooks and glove hooks now at prices of from around a dollar to about $10. One of the country's top button hook collectors, Bertha L. Betensley, wrote a booklet about these interesting devices just a few years ago. It is entitled *Buttonhooks to Trade — to Treasure* (published by the author, 5042 North St. Louis Avenue, Chicago 25, Illinois). Miss Betensley points out in her booklet that almost all of the wooden handles on button hooks were hand-turned so that no two are precisely alike.

Giveaway button hooks, mentioned earlier, sometimes had the names of the dealers stamped on them. These are much more desirable than the unidentified giveaway devices. A fair-sized collection of these could be assembled; and while they might not be particularly valuable from a monetary standpoint, they could compose an interesting collection.

Anyone interested in collecting button hooks may also be intrigued by shoe horns and glove hooks. In its 1900 catalogue, Otto Young & Company offered an attractive ebony-handled button hook at 54 cents, wholesale. This company featured a set consisting of a steel button hook and nail file and an ivory tooth brush—all mounted on a card—at $2. It sold truly elegant shoe horns with nickel-plated steel blades and an imitation amethyst setting in the handles at $12 a dozen. In its 1892 catalogue, B. F. Norris, Alister & Company depicts an extraordinary button hook with a silver-plated handle in the shape of a mythical creature with wings and long claws. The price to the retailer was $1.50.

Other generally less interesting types of hooks include gate hooks and cabin hooks; also those for holding hammocks, clothes lines, and harnesses.

9

Decorated and Decorative Stands

ORNATE METAL UMBRELLA STANDS, WHICH STOOD IN THE ENTRANCE HALLS
to most middle- and upper-class homes in this country from the period of the
last half of the nineteenth century through World War I, have now largely
fallen into disuse. The fact is, however, that they can serve a most useful purpose today on almost anyone's porch or entrance stoop or outside the entrances
to apartments. They are among a group of special types of metal stands, which
also include fireset, blower, match and display stands, for which tomorrow's
collectors are likely to be on the lookout.

Brass and bronze are probably the most desirable umbrella stands, and
because they are currently largely unloved and unsought, you may be able
to pick some of them up for a trifle—at least in comparison with what you
may have to shell out for them a few years hence.

One type of umbrella stand closely resembles the early fire iron stands:
it consists of a metal upright, usually handled. Near its top is a series of circular openings through which the closed umbrellas may be placed; at its bottom is a trough-like base, often footed, which receives the umbrella tip and
allows the water to drain into it. These customarily were a bit less than three
feet in height. Those the collector will be interested in are of decorated metal
—often in solid colors, including green and gold. In 1885, these sold for
around $5 each at retail, sometimes a bit less.

More commonplace types consisted of a hollow cylinder of metal, most
often brass, sometimes plain and sometimes decorated with embossing. The
bottoms of these were weighted so they could not be easily overturned. The
majority stood 20 to 24 inches high and were capacious enough for half a

Umbrella stand

Umbrella stand

dozen or more umbrellas. As late as 1915, this type was being advertised by retail stores for $1.65 to $2 each.

In addition, there were umbrella stands of stoneware and pottery, some gaily colored and others bearing modeling in relief. Some of these stands were produced by potteries which were either then or have subsequently become famous. For example, there was advertised some time ago a majolica-type umbrella stand made by Wedgwood which featured a modeled likeness of Neptune's head and with glazes of turquoise, rose olive, white, and lavender. Not only was the stand fancy; so was the price: $200.

A pottery stand made by the pottery firm founded by Samuel A. Weller in Zanesville, Ohio, and decorated with yellow and gold flowers is offered at $85—with a few chips.

A number of pottery umbrella stands were imported from the Orient. An Imari stand, decorated in dark blue, gold, and orange-red, is tendered at $95. An old blue-and-white Canton china stand is offered at $35. Sixty-five dollars is the asking price for a celadon holder and a footed celadon jardiniere to match.

Some inexpensive umbrella stands were made of bamboo with a metal holder at the bottom, and these can often be picked up at prices of $7.50 to $15.

A majolica-type stand decorated with a likeness of Independence Hall in Philadelphia and the Liberty Bell is advertised at $30. And a stand made in the Staffordshire pottery district of England, embellished with Chinese waterfall scenes, bears a $50 price tag.

On the other hand, numerous American metal stands well worth salvaging have been tendered of late at prices of from $10 to $15, and the better of these could be "sleepers." One quite popular type of brass stand was adorned with lion-head handles on opposite sides. Others were decorated with such things as birds (including storks), animals, and flowers.

Bases of the old umbrella stands can be used for plants if you simply must have another planter—but why not use the stands for their original purpose?

You're likely to find a good many umbrella stands in old homes, and you may find some in the junk and salvage yards.

Also available in some quantity are attractive metal stands designed to hold fire irons—shovels, pokers, and tongs. These often bore quite sprightly decorations, and some are strikingly handsome and would grace the prettiest fireplace. Those of bronzed metal proved to be both utilitarian and decorative accessories in the homes of a few generations ago, and could serve the same purposes today.

Although a great many fire iron sets were originally sold with stands, many stands were also sold separately and in a very wide range of prices, depend-

Collectible stands. At top, left to right, a fire iron stand, a cottage fire iron set on a stand, and an umbrella stand. Below: two pickle caster stands and a caster stand with individual pepper, salt, butter plate, and napkin ring.

ing upon their quality. They varied in height from around 23 to 32 inches. In 1884, prices of these on a wholesale basis ranged from $17.50 to $192 a dozen. The highest-priced were made of heavy bronze and were beautifully decorated.

Many less expensive stands were made as a part of cottage fire iron sets during the same period. Sometimes these stands were sold separately from their sets of tools. A Tuscan bronzed stand of this type with open metalwork wholesaled at $14.85 a dozen.

In a similar category were blower stands, made to hold fire bellows. Some of these were in the shape of lyres and could be bought in Berlin bronze or green or gold bronze, among other finishes. Wholesale prices in 1884 were from $6.50 to $17 a dozen.

Match stands, discussed briefly in an earlier chapter, should ensnare some collectors because they were produced in so many designs, and also because they are relatively so small that a large collection of them can be assembled in a small display area. Thousands were made in cast bronze, bronzed iron, and spun brass.

And, of course, in the category of very small stands, there are the inkstands, already being earnestly collected by a dedicated band of men and women, most of whom also seek inkwells, pens, and some allied writing paraphernalia.

Stands for accommodating inkwells and pens were among the abundant productions of a century ago and were made in scores of shapes, not all of them with an eye solely to utilitarian value. The inkstands were made of Britannia metal, iron, porcelain, pottery, papier mâché, glass, and other materials. They were square, oblong, oval, round, octagonal; they were manufactured with feet, pedestals, and flat bases. Beyond the pale of the impecunious are those made of silver and other precious metals. Many, naturally, came equipped with their own ink bottles and some with even stamp boxes and pen wipers.

Some rather fantastic inkstands were made of such things as yak horns, deer's heads, and horses' hooves. Inkstands are available today at prices of from a dollar or two up—the desirable ones often being quite costly.

Small display stands such as were used in numerous types of mercantile establishments not only are collectible but will serve a very useful purpose for collectors of such things as hatpins, fans, tableware and certain other small objects.

For example, hatpin stands once used in jewelry stores and other shops held 25 to 50 hat pins for display to customers; and if you're a hatpin collector, they will make ideal display stands for your own collection. Normally, these stands consisted of a plated upright rod to which were attached one or more arched crossbars, each with small depressions into which the hatpins were inserted, point down.

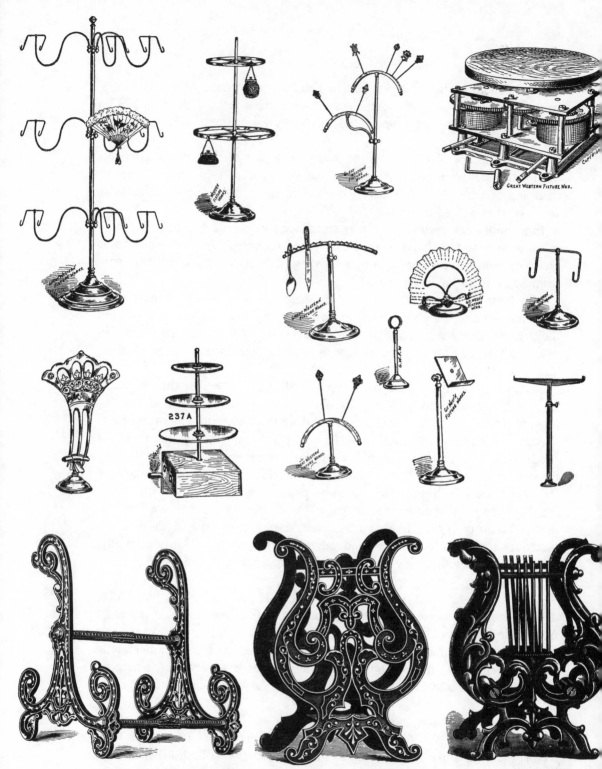

Miscellaneous display and blower stands. Left to right, top: fan, chatelaine bag, and tier hat pin stands, and motor with turn table for display uses. Second row: comb stand, display stand with motor, knife-fork-spoon-scissors, and two fan stands and (center) miniature card, and stick pin and (below) hat pin, tilting top boxed goods, and telescoping glass shelf stands. Bottom row: blower stands. The majority of the display stands were made by the Great Western Fixture Works.

Inkstands produced between 1893 and 1907.

Inexpensive library inkstands of 1908.

Though still available, these lovely plated fruit stands with their delightful colored glass bowls are growing scarcer — and costlier. They were used interchangeably for fruit and berries.

Handsome stands once held such things as berry bowls, vases, and toilet sets. The two quadruple-plated ones shown at top and center held berry bowls of decorated glass. The one at top right is a vase stand and the two at bottom hold toilet sets of decorated glass.

Choice late nineteenth century fruit or berry stands with glass baskets.

Fan stands—for use on store counters or in display windows—were made by attaching a series of nickel-plated or brass holders on arms to an upright post with a flat base. Fan collectors can use these for their collections. Some held a single fan; others several.

Stands for displaying knives, forks, spoons, and scissors consisted of an arm attached to a telescoping base. The arms had slots into which the tableware or scissors could be placed. These can be used to show off one's choice items of tableware, souvenir spoons, or scissors. A similar type of display rack for these items consisted of an arm screwed to a wall, but this was not properly a stand.

Also available are comb stands, stickpin and baby pin stands, and even chatelaine bag stands. And of interest to collectors of dozens of types of small antiques are the metal stands with glass shelves graduating toward a smaller size at the top.

Some display stands were equipped with clockwork motors, which would keep them revolving for several hours with a single winding. Early in this century, small ones of this type could be bought for $5 or $6—but don't bother with trying to find them at such prices today.

Ring and watch stands are discussed in Chapter 19.

10

Buy the Case

IT MIGHT SURPRISE YOU TO LEARN BY HOW MANY YEARS THE VOGUE FOR carrying cigarette and cigar cases predated the discovery of the alleged relationship between smoking and lung cancer.

The cigar case was only one of many types of small cases which were fashionable in the nineteenth century. Others included cases for calling cards, spectacles, matches, jewelry, court plasters, combs and brushes, and face powder. They have been made for more than a century and a half, but those specifically for cigarettes weren't manufactured in this country until after 1867, which marked the beginning of commercial cigarette production here.

The earliest cigar cases were of decorated papier mâché and were relatively small, because cigars in those days were small. In the latter part of last century cigar and cigarette cases of leather were turned out in some abundance. Some leather cigarette cases resembled card cases, and in fact many were used interchangeably for these two purposes. Some cases folded over and were closed with a button lock; others were two-part affairs with the case made to fit inside an outer cover. Seal-leather cigar or cigarette cases could be bought at the opening of this century for $1 to $2, including those with little silver shield decorations or corners.

Silver and silver-plated cases became popular a little later. Some of these were lavishly engraved or decorated with repoussé work and were much costlier than the leather case. In its catalogue for 1908, A. L. Jordan Cutlery offered a silver case in French gray finish with a lion's head covering the front for $16.88, wholesale. There were silver cases with gold-washed chased interiors.

111

Less expensive silver-plated cases flooded the market about the time of World War I. Marshall Field & Company offered them at prices of $2 to $10.50. Some had separate compartments for each cigarette. They were closed by means of little clasp locks.

Marshall Field's sterling silver cases, on the other hand, were selling for as much as $43 in 1919. Some were embellished with hand-engraved, engine-turned, or hammered designs. Most of these cases had plates on which the owner's initials or name could be engraved.

Some manufacturers made identical cases in nickel silver and sterling silver with a rather substantial difference in price between the two. Some of the older sterling silver cases are selling now at prices of $15 or more. The earlier leather ones are cheaper, but there hasn't been as much interest in them.

Cigar and cigarette cases are still being produced and sold in some quantity, but far fewer persons today carry metal calling-card cases, although a good many businessmen use small leather containers for their business cards. But in the last quarter of the nineteenth century handsome calling card cases of silver and even gold were quite the fashion and the lady who went visiting without one was hardly in style. The best of these little cases were far from cheap, even in those days, and this was particularly true for those set with semi-precious stones or tiny medallions. In addition to silver and gold, these cases were made of ivory, tortoise shell, papier mâché, Sheffield plate (before it was displaced by electroplating), beadwork, and mother-of-pearl. The last-named were quite handsome and also highly popular, and they made charming accessories when decorated in patterns.

Nearly all of the card cases were hinged so they opened at one end or so that a top could be lifted off. Although a great many plain cases were utilized, patterned ones were popular and were sold in abundance to both men and women. It is the decorated ones which are of prime interest now, and particularly those made of mother-of-pearl.

Small engraved white cards bearing the owner's name were always used on formal visits, but cards in colors were often utilized on less formal occasions. Also in use in the latter part of the century were cards decorated with embossed flowers or scenes; there were hand-painted cards, too, most of which were done to order by professionals. Decorated cards also utilized decalcomania and chromolithography. Not only the card cases but the cards themselves are worth collecting today.

Around the turn of the century, some folk turned to the leather calling-card cases, and prior to World War I, combination vanity and calling-card cases of silver and silver-plate were in use. These employed a little spring holder to keep the cards in place.

An ivory card case adorned with a group of carved monks was advertised not long ago at $50. One of sterling silver with repoussé work depicting a battle was tendered at $22.50. Other silver and silver-plated cases are worth about a minimum of $5 up, and the nicer ones may be considerably "up." Calling cards were frequently pasted in scrapbooks and albums, some of which may yield these treasures today.

A promising new field for collectors is that of early spectacle or eyeglass cases. Few persons have paid any attention to these, and yet the papier mâché spectacle cases of the 1880's could provide a fertile source of interest.

Most of the papier mâché cases, oblong in shape, had one end open for inserting the eyeglasses and were decorated on their exterior surfaces. Some were made in Japan and were hand painted; others were decorated in China and imported into this country.

In addition to the open-end cases, there also were spectacle containers, which although closed at both ends, opened on one side. Floral and geometrical patterns on the outside of the cases predominated, but were not exclusively used. One early case bears a depiction of a bird among the leaves of a tree.

In addition to papier mâché, early spectacle cases—"early" in this case referring to the nineteenth century—also were made of leather (often stamped with a design), velvet-lined nickel-plated, tin, coquille (a type of wood named after the town of Coquille in Oregon, which was well known for its production of wooden novelties), silver, and plated silver; later, imitation leather, aluminum, and plastics came into use.

One type of case made in nickel-plate, and also in nickeled tin, was designed so that one side of the top half opened to permit the insertion and removal of the spectacles. Early in the twentieth century, cases were produced with patented self-closing springs, similar to those still in use in some of today's cases. Most cases were lined with velvet or velveteen to protect the lenses; half-size cases were made for the so-called "Oxford" folding glasses. What is more, many cases early in this century displayed the name of the dispensing optician lettered in gold leaf.

Cases of leather and pressed paper were also produced with button flaps.

(Other eyeglass accessories, including lorgnette chains and reels, are discussed later in this book in Chapter 20.)

Early eyeglasses themselves are just now beginning to be collected by a few persons, and here's an excellent field for research, because eyeglasses and reading glasses of various types go back many years.

Match stands were discussed earlier, but match cases of 50 and 75 years ago offer many opportunities for assembling an outstanding display. Cata-

logues of the early 1900's display numerous perfectly delightful match cases in quadruple-silver-plate. Most of these had covers embossed in designs ranging from the rococo to the patriotic. One 1900 case bears on its cover an enameled replica of the United States flag. Others were decorated with, for example, hunting scenes, flowers, and vines.

Most cases of this type had a hinged top consisting of about the top quarter of the case itself. Some were covered with leather or alligator hide. The simpler cases wholesaled for 30 to 40 cents, but the more decorative ones were priced at a dollar or two.

Cases in sterling silver and nickel silver abounded about the time of the first World War. A good many were made in shapes and designs similar to those produced at the turn of the century, but the majority—made for safety matches, which were then already in use—were thinner; they were opened and closed by means of snap locks. A large percentage of the higher-priced ones were hand-hammered or had hand-engraved designs, largely restrained in character as compared with earlier decorative devices.

Prices of those in sterling silver in 1919 ranged from around $2 to $10 at retail. In shape, design, and appearance, they were similar to the larger cigarette cases of the period.

The more affluent collector may wish to venture a bit further back in time to collect match cases or boxes made prior to and during the middle of the nineteenth century. Many boasted gold or precious and semi-precious stones. Incidentally, these cases (the word "box" is used interchangeably) also have been made of such materials as horn, ivory, brass, and tortoise shell.

Special match cases were frequently made: sometimes they would be decorated with the insignia of fraternal orders, while others were issued in connection with fairs, expositions, and other celebrations. Some businesses had special advertising match cases made for them.

Match cases from collection of Ray E. Wentworth, San Leandro, California. Top to bottom, left to right: gold-plated case with dancing figures, watchfob type; embossed sterling with a secret window which can be opened by pressing tiny button below monogram; sterling with embossed rooster; sterling with secret window, hinged from lower triangular face and activated by a match end from inside; metal with raised wishbone and cupids on both side, fob type; Elks box, in shape of elk's tooth and with rare blue enameled clock; sterling with English hallmark; World's Fair souvenir case; brass with hinged head, scratcher on belly and tail forms ring for watch chain; sterling with coat of arms and fleur de lys; sterling with raised stag design; fine silver with raised Chinese girl with musical instrument; sterling, shaped to fit hand; metal with hinges on back and mythological raised heads; solid gold with inlay; nickel-plated souvenir of Alaska-Yukon-Pacific Exposition; metal with raised figure of buffalo hunter, advertising souvenir of Buffalo Brewing Company, Sacramento; and sterling with English hallmark, combination match and coin holder and designed for wearing on chatelaine. (Photo courtesy of Mr. Wentworth.)

A splendid collection of match cases is owned by Ray E. Wentworth, of 976 San Jose Street, San Leandro, California, who operates an insurance business in Oakland. His collection embraces a number of rarities. Mr. Wentworth started collecting, virtually by accident, about 1955. He wrote an article for the October, 1965, issue of *Western Collector* that describes his exceptional collection; it is illustrated with some excellent photographs by Thelma Winnie.

An elaborate sterling-silver match case adorned with a woman's head in raised design and with a striker on the bottom is priced at $7. One of brass, decorated with the likeness of a trotting horse, is tendered at $6.50. Similar prices have prevailed recently for the more commonplace types but are likely to ascend with the diminishing supply. Truly fine and rare match cases cost a good bit more.

Fine match cases. Top (left), heavy brass with raised Chinese figure, finished front and back; and (right), case with snap top forming frog's head, known as "The frog who would a' wooing go." Below, left to right: fine brass with heavy embossed design of vines and insects (photographed upside down); sterling with decorative embossing on sides and top and scratcher on base; and brass with raised Chinese figure. (From the collection of Ray E. Wentworth, San Leandro, California, by whose courtesy this photo is used.)

Vanity cases do not date back to antiquity, but examples of the relatively early ones are of interest. Those produced early in this century were small oval or square metal ones designed to hold a dab of face powder and a very small puff or applicator, and, often a small mirror. Many dated prior to 1910 were of sterling silver with repoussé work. They were sold in jewelry and other stores at prices from $3 to $5.

By the time of World War I, no woman's purse was complete without a vanity. Nearly all of them by this time were oval or rectangular in shape, though some few were square. They had hammered or engraved designs, usually quite chaste and restrained. The more expensive ones featured 14-carat gold inlay and were priced as high as around $65. Thousands, however, in plated silver were available at prices of $4 to $10.

Cases were produced which not only held powder, a puff, and a mirror, but also contained coin holders and tiny memo tablets. Others were combination vanity and card cases. The most commonplace size was around 2½ by 3½ inches.

Some metal cases were made with ivory ornamentation and others were decorated in colors. Any with good cameo-type decorations on the covers are quite desirable. Most of these cases around the time of World War I had a chain handle and were opened and closed with a metal clasp-type lock.

Dorine boxes were very small round cases, in silver or plated silver, for powder, puff and mirror. They usually had a chain with a round metal ring attached at one end.

Fine combs have been collected for some time, but there also are collectible comb cases of sterling silver and silver-plate. These were designed primarily for small, straight combs rather than those elaborate ones which in earlier years composed a part of milady's hairdo. Many of these smaller comb cases were made for men and came equipped with a man's hair comb. These cases date back to the latter part of last century and were embossed with curlicues or miniature scenes and sometimes with figures. One embellished with a figure of a cupid was advertised in 1900 at $16.50. Sometimes the combs were attached to one end of the case. Some sets also included nail files.

In addition, embossed comb-and-brush cases with mirror centers were made. There was a pocket on one side of the case for a comb and on the other side for a brush. Made in nickel and white metal, these were quite inexpensive. Some are pictured in a 1906 catalogue of the W. H. Sweeney Manufacturing Company and are priced at only $1.75 a dozen, wholesale. They came cheaper by the gross! Earlier comb cases were made of tin and were often designed to be hung on the wall. Some of these tin cases have been advertised recently for $3 to $7 each. A few of these tin cases had tiny mirrors on the outside.

An early hand-carved wooden comb case was advertised not long ago at

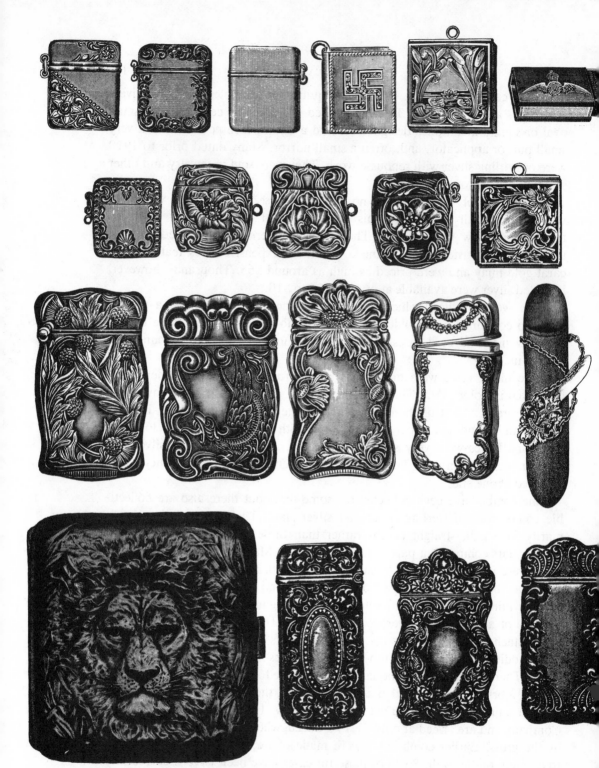

Group of sterling silver stamp cases, match cases, a lady's chatelaine spectacle case (third row right), and a cigarette case (bottom left).

A variety of cases. From left to right, top row: playing card, calling card, two court plaster cases, and papier-mâché spectacle case. Second row: two stamp cases and a group of small dorine cases. Third row: three vanity cases and a tobacco case. Bottom: match, comb, spectacle, vanity and calling card cases.

$17. It was adorned with open-work flowers and leaves and measured 15 by 20 inches. An early combination tin-and-wood case decorated with a cherub is offered at $12. One dealer advertises a tin case at $2.50. A comb case made of bone trimmed with brass is advertised at only a dollar. A combination comb case annd towel rack of wood is listed at $10; this one is decorated with half-round turned pillars on each side.

Numerous attractive embossed stamp cases of sterling silver were in use early in this century and for several years previously. Most had hinged covers and could easily be carried in one's purse. Their covers, too, were embossed and otherwise ornamented. There usually was a metal link on one side for attaching a chain. In 1900, these cost from about $8 to $16, but similar ones had dropped in price by 1907 to $1.50 to $3.

Sterling silver toothbrush cases can be collected. One type came equipped with a threaded end, in order to hold a toothbrush having a screw end. When not in use, the brush was housed inside the case; for use, the case and brush were screwed together and the case served as the handle.

Other cases that could well be collected include those made for court plasters (or "beauty spots"), tape measures, playing cards, cigar cutters, and collapsible cups. Thimble cases are discussed in Chapter 21.

11

Some Clocks - And a Few Accessories

THERE ARE CLOCK AND WATCH COLLECTORS ALL OVER THE WORLD. SOME OF the most dedicated of them in the United States are members of the National Association of Watch and Clock Collecors, one of this country's outstanding collector organizations. Its headquarters is in Columbia, Pennsylvania.

For the collector who doesn't have a fortune to spend but who would like to invest a smaller sum in the highly intriguing field of clocks and watches, novelty clocks of the late nineteenth and early twentieth centuries can offer exciting fun. So can early alarm clocks. For those with still less money to invest, there are hundreds of fobs, charms, and chains that are fascinating.

Dozens of excellent books have been written about early clocks and clock inventions, but little research in depth has been done by the experts in the field of novelty clocks. One reason is that the advanced watch and clock collectors prefer to occupy their time with older types of horological devices. But the fact is that hundreds of thousands of novelty metal and porcelain clocks were made between the beginning of the final quarter of the 1800's and about 1915. These were relatively inexpensive and had the added advantage of being quite decorative. If you need a bit of dash and ginger in your living room, look around for an ornately-ornamented eight-day mantel clock with a case of bronze or porcelain. You name the shape, size, and design—and you'll probably find a clock made to those specifications.

Dozens of pages are devoted to this type in the early catalogues of watch and clock jobbers, manufacturers, and jewelry wholesalers and retailers. Some were gold-plated with ivory dials and cast gilt sash and bezel (the rim around the glass over the dial). There were some with porcelain dials. Many were

Late-nineteenth and early-twentieth-century novelty clocks. Top row: Flashlight Electric Alarm, and Get-up Electric Alarm. Center row: Cuckoo, gold-plated clock, and Seth Thomas electric alarm. Bottom row: Music, Volunteer, Bicycle Girl, and gold-plated clocks.

The fancy bronze and gold finish clocks shown at the extreme left in top and middle rows featured ornaments representing classic and mythological figures. At right, top, is the Globe Clock. The globe made a complete revolution every 24 hours, showing the correct time in cities all over the world. Bottom left is the Negus Clock. The eyes in the face moved when the clock was operating. Bottom center is a novelty clock, whose bell was rung by the Monk to sound the alarm. An automobile clock with eight-day movement is shown at bottom right.

mounted on bronze or white metal bases which held both the clock and a cast figure or figures. Figures on these metal clock bases range from those of sword-flourishing cavaliers to demure maidens and include also winged angels, armor-clad warriors, cupids, unadorned ladies, pipe-playing shepherds (usually modelled after accepted likenesses of Pan, the mythological god of forests, fields, flocks, and shepherds), painters with palettes, long-antlered deer (and other animals), composers, writers, and historical personalities.

The cases were fitted with American-made movements by various manufacturers, and many had gong strikes which operated on the hour or the half-hour. Most of them ranged in height from 8 to 16 inches, and some measured as much as 20 inches in length along the base. A 1907 catalogue pictures a gold-plated clock 11 inches tall and 6½ inches wide with a 2½-inch ivory dial and a porcelain child seated atop the case at a wholesale price of $12.65. Other gold-plated ones ranged up to $26.65.

Prices of long, fancy clocks with bronze bases, ornaments, and cases—and gong strikes—ranged, at wholesale, in the same catalogue from $22.65 to $44.50. The shipping weight of some of these was 50 pounds or more.

Many of the bronze clocks bore names, usually associated with their cast figures. Among many others were Orpheus, Vinola, Brennus, Gaul, Cavalier, Tempest, Cinderella, Mignon, Eveline, Cupid's Dart, and Arverne.

On some bronze bases, the clock case occupied one end and the cast figure the other; but on other bases, the cast figures held up the clock case, and on still others they reclined upon or rested against the case.

During the lattter part of the nineteenth century several lines of quite inexpensive novelty or fancy clocks in bronze finish and with cast figures of white metal were produced to wholesale for as little as $3 to $7. It would cost considerably more than that to produce them today. Most of these inexpensive clocks were fitted with New Haven or Waterbury movements.

Other fancy mantel clocks of the early twentieth century were produced in onyx and porcelain, decorated in colors with flowers, scenes, scrolls, and animals. Movements were made by Waterbury, New Haven, Gilbert, and other clock companies. In 1900, prices of these at wholesale started at about $2.15 for very small ones and ranged up to $40 for the better ones. Of course, clocks of much higher quality were made at much higher prices.

Enameled iron clocks also were turned out by the thousands late last century and early in this one, and a great many of these featured cast metal ornaments. However, there has been little demand for this type. Neither has much interest been shown among collectors thus far in the enameled wood mantel clocks of the same period. On the other hand, there seems to be a mounting interest in the elaborately scrolled wooden mantel clocks, once largely used in kitchens and in rooms other than the parlor or living room. These were

Decorative novelty clocks of 1900 and their wholesale prices at that time are shown here in a page from the catalogue of Otto Young & Co.

NOVELTY CLOCKS, FINE BRONZE AND GOLD FINISH.

PUTNAM

Height 11¼ inches, width 5 inches, 2-in. porcelain dial.
Rich gold or dark bronze finish.

No. 625. 1 day time, gold........ ....$6 00
" 626. " " bronze......... ... .5 40
Jeweled sash, extra.................................... 2 00
Fitted with eight day movement, extra.............1 50
(New Haven.)

MAINTENON

Height 7⅝ inches, width 3½ inches, 2-in. porcelain dial.
Rich gold or dark bronze finish.

No. 627. 1 day time, gold.........................$4 90
" 628. " " bronze......... ....4 40
Jeweled sash, extra................................. 2 00
Fitted with 8 day movement, extra 1 50
(New Haven.)

No. 629. HIT. $5.50

Rich Roman, gold plated.
1 day lever time.
Gilt center, beveled glass.
Height 7¾ inches, 1½-inch ivory dial.
(Waterbury.)

ARIEL

Height 8 inches, width 4½ inches, 2-in. porcelain dial.
Rich gold or dark bronze finish.
Jeweled or plain sash.

No. 630. 1 day time, gold...........................$7 00
" 631. " " bronze...................... 6 30
Jeweled sash, extra.................................... 2 00
(New Haven.)

BELLONA.

Height 9¾ inches, width 6½ inches, 2-in. porcelain dial.
Rich gold or dark bronze finish.

No. 632. 1 day time, gold............ ....$7 65
" 633. " " bronze...................... 6 90
Jeweled sash, extra................................. 2 00
Fitted with eight day movement, extra............. 1 50
(New Haven.)

No. 634. PALM. $5.00

Rich Roman, gold plated.
1 day lever time.
Gilt center, beveled glass.
Height 6⅜ inches, 2 inch ivory dial.
(Waterbury.)

Ansonia and other makes of novelty clocks and alarm clocks popular at the turn of this century. The novelties wholesaled at prices of from $4.20 to $8.50 with the exception of the "Trianon A" clock (second from left on third row), which sold for $25. The alarms were priced at $1.80 to $3.60.

quite inexpensive in 1900, a large number having been available at whole-sale prices of $4.50 or $5. They are now being sold at prices of $25 to $50. Some wooden scrolled case clocks had metal trimmings and utilized pendu-lums which could be seen through the glass case. The glass was frequently decorated with painted scrolls. Most of these clocks are rather atrocious in appearance, but they were popular when first made, and for some reason which we will not attempt to explain, are becoming popular again.

This is an expression of purely personal opinion: every clock collector should have a Cuckoo clock. These have been made for more than 225 years and are largely associated with the Black Forest region of Germany. They provide a constant source of mystery and delight for children and adults alike. Most Cuckoo clocks were designed to be hung on the wall and are operated by the use of weights. Cases were carved in charming and intricate designs by skilled and apparently indefatigable artisans. Although the cases were made of various types of wood, they usually were finished in dark walnut or oak and had arbors made of iron.

On the strike, a tiny door at the top of the clock would fly open and a bird would pop out, frequently flapping his wings; he would emit a "cuckoo" song. Some of the clocks of this type were equipped with two mechanical birds: one a cuckoo and the other usually a quail. Others had different musical at-tachments, but all were activated by a bellows.

The better Cuckoo clocks, having excellent brass and steel movements, are good timekeepers. The clocks were originally priced according to the ex-cellence of their carving. An early-nineteenth-century American trade cata-logue lists a large group of these clocks at wholesale prices of $15.40 to $56.70. Some sounded on the hour, the half-hour, and the quarter-hour. The carving, incidentally, virtually always featured leaves, and sometimes also flowers and grapes.

Cuckoo clocks are still being made, but the older ones are getting scarce. Some from the Black Forest and some American-made ones are occasionally found in antique or clock shops at prices now of $25 to $75 or more. This seems quite low in view of their original cost.

Early alarm clocks in good condition are rarely seen today, but whether this is because they actually are scarce or because nobody collects them yet is open to question. Yet, many late-nineteenth-century alarm clocks are prac-tical as well as decorative.

Of interest is a group of nickel-plated frame clocks with metal handles which were used as alarm clocks as this century opened. They were available in both square and round cases, some with the alarm bell or gong inside the case and some with the bell on top. Others were made without handles but with metal rings at the top by which they could be lifted. Some were equipped

2145
Rolled Gold,
Ruby Eyes.
$0 58 each.

2146
Gold Filled,
Bright Polished,
$1 00 each.

2147
Gold Filled,
$2 85 each

2148
Street Car,
Bright Finish,
$0 58 each.

2149
Rolled Gold
Brown Sardon
Intaglio Seal
$0 58 each

2150
Fine Cut Topaz
Intaglio
$0 58 each.

2151
White Crystal,
$0 58 each.

2152
Black and White
Stone,
$0 58 each.

2153
Pig and Corn,
$0 58 each.

2154
Shoe,
Bright Finish,
$0 58 each.

2155
Bright Finish
$0 58 each.

2156
Horse, Garnet Eyes
$0 58 each.

2157
Dog, Bright Finish, Garnet Eyes.
$0 58 each.

2158
Base Ball,
$0 58 each.

2159
Opera Glass with
$0 58 each.

2160
Telephone, Bright Finish,
$1 00 each.

2161
Rolled Gold and Pearl
$0 58 each.

2162
Green Globe,
$0 58 each.

2163
Canteen, Bright Finish,
$0 58 each.

2164
Painter, Bright Fini
$0 58 each.

2165
Ear of Corn,
Rose and Green Finish,
$1 25 each.

2166
Fish,
Bright Finish,
$0 58 each.

2167
Saw, Polished Handle
Steel Blade.
$0 58 each.

2168
Revolver, Silver Finish,
Pearl Set Handle,
$0 58 each.

2169
Cleaver,
Coral Handle,
$0 58 each.

2170
Cigar, Natural
Ruby Setti
$0 58 ea

A group of novelty rolled gold charms with their wholesale prices early in this century. These are indicative of the "gadget" craze of that era.

with double alarm bells with a gong between, which struck against each outer bell surface when activated. A standard diameter for many dials was 4 inches. Produced largely between 1875 and 1910, these nickel-plated clocks sold at wholesale for $1.28 to $3.90 in 1900.

The alarms of some types sounded intermittently every few seconds for as long as 15 minutes, which should have been sufficient to awaken the soundest sleeper; others alarmed steadily for five to seven minutes with each winding. Nearly all of these had 24-hour movements.

Waterbury made a clock of this type with a perforated gilt-decorated dial and an alarm bell on top of the case. It was 6½ inches high and wholesaled for $3. Gilbert produced one with a similar dial, a second hand set in the lower part, and twin alarm bells, which wholesaled for $2.60. The latter alarmed for eight minutes with each full winding.

Seth Thomas produced a clock on a small decorated metal base which would alarm for 20 minutes. Its wholesale price was $4.16. Parker, Ansonia, New Haven, and other companies turned out similar types. Some were combination alarm and calendar clocks, an extra hand keeping track of the date on the dial face. Various models bore interesting names, including Wasp, Bee, Tocsin, Pet, Get Up, Tattoo, Mustgetup, Trolley, Buzz, Omar, Fez, Monitor, Roy Rob, Nutmeg, Wecker, Caliph, and Sunrise.

Novelty alarm clocks were on the market a few years later. One of these was a Flash-Light Electric with a stamped steel savings bank attached, complete with lock and key. Operated with two dry batteries, this contrivance had a small light in front of the clock case. A long cord with a push knob attached enabled the sleeper to turn on the light so he could see the dial and ascertain the time without moving from his comfortable place in bed. Not only that, but the clock would ring if you touched the knob to any part of the clock or frame, thereby converting it to service as a call bell. This was patented in 1904 and was priced at $11, wholesale.

Alarm clocks also were made early this century in marbleized wood cases and in bronze cases. One bronze-case alarm, which was advertised as being made for "very heavy sleepers," had an extra-strong alarm spring; the sound was emitted through open work in the base. It alarmed for 30 seconds at 30-second intervals, continuing for 12 to 15 minutes on a single winding.

One novelty alarm was made in the shape of a watch and could be used either as a hanging or standing clock. Various other novelty types were made and are worth searching for. Since little interest has been awakened thus far, you may find clocks of this type in old homes whose owners may be induced to part with them in exchange for a new alarm clock—and you undoubtedly would be getting the better of such a bargain.

The collector can have a field day in the area of watch accessories. Fobs,

PRICES EACH.

Polished, tiger eye handle.
No. 4076 Each....$2 00

Pearl handle, fine steel blade.
No. 4077 Each....$2 00

Polished, pearl handle.
No. 4078 Each 70c

Polished.
No. 4079 Each......70c

Crystal, rolled plate tongs.
No. 4080 Each 75c

Polished.
No. 4081 Each........$1

Polished.
No. 4082 Each $1 10

Polished.
No. 4083 Each......70c

Chased head, polished base, ruby eyes.
No. 4084 Each....$2 00

White pearl, rolled plate trimmings.
No. 4085 Each....$1 50

Chased, 2 views.
No. 4086 Each....$1 00

Chased, 2 views.
No. 4087 Each......

Polished, stone base.
No. 4088 Each 80c

White stone headlight, green and red stone sidelights.
No. 4089 Each...... 70c

Polished, red globe.
No. 4090 Each....$1 35

Polished
No. 4091 Each......70c

Polished, tan colored or all black
No. 4092 Each 70c

Polished.
No. 4093 Each....$1

Polished with assorted views.
No. 4099 Each......70c

White ivory, rolled plate trimmings.
No. 4100 Each....$1 75

Genuine ivory, rolled plate trimmings.
No. 4101 Each....$3 00

White ivory, rolled plate trimmings.
No. 4102 Each....$1 75

Polished, satin and chased.
No. 4103 Each....$1 60

Polished, onyx base.
No. 4104 Each..........

Polished.
No. 4105 Each........$1 10

Polished.
No. 4106 Each 70c

Chased.
No. 4107 Each 70c

Polished, intaglio stone base.
No. 4108 Each 70c

White ivory, rolled plate trimmings.
No. 4109 Each....$1 75

Polished, raised band.
No. 4110 Each ......

This group of rolled gold novelty watch-fob charms was advertised in 1906. Prices shown were retail.

charms, and chains have been produced in such abundance and variety over the years that an enormous collection of them can be assembled without duplications.

Watch charms, along with other types, are holdovers from the days when charms, or amulets as they usually were called, were used to ward off evil. Charms could be attached either to fobs of silk, leather, or other material; or directly to fancy chains. Watch chains were made so that they could be fastened by one end on the outside of the watch pocket or inside the male vest. However, use of the fob and charm was not limited to the male of the species; relatively small ones were made for the use of ladies to help them secure their small watches to their persons. Watches thus securely attached to the owner's person discouraged pickpockets. This in itself constituted substantial good fortune. Since the wrist watch has, in so many cases, supplanted the pocket watch, its fobs, chains and charms are now rarely encountered; it is no wonder that so many evils befall us.

In addition to silk and leather, fobs and fob chains were made of such materials as white metal, gold, silver, nickel, bone, horn, and woven wire.

In the late 1800's a gentleman wasn't well dressed unless he wore a vest chain, one end of which could be attached to a watch and the other end terminating in a small metal bar which could be secured through a buttonhole in the vest. The more affluent sported vest chains of solid gold, some of which cost $75 or more in the early 1900's. The cost of the chain was based upon the fineness of the gold and the weight, and a 1900 wholesale catalogue offered 14-carat gold chains at $1.75 per pennyweight, and 10-carat chains at $1.36 per pennyweight.

Vest chains were made in dozens of shapes and designs. Some links were oval, some oblong, some square. Some chains were made in mesh form, some as rope links, some as trace links. There was the "Boston link," the "California link," the "Double curb link," and the "open curb link."

Double chains were made with slides of gold and other materials. Even the end bars varied in shape. Some were round, others square; some resembled rope, others were chased or otherwise decorated. Although the vest chains varied in length, the majority were from 11 to 12½ inches long.

Nickel-plated steel vest chains with charms wholesaled in 1900 for as little as 84 cents a dozen, and heavy leather pony chains cost only 50 cents a dozen. Gold-plated chains ranged from $11.50 a dozen up.

Popular, too, were short chains attached to long silk braids with gold-filled and other types of mountings. These included the hair braid chain made of imitation hair in various colors. All types of charms were attached to the chains and braids, including cameo types made of precious and semi-precious stones, among them: bloodstone, a greenish variety of chalcedony, or trans-

FINE SILK FOB CHAINS, WITH SOLID GOLD R. P. MOUNTINGS.

CUTS SHOW EXACT SIZE.   PRICES PER DOZEN.

No. 651. $14.00
Rolled plate mountings.
Fine Im. opal in charm.

No. 652. $12.50
Rolled plated trimmings.
Imitation topaz charm.

No. 653. $12.00
Rolled plated trimmings.
Intaglio charm.

No. 654. $12.00
Rolled plated trimmings.
Imitation pink diamond.

No. 655. $8.00
Rolled plated trimmings.
Intaglio charm.

No. 656. $102.00
Solid 10k gold mountings,

No. 657. $72.00
Solid 10k gold mountings.

No. 658. $27.00
Rolled plated trimmings.

No. 659. $27.00
Rolled plated trimmings.

No. 660. $27.00
Heavy gold front, 8 fancy

448

Collectible watch fobs are available in profusion and variety. This page, from the catalogue of Otto Young & Co. shows wholesale prices in 1900.

GOLD FILLED NOVELTY VEST CHAINS.

FOR LADIES' OR GENTS' USE. ALL SOLDERED JOINTS EXCEPT Nos. 592 and 595. PRICES EACH.

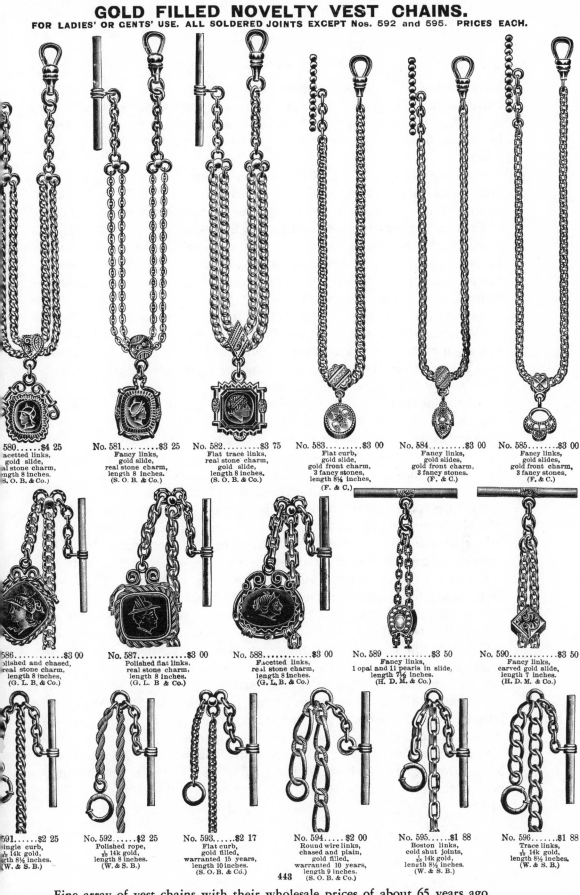

No. 580......$4 25
...acetted links,
...gold slide,
...al stone charm,
...ngth 8 inches.
(S. O. B. & Co.)

No. 581........$3 25
Fancy links,
gold slide,
real stone charm,
length 8 inches.
(S. O. B. & Co.)

No. 582........$3 75
Flat trace links,
real stone charm,
gold slide,
length 8 inches.
(S. O. B. & Co.)

No. 583........$3 00
Flat curb,
gold slide,
gold front charm,
3 fancy stones,
length 8½ inches.
(F. & C.)

No. 584........$3 00
Fancy links,
gold front charm,
3 fancy stones.
(F. & C.)

No. 585........$3 00
Fancy links,
gold slides,
gold front charm,
3 fancy stones.
(F. & C.)

No. 586........$3 00
...lished and chased,
...real stone charm,
...length 8 inches.
(G. L. B. & Co.)

No. 587........$3 00
Polished flat links,
real stone charm,
length 8 inches.
(G. L. B & Co.)

No. 588........$3 00
Facetted links,
real stone charm,
length 8 inches.
(G, L, B, & Co.)

No. 589........$3 50
Fancy links,
1 opal and 11 pearls in slide,
length 7½ inches.
(H. D. M. & Co.)

No. 590........$3 50
Fancy links,
carved gold slide,
length 7 inches.
(H. D. M. & Co.)

No. 591......$2 25
...ingle curb,
... 14k gold,
...gth 8½ inches.
(W. & S. B.)

No. 592......$2 25
Polished rope,
¹⁄₂₀ 14k gold,
length 8 inches.
(W. & S. B.)

No. 593......$2 17
Flat curb,
gold filled,
warranted 15 years,
length 10 inches.
(S. O. B. & Co.)

No. 594......$2 00
Round wire links,
chased and plain,
gold filled,
warranted 10 years,
length 9 inches.
(S. O. B. & Co.)

No. 595......$1 88
Boston links,
cold shut joints,
¹⁄₂₀ 14k gold,
length 8½ inches.
(W. & S. B.)

No. 596......$1 88
Trace links,
¹⁄₂₀ 14k gold,
length 8½ inches.
(W. & S. B.)

443

Fine array of vest chains with their wholesale prices of about 65 years ago.

lucent quartz, with bloodlike spots of jasper scattered through it. Other charms were made of, for example, pearl, horn, amethyst, garnet, carnelian, or opal. Shorter, so-called "pony" chains were made of similar materials. Classic heads were favorite designs for the intaglio-type charms over a period of some years.

Fob chains of woven wire, silk, and other substances were frequently decorated with buckles of one kind or another in the center; most buckles contained a plain surface on which the owner's name or initials could be engraved.

The charms themselves were produced in literally thousands of designs and dozens of shapes. Among them were charms resembling hearts, cow horns, colored balls, stars, bells, compasses, animal heads, anvils, horseshoes, skulls, baseballs, telephones, opera glasses, fish, tools, cigars, fruits and vegetables, lanterns, shoes, trains, and street cars.

Special charms were made for various fraternal organizations, including the Masonic groups, Benevolent and Protective Order of Elks, Odd Fellows, Woodmen of the World, and Fraternal Order of Eagles. Special charms also were made for various labor groups, including types for telegraphers, conductors, engineers, firemen, and pharmacists.

Advertising charms are of special interest: a number of companies produced them in the shape of their product. Typical of these was one in the shape of a cake of Ivory soap made for Procter & Gamble. Firms often offered these as premiums in exchange for wrappers and box tops. An excellent and rewarding collection could be built of advertising watch charms alone.

Novelty charms were predominant from about the final quarter of the 1800's through the opening years of the present century. About the time of World War I, fobs with the initials of the owner in rather large sterling silver letters gained considerable popularity. Vest chains became more sedate too. One particularly popular type of chain was worn across the vest, looped in the center with a charm or locket suspended from the center bar. These were available at retail prices of from around $3 to $50 each.

Naturally, the value of fobs, chains, and charms should depend upon the value of the material of which they are made. Those of precious metals or set with jewels will fetch substantial prices, while inexpensive types may be picked up for a dollar or two. To give you an idea of some current values, here are some recently asked prices of watch fobs:

Leather with baseball charm in custard glass attached, $5; fob with red intaglio charm, $4; leather strap with metal stirrup, $1.50; Bush Motor College fob with charm in the shape of a miniature touring car, $4; Harley Davidson advertising fobs, $3.50 and up; fob with a charm of the Ohio state seal, $4; gold-filled chain with barber's charm, $7.50; silver-plated chain with caterpillar charm of bronze, $2.50; and lady's chain of gold with a crystal slide, $10.50.

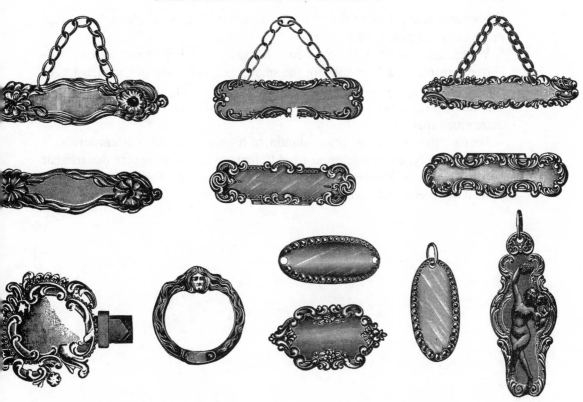

Left to right, top: sterling silver coat hangers. Second row: sterling hat marks. Bottom: umbrella clasp, figured key ring, two cane or umbrella plates, and two key checks.

One of the best ways to locate watch chains, fobs, and charms is to advertise for them in one or more of the collector periodicals and to search through the small lots of miscellaneous costume jewelry that so often are offered for sale at flea markets and auctions.

In a somewhat allied category are key rings and chains, name plates, metal coat hangers, and hat marks. About 70 years ago these were manufactured in some abundance in sterling silver and even, to a much lesser extent, in gold.

Novelty key rings were made in the shape of birds, animals, and other figures. Most of the small silver coat hangers and hat checks, (made to be placed with these garments when they were checked in restaurants and public places so the owner could readily identify his property) had borders embossed in rococo designs. So did the silver nameplates. A good many key rings were made with nameplates attached. The nameplates were round, oval, square, and oblong.

These little items were not inexpensive when made in sterling silver or gold.

Their wholesale prices at the turn of the century started at about $3.50 and ranged upward to around $20.

Watch accessories, key rings, coat hangers, and hat checks can be displayed advantageously in some of the small cases discussed in Chapter 4. An eye-catching display of them also can be arranged along a portion of a wall. The items themselves are so small that even a sizable collection doesn't require much space.

Here's a field to watch: prices should go higher than their current levels.

(Incidentally, those interested in old clocks will find a regular department on time-pieces in *Hobbies* magazine of much interest. For the past several years it has been conducted by L. W. Slaughter.)

12

Hardware: Door Accessories

FANTASTICALLY EFFICIENT MACHINES TODAY TURN OUT HARDWARE — particularly builders' hardware — by the ton and carload to supply the demands of the greatest building boom in history. Much of it is of fine quality, but because such quantities are needed and because of the necessity for holding prices as low as feasible, much of this mass-produced hardware lacks the extra embellishment that characterized its counterpart of earlier years.

Some decades ago the designer of builders' hardware was concerned as much with decoration as he was with utility, and some hardware of earlier years obviously was designed by craftsmen who strove to create "art." Many early hand-wrought items which have come down to us were fashioned with loving care — a care that is particularly noticeable in such items as keyhole escutcheons, door knobs, and certain types of hinges. But even when the machine had largely replaced manual labor during the nineteenth century, scores of items of hardware were still produced which featured design with "eye appeal." This was true of hardware used in the erection of doors, the installation of windows, and the embellishment of chests, cabinets, and other articles of furniture. Hardware of this type imparted to the beholder a sort of aesthetic satisfaction — a sensation not too often experienced today — and this is one of the reasons why nineteenth-century hardware has become collectible and is likely to be increasingly treasured in the years ahead.

Embellishment of hardware attained a high-peak, from the collector's standpoint, in the Pennsylvania Dutch country a good many years ago; but today, collectible hardware is by no means limited to those hand-made items which required both a fertile imagination and considerable physical labor.

137

Fancy door hardware of the late 1800's — wrought barrel bolts, chain door fast, glass and wrought bronze knobs, two door pulls (the one at bottom left designed for use on banks), and a loose pin bronze butt.

Hardware designers during the latter half of the nineteenth century leaned heavily toward fancy embellishment of such otherwise mundane articles as door pulls, butts and hinges of various types, door and window bolts, chain lock hardware, cupboard catches, letter box plates, sash lifts, transom catches, and numerous other hardware items and accessories. Decorations with scrolls, flowers, and geometric designs were widely used on such hardware not only during a large part of the nineteenth century but for some years into the present century, until simplification and standardization largely took over.

If you have observed from close by the dismantling of a fine old Victorian home, store building, or hostelry erected a century ago or a little less, you undoubtedly will have seen some of the intriguing hardware of the type we are discussing here. The truth is, however, that few persons other than the employees of house-wrecking firms and the occupants of the structures themselves have had an opportunity to inspect this hardware at close range; and even many of those who have may have found the surfaces so covered with rust or dirt that they could not recognize the fascination of the design beneath the layers of grime.

Right now, few persons collect this hardware — but it definitely is collectible and, cleaned up, will make an interesting and informative display in one's home or office. The small hardware items may be mounted on walls, singly or in groups, or on large boards or small panels with a good lighting arrangement; this will show off their designs to advantage. Cleaned up and given a light coating of linseed oil, the metal items will resist additional corrosion.

The ornate hardware of the nineteenth century was not a Victorian innovation but a throwback to the Middle Ages when such things as hinges were designed to be not only utilitarian but beautiful as well. This medieval ornamentation was achieved largely by door embellishments surrounding the hinges; and incorporation of the decoration within the hinges themselves was made possible in the eighteenth and nineteenth centuries by improvements in iron and steel work.

A striking advance in hinge design was made last century with the perfection of "spiral spring butts" by the American Spiral Spring Butt Company, of New York City. In this the spring and hinge were combined, and the rod, which normally ran through the alternate cylindrical flanges of the two portions of the ordinary butt, was replaced by a cylindrical sheath containing a spiral spring. The arrangement of the spring was such that when the door was opened, the spring would be pushed backward in the direction of the coil; as a result, it would be partially uncoiled. When the door was turned loose, the spring returned with some force to its original position, pulling the door shut with it.

Increasing attention was given to ornamenting hardware by manufacturers

Ornamental turn plates for rotary door bells, and push button cases for push button door bells.

throughout the last half of the nineteenth century, and even the over-decorated items will add interest to a collection. Over-ornamentation was somewhat of a habit during the Victorian era, but it was not always necessarily a vice.

You may be able to make an arrangement with the operators of house-wrecking firms whereby you can obtain desirable hardware on houses or other structures being wrecked at very little cost. And, of course, if the idea appeals to you at all, the salvage and junk yards should be placed on your regular foraging itinerary.

There are a few individuals now who collect fancy old glass door knobs and knobs of the so-called "Bennington type." Glass door knobs were among the first pressed glass articles, dating back at least as early as the first quarter of last century. They were made by a number of well-known manufacturers, including the New England Glass Company, Bakewell & Company (which subsequently became Bakewell, Pears & Company), and the Boston & Sandwich Glass Company. The famous factory at Sandwich produced pressed glass knobs with glass screws, according to George P. and Helen McKearin in their exhaustive study *American Glass* (Crown Publishers, New York City). Free-blown and pattern-molded knobs will be difficult to find today; but there are literally thousands of other intriguing types around, many of which can be cleaned up and, if you wish, substituted for some of the less interesting door knobs now in use inside your home.

Several manufacturers made appealing door knobs in the last half of the nineteenth century. Among those producing them in fancy art metal work was the Yale & Towne Mfg. Co. (now Eaton Yale & Towne, Inc.), with general offices in New York City. An 1897 catalogue of this company illustrates art-metal door knobs as parts of doorsets which reflected the influence of the major schools of ornamentation. Most of the work was done either by the company's own designers or by outstanding architects for the company's exclusive use. The company claimed at that time that its collection of art-metal work of this kind constituted the largest line in the world.

In the catalogue referred to, the company said:

The tendency to regard the Hardware of Ornament as an important element in the general scheme of decoration of a building is steadily increasing, as is also the resulting tendency to omit such hardware from general specifications, and to reserve it for selection by the architect or his client, in the same manner as other details pertaining strictly to matters of taste and decoration. Heretofore the selection of such metal work has been confined necessarily either to special designs made to order, and therefore necessarily expensive, or to limited lines of· conventional design, of doubtful merit and of such commercial character as to be objec-

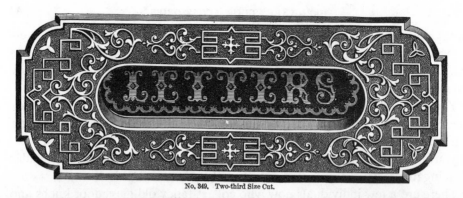

Fancy letter and newspaper door drop boxes made of bronze metal with lettered inner plates. These date to 1884.

tional to those who prefer a reasonable degree of exclusiveness in such matters. The scope of the line herein presented is so broad and varied as to meet almost every requirement of individual taste or preference and to avoid the objection of commonplaceness so justly urged against work of merely commercial character.

The Yale & Towne doorsets were available in cast brass, cast bronze, cast iron, steel, and gold- nickel- or silver-plate on bronze metal. Schools of ornamentation represented in the designs ranged from the Byzantine to the Romanesque — including in between such varied designs as, for example, the Colonial, East Indian, Elizabethan, Empire, Flemish, Gothic, Greek, Moorish, French, English, and German Renaissance. Many of these Yale & Towne sets consisting of door escutcheon, knob, letter-drop, and sometimes push-button sets reflected the grand taste in no uncertain manner, and a magnificent collection of them could be assembled with a little luck and some cash.

Door handles, latches, and pulls made also by a number of other manufacturers in the last quarter of the nineteenth century display some elaborate and appealing decoration.

A beautiful array of bronzed thumb latches, home and store door handles, locks, and pulls are pictured in the 1884 catalogue of Sargent & Co., of New York and New Haven. The plain japanned hardware of this type pales into insignificance in comparison with them, even though it served the purpose for which it was intended equally as well. Only an illustration can reveal just what fascination they possessed, unless you happen to have some of the original articles.

An examination of some of the delightful escutcheons made by Yale & Towne and other manufacturers should make us think a bit more highly of the creative imaginations of many of our nineteenth-century designers and should serve as further evidence that our ancestors were not nearly so stodgy in their tastes as we may have imagined them to be. And even though some of this hardware may strike you as being excessively gaudy, you'll hardly deny its piquancy.

Door chain and bolt fasteners of the 1880's and 1890's also reflect an imaginative bent on the part of their designers. Some spring-foot bolts could be used either at the top or the bottom of doors, and others were made for use only as door-bottom bolts. They were made in japanned iron, bronze, and cast brass.

Many barrel bolts with their round metal locking rods, which were pushed forward to lock or pulled in the opposite direction to unlock, were highly ornamented; and the knobs themselves were made of iron, bronze, brass, and porcelain. There were square bolts, which were operated either with a knob or a curved metal extrusion at one end, and chain bolts, which were unlocked by pulling the chain attached to one end. There also were mortise door bolts, which were opened by turning a key knob attached to an escutcheon or by a round knob; and flush door bolts were made with either knobs or sunken thumb pieces, which were pushed forward or pulled back to lock and unlock.

Chain door fastenings (as differentiated from chain bolts) also were often elaborately decorated affairs. Some chains were made as round links, others as square or oblong links. Their modern counterparts, which are used in some homes and many hotels and motels, are for the most part quite plain. These handsome earlier chain fastenings could perform yeoman service in today's homes, not only by keeping out intruders but also by serving as decorative accessories.

Decorated bronze butts and door hinges were made in profusion during the latter part of last century. Screws were made to match. That is, screws of

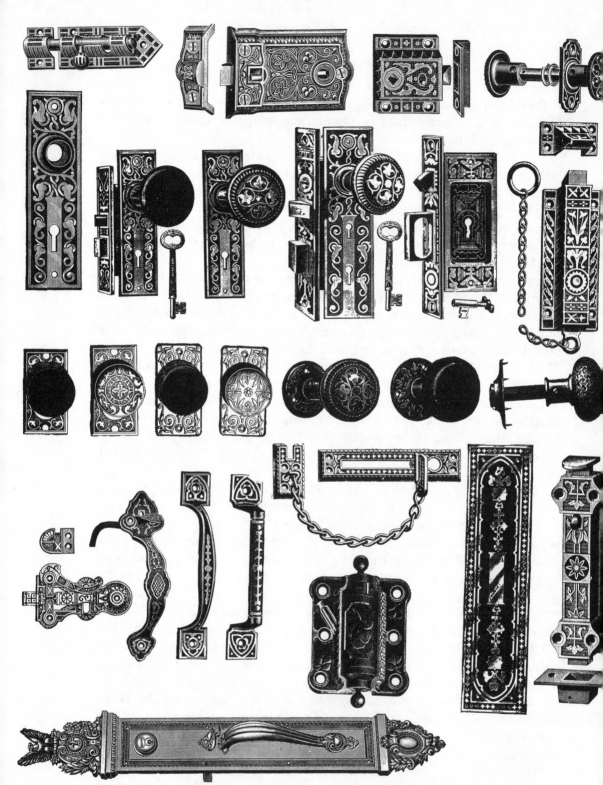

Door hardware and accessories. Left to right, top: decorated barrel bolt, two
screen door catches and an ornamental rim knob latch for screen doors. Second
row: embossed escutcheon, two embossed inside door sets, a bit key front door
set, and a sliding door set, all in Oriental design, and an ornamental chain bolt.
Third row: decorated door sets with escutcheons and knobs, and ornamental door
knobs. Fourth row: thumb latch, two door pulls, decorated chain door fast and
(below) spring hinge for screen door, door push plate, and foot bolt. A cylinder
door set with an eagle finial is shown lengthwise at the bottom.

bronze were made for the bronze metal butts and hinges, and screws plated on brass accompanied the hardware that was silver-plated or nickel-plated. The loose pins on the butts were sometimes round, sometimes acorn-shaped, sometimes grooved, with ornamentation to match that displayed on the plates. Spring hinges were decorated in much the same way as were the loose pin butts.

Door push plates came in a great variety of ornamental designs. The 1884 Sargent & Co. catalogue shows one graced with butterflies and birds. Some plain plates relieved by incised lines near the borders were lettered with the word "Push."

Letter box plates or drops — the metal plates with hinged inside plates through which the postman pushed mail, and which years ago were attached to thousands of front doors — are still found on some older homes, but their use today is limited largely to offices. They could be attached to the door with screws, either horizontally or vertically, and the inner plate of many of these bore the single word "Letters." Drops of similar shape and design, but larger, were used for newspapers, and some of these bore the lettering "For Newspapers." Some of the letter drop plates were made to match the door escutcheon plates and knobs.

Ornamented screen door catches shouldn't be neglected either, nor should inside door catches. Handles and knobs of these were made in varying sizes and several shapes. And don't overlook such interesting door accessory collectibles as transom catches and transom lifters.

13

Hardware: Window Accessories

WHEN IT COMES TO COLLECTIBLE HARDWARE, DON'T STOP WITH THE DOOR OF the old house. Take a close look at the windows too.

Window sash lifts, pulls and fasteners, and pull plates offer a host of interesting designs. Sash lifts were made primarily of steel, cast brass, bronze metal, and iron. But the metal was often electroplated with copper, or occasionally with silver. It also was often nickel-plated. Lifts were made with a finger catch so that the forefinger could be hooked beneath it and the window, or with a depressed area in the sash plate so that the fingers of both hands could be inserted.

The small lifts, made chiefly for smaller windows, usually measured 1½ to 2 inches in width, but the larger flush sash lifts ranged from 3 to more than 4 inches in length. During the nineteenth century, both types were decorated with rococo designs. The finger catches on the small lifts varied in shape; and in the combination sash lift and lock, the finger hook was pressed down to lock the sash tight. A smaller ornamental surface sash lift was made for window screens, and these are no less collectible than the window lifts.

Some of the decorated window pulls on the old houses were quite handsome indeed. They also varied in size, but not much. Some were attached to the window with two screws, others with four. Of course, plain metal sash lifts and pulls were made, but it is those with ornamentation which will attract the collector's attention.

Decorated window pulls of bronze with bronze metal screws wholesaled for $4 a dozen in the final quarter of last century. As soon as collectors

146

Window hardware and accessories. Left to right, top: 1893 opaque window shade, decorated sash lifts, side lock, two Oriental design sash locks and an Ives' Patent Oriental sash lock. Second row: Gardner's burgler proof sash lock, bar sash lift, two hook sash lifts, and sash lift and lock. Third row: shutter knobs, shutter bars, and hook sash lift. Fourth row: wood cottage curtain pole, and curtain pole trimmings. Bottom: curtain pole sets.

generally become aware of their interest, they are likely to be selling for about that much each.

A wide variety of sash fasteners or locks was produced between 75 and 100 years ago. The simplest of these were of undecorated metal (except for polishing and electroplating), but others matched the sash lifts in ornamentation. One brand, Ives Patent sash locks, was made with either an ogee or a bell tip. Still others were made with porcelain, bronze, brass, and other metal knobs. In addition to ogee and bell, the knobs and tips were designed in other fanciful shapes.

One patented fastener was known as the Crescent. A quite heavy and elaborate fastener was advertised as "Burglar Proof." The latter ranged in wholesale price in the 1880's from $2 to $30 a dozen. The simplest types of fasteners were priced as low as 47 cents a dozen! Yale & Towne made flush sash lifts to match their art door escutcheon and lock sets.

French window catches were manufactured with both metal and porcelain knobs and were similar in general appearance to many cupboard catches of the day. Sets of these early decorated catches can be cleaned up and used today as catches for the built-in cupboards in your kitchen or elsewhere in the home.

Progressing from the window to the shutter, we find a delightful array of shutter knobs in bronze, japanned iron, and other metals that can be used on today's cabinets to advantage. Some also were made of porcelain. In shape and general appearance, they were similar to picture knobs. Some had tinned bases, but better ones had silver-plated bases and naturally cost a bit more.

You should be on the lookout, too, for ornamented shutter bars, used for hooking the shutters — especially those of cast brass and bronze. What is more, wrought iron shutter bolts, although not very decorative, can still be used to bolt shutters. And both shutter screws and window sash props are of passing interest.

We can't leave the window without mentioning the hand-painted window screens of a little less than a century ago. These were originally sold in widths of from 12 inches to 48 inches, the most interesting window screen cloth being decorated with landscapes. Others had figured designs on the screen. Decorated wire cloth made by the New Jersey Wire Cloth Company was sold 70 years ago by the square foot. The same firm also made window-screen cloth in solid colors of green, black, and drab.

As this century opened, the Pennsylvania Screen Company was manufacturing its handy automatic window screen, first patented in 1895. This was made in hand-painted panels and also in solid green or black. The screen was made of hard wood, finished in oil, and when placed under the sash it adjusted itself

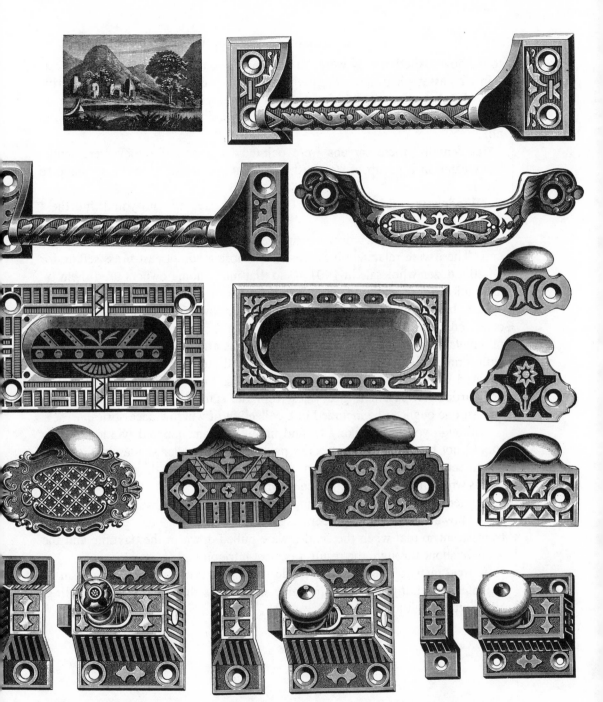

Window accessories. Left to right, top: the New Jersey Cloth company's landscape window screen cloth, and an embossed large bar sash lift. Second row: two bar sash lifts or window pulls. Third and fourth rows: window sash lifts in various designs, and bottom: French window catches.

to windows, whether they were "in square" or "out of square." This was certainly an asset when they were used in older homes, which had settled a trifle and whose windows would often be "out of square." The Pennsylvania Screen Company's automatic window screens had box panels, making both sides alike.

Incidentally, these screens were painted by hand after they were made. They came in a group of standard sizes, but special sizes could be made to order.

(Window screen brackets were frequently intriguing, and you'll find these discussed in Chapter 17.)

To deter burglars, window alarms were in use in many homes some years ago. These were relatively inexpensive — those made of cast brass selling for $4.20 a dozen wholesale in 1901 — so that many home owners used them on all windows on the ground floor. The alarms were used in connection with an electric bell; the alarm would sound if the window were opened. The device consisted, in addition to the bell — which usually was purchased separately — of a metal strip about 4 inches long, which was attached to the window frame with screws. A small protruding piece of metal attached to the alarm bar was released when the window was opened, thus setting off the bell. These were not particularly fascinating devices from the standpoint of appearance, but at least one ought to be included in a collection of window accessories.

Although you aren't likely to find many of them, painted window shades should not be ignored. The scenes painted on the roller shades in the nineteenth century may not have been great works of art, but they added color to rooms when the shades were pulled down.

Numerous shades bore paintings of outdoors scenes, still life featuring fruits, flowers and vines, seascapes, and historic places. The paintings were transparent so that when the shades were pulled down in the daytime and the sunlight shone through, the result was most intriguing.

A great many of these painted shades are worth preserving, and they can be mounted and hung in much the same manner as the ordinary oil painting, either with or without a frame.

14

Furniture Hardware

MANY ANTIQUE SHOPS TODAY CARRY AT LEAST A SMALL AMOUNT OF HARDware from early pieces of furniture. Some stock reproduction hardware to help collectors restore such missing items as pulls, knobs, and locks to their antique cabinets, chests, or desks.

But a collection of miscellaneous furniture hardware of the nineteenth century can in itself provide an informative and a most interesting display. And collecting furniture hardware can help provide an education in identifying periods and styles. This is particularly true of hardware from the Victorian period because so many earlier styles and designs were adapted and used in this country as well as in England during Victoria's long reign.

You can arrange your collection by types: drawer pulls, handles, knobs, and locks; chest hardware; cabinet bolts and locks; wardrobe and cupboard locks; desk locks; miscellaneous ring, drop, and lift handles; and even refrigerator hinges and stair buttons can be placed by a stretch of the imagination in the category of furniture hardware.

Metal drawer pulls were manufactured in remarkable variety throughout last century. In addition to the conventional period types, novelty designs were produced. Pulls were made in the shape of oak tree twigs with leaves and acorns; others were decorated with a variety of raised designs (one was in the shape of a lyre); and still others were fashioned in openwork.

One category in which a fine collection can be assembled is that of druggists' drawer pulls, many of which were turned out in fancy shapes: some with drop handles and others with finger pulls. The majority were provided with a recessed area in which identifying file labels could be placed. Some were designed for the insertion of labels from the underside after the pulls had been attached to the drawers with screws.

Intriguing drawer pulls (top left and right), drop handles (Center left and bottom right), and piano handles (center right and bottom left).

Fancy metal drop handles abounded in the late nineteenth century and came in numerous shapes and with a variety of decorations on their surfaces. Widely used was the period-brass ring handle in the shape of a lion's head with the ring in its mouth; these sold in the 1880's for only $12 a gross.

Numerous special design drop handles were manufactured for use with special design hardware but also could be used on other hardware types. For example, one flush drawer handle, made around 1900, bore on its surface a depiction of an arm and a hammer surrounded by scrollwork. It can be fun to search for types with unusual decorations such as this.

There are thousands of collectible drawer knobs around, including those of porcelain, which were often used interchangeably as shutter knobs. Fully as fascinating, if not more so, are the glass knobs, which were pressed by the leading glass factories of the middle and late nineteenth century. These were made of clear glass, milk-white glass, and in so-called vaseline, as well as in other colors. Prior to the middle of last century, blown, cut, and engraved furniture knobs were made, and there were even some in which paperweight techniques were utilized. These are far scarcer than the pressed knobs. The famous Boston & Sandwich Glass Company at Cape Cod is said to have produced literally millions of pressed-glass furniture knobs. Of course, glass knobs are still being manufactured. The old ones, depending on type, will fetch several dollars each as a rule with those in color bringing more than the ones in clear glass. Some Sandwich pressed knobs in vaseline color have recently been selling for about $5 each and up.

Chest hardware, including locks, is a fertile field for collectors. Various types of chest handles were made in bronzed and japanned metal. These were often fairly large, measuring 3 or 4 inches in both width and depth. They were heavy and sturdy because of the weight of so many chests.

Plain wrought iron chest handles were made, but most of these are not particularly interesting.

We shall discuss miscellaneous locks and keys in a separate chapter, but numerous interesting chest locks from the late nineteenth and early twentieth centuries are available for the hardware collector. They were made primarily of iron or brass with flat or round steel keys. The pin-tumbler chest locks are among the more interesting types. Drawer locks were similar. Most locks originally came complete with two sets of keys — but you'll be lucky if you find one of the original keys with the older locks.

An array of cabinet and cupboard bolts, locks, and latches is available, and many of these are quite handsomely decorated. The types popular in the late nineteenth century included square bolts, with end pull mechanisms; square cased bolts, with knobs of metal or porcelain; cupboard turns, with porcelain or metal knobs or turns, and triangular bolts; and brass pin-tumbler locks.

No. 800 AC.
ANDOVER DESIGN.

No. 800 CD.
COPLEY DESIGN.

No. 800 CC.
CHESHIRE DESIGN.

No. 800 CR.
RANDOLPH DESIGN.

No. 800 AF.
ARNON DESIGN.

No. 800 VR.
VERONA DESIGN.

No. 800 LG.
LEMNOS DESIGN.

No. 800 BG.
BULIS DESIGN.

No. 800 RG.
ROYALSTON DESIGN.

No. 800 R.
RICHMOND DESIGN.

No. 800 MC.
MILFORD DESIGN.

No. 800 RK.
ROANOKE DESIGN.

No. 800 PG.
PAROS DESIGN.

No. 800 SR.
SAVONA DESIGN.

No. 800 BF.

No. 800 TR.
TOURS DESIGN.

No. 800 MF.
MONTFORT DESIGN.

No. 800 DG.
DELPHI DESIGN.

No. 800 KG.
KIRKBY DESIGN.

No. 800 Y.
VGRANDE DESIGN.

Furniture hardware. Left to right at top: group of brass ring handles and a brass drop handle. Second and third rows: four drawer pulls. Below: group of special drop handles with their early-twentieth-century catalogue designations and names.

Furniture hardware of the late nineteenth century. Two top rows: brass drawer pulls. Third row: glass furniture knobs. Fourth row: two cupboard turns and two drawer pulls. Bottom row: two refrigerator hinges and a file drawer pull.

Furniture and window hardware. Left to right, top: three cupboard catches and two French window catches. Second row: cupboard catch, transom catch, and cabinet escutcheons of wrought and cast brass. Third row: drawer drop handle, desk knob, ring drawer handle, and drawer knob.

There also were level cupboard catches in brass, bronze, or cast iron; these operated by means of a spring. You may find you can clean up some of these ornate locks and catches for use on your contemporary cupboards or drawers. They'll add a note of liveliness.

The hinges used on some early refrigerators also were intriguingly decorated and are worth looking around for and placing in a collection. You may still be able to obtain some of these from salvage or junk yards.

And some handles for upright pianos of the nineteenth century were fabulous. If you appreciate gargoyles, you won't want to neglect these; they were made of both nickel and gold-plate.

15

Undertakers' Hardware

THE SUBJECT OF UNDERTAKERS' HARDWARE ISN'T GRUESOME AT ALL. IN fact, some of the most beautiful hardware ever made was designed for use on caskets and vaults. You probably haven't noticed this, because you normally don't spend time at funerals admiring the ornamentation of caskets. Nevertheless, coffin makers' catalogues of the late nineteenth century illustrate some strikingly beautiful designs in such things as silver-plated handles, nameplates, ornaments, and trimmings.

Engraved, embossed, and otherwise embellished coffin handles often featured metal tassels, bells, flowers, leaves, and hands. Specially-designed handles for fraternal orders included the organizations' emblems on the attached plates that held the screws.

For some reason, hands seemed to be a favorite motif for designers of casket hardware, and numerous handles utilize metal hands extending down from the screw plates to grasp the handle itself. The hands give the impression of being encased in mailed armor. Handles for children's caskets often featured representations of lambs.

Screw plates attached to the handles quite frequently took the shape of crosses, decorated with leaves, vines, and scrolls. Bars of handles were sometimes decorated with a ropelike twist.

Stock casket name plates for children bore phrases such as "Sweet Babe" and "Our Darling," lettered amidst designs of flowers. Although some silver-plated nameplates were in the shape of crosses, numerous others were round, oval, or oblong and were decorated with flowers, leaves, and birds.

There were relatively large silver-plated casket ornaments with sculptured

A group of coffin handles, ornaments, and tacks. Rose ornaments, several of which are pictured here, were favorites. Some of this coffin hardware was patented in 1875.

Silver-plated casket ornaments.

figures of Christ on the Cross, some as much as 9 inches long. Other ornaments included a hand holding a large rose, wreaths of flowers, crosses with wreaths and anchors, and long horns of the type pictured in some Biblical illustrations; and of course some ornaments were in the shape of fraternal emblems.

There were all types of silver-plated small trimmings with rococo and other designs, some in the form of stars, acorns, or roses with leaves, crosses, and rosary beads. These trimmings embraced the studs and escutcheons.

The trend in this century has been toward a simplification of casket hardware design. Nevertheless, you aren't going out digging up graves to search for casket hardware, but you may occasionally encounter stocks from manufacturers who have gone out of business.

Just the other day we chanced across a display of about half a dozen fine small items of undertakers' hardware in a newly-opened antique shop. The hardware had been mounted in an oblong frame and hung on the wall. It made a striking appearance. This is one interesting way to display these items. A glass in the front of the frame is satisfactory but not essential.

(Quite apart from casket hardware, but perhaps of interest, is the fact that "corpse preservers" were offered in the nineteenth century. The Cincinnati Coffin Company, of Cincinnati, Ohio, in its 1877 catalogue offered one divided into two sections — the upper containing a galvanized iron chamber for ice and the lower one a cooling board, slightly raised, on which the corpse was placed.)

16

Keys and Locks

MAN'S MISTRUST OF HIS FELLOW MAN EXTENDS BACK TO PREHISTORIC DAYS. And the lock — of one sort or another — extends back about as far. Literature through the ages is filled with references to locks. The earliest ones indeed were crude; but as man's appreciation of the beauties around him increased, he turned his ingenuity to the provision of locks — and, later, of keys — that not only would serve the purpose of safeguarding property but would appeal also to the aesthete which lurks somewhere within most of us.

In case you think interest in these latter days has lagged in keys and locks, be advised that one of the most fascinating collections in this country is an array of just such security devices assembled over a period of many years and section includes locks and door ornamentation created for Eaton Yale & & Towne, Inc.

The collection really dates back to 1868 when Linus Yale, Jr., and Henry R. Towne formed a partnership to manufacture the pin-tumbler cylinder lock invented by the former. The display contains scores of early security devices, including antique locks and door ornamentation originally in a collection assembled in 1883 by Andreas Dillinger, a Viennese locksmith and historian.

It also contains ancient Roman keys acquired by Nathaniel Meyer Rothschild, antique locks once owned by Kaiser Franz Joseph I of Austria-Hungary, the Emery collection of European and Asian locks, art hardware and tools owned by Ohio Mechanics Institute, and American antique locks comprising the Gillian W. B. Bailey Collection. The collection's Modern Art Hardware section includes locks and door ornamentation created for Eaton Yale & Towne, Inc., by a number of noted artists.

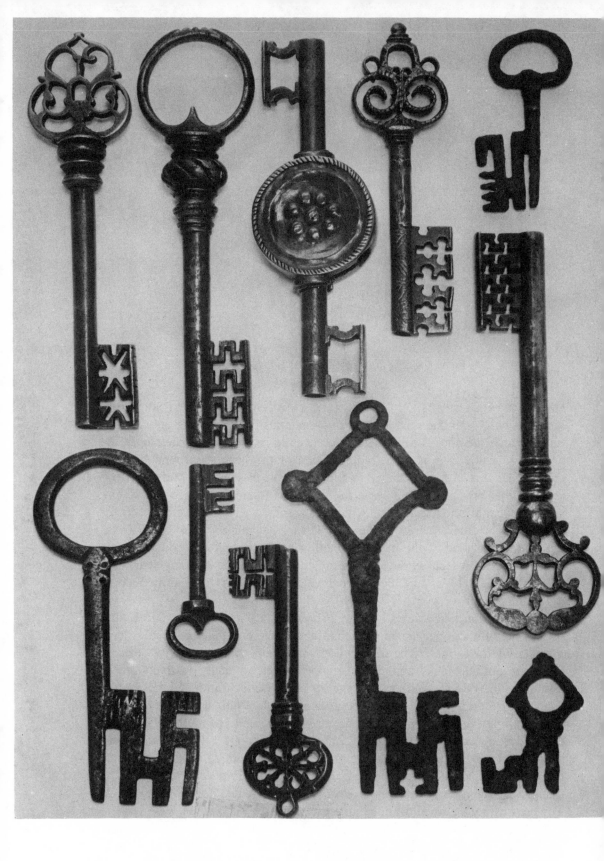

Group of ancient keys from the extensive Yale Lock Collection presented by Eaton Yale & Towne, Inc., by whose courtesy this photograph is reproduced.

Among the historical locks in this fabulous assemblage is an example of what is believed to be the oldest type of mechanical locking device. The oldest known lock, which is of this type, is reported to have been found by Joseph Bonomi in the Halls of Sargon at Khorsabad, near Ninevah. This is known today as the "Egyptian type" lock, because similar ones were depicted in tomb frescoes in the Nile Valley; it is said to date back at least 4,000 years.

Made of wood, the Egyptian locks were fastened on the exterior of gates. Pegs on the end of a large wooden key corresponded with wooden pins in the lock, which kept the bolt from moving. The pins were raised flush with the top of the bolt by lifting the key (which also served as a handle). When the pins were thus raised, the bolt was free and could be withdrawn from the staple.

The first keyhole is reported to have been developed by the ingenious Greeks, who also invented the first lock that made it possible to lock or unlock a door from either side. The Yale Lock Collection contains a model of a Greek lock, which was opened from the outside by inserting a large key through the hole and pushing back the bolt on the inside. The door was locked by pulling the bolt shut from the outside with a latch string, which was then removed.

The Greek key was in the shape of a clavicle and was quite cumbersome and large. Early keys devised by the Romans were a good bit more elaborate than those perfected by the Greeks. Roman locks utilized obstructions of various sizes and shapes to stop keys, which meant that keys could not retract the bolts unless they were precisely shaped to pass these obstructions. The Romans made numerous small keys which many women wore on their fingers as rings. Most of the Roman iron keys have long since been lost to the ravages of time, but the Yale collection has some made of bronze dating back to 100 B.C.

In the Middle Ages, locksmiths employed such devices as hidden keyholes or studs placed on the exterior decoration to foil would-be thieves. In some cases, sculptured decorations at the entrance had to be pushed back in a specific sequence in order to retract the bolt. Many beautiful locks were produced during this period.

Lever tumbler locks — the first truly basic improvement in technical design since the Roman's warded lock — were devised in the eighteenth century. These were operated with a key that had to raise a lever to an exact height before the bolt could be removed. Early American keys had flattened oval rings and a plain baluster shaft.

With the continued trend toward apartment dwelling, the collecting of locks and keys should appeal to an increasing number of persons who have little room for bulkier objects in their collections. From the artistic stand-

This wooden lock is reported to have been placed on the west gate of the Holy Sepulchre by the Crusaders of the twelfth century. It is one of several Egyptian-type locks in the historic "Style and Security" collection of the noted Yale Lock Collection presented by Eaton Yale & Towne, Inc., by whose courtesy it is shown here.

point, the study of keys and locks thus far has received from neither antiquarians nor collectors the consideration and attention it deserves. The majority of locks easily accessible to the average American collector today were made in this country in the eighteenth and nineteenth centuries. There are, however, records of ironsmiths who made keys and locks in America in the seventeenth century.

If you attempt to collect keys and locks, give consideration not only to their historic interest but to their aesthetic appeal, remembering that many of the early devices were beautifully decorated.

Incidentally, the lock which Linus Yale, Sr., invented was based on a principle similar to that of the ancient Egyptian locks and was radically different from those which were being produced by other locksmiths in his day. It was this device that led to the invention by his son, Linus Yale, Jr., of the pin-tumbler cylinder lock.

Collections certainly need not be limited exclusively to entrance locks and their keys. Collectible locking devices extend to those made for bicycles, luggage, dog collars, clocks, desks, chests, pianos, railroad switches, and even parcel checking compartments. Restraining devices, such as handcuffs and leg irons, offer a challenging collecting field in themselves.

You can of course utilize some of the beautiful old locks and keys in your home or apartment, and a diversified group of them displayed along a wall will intrigue your visitors. Some antique shops are now beginning to stock interesting nineteenth- and even twentieth-century locks and keys. A collection doesn't have to begin with great rarities, and a variety of types can be obtained with a fairly small outlay of cash. Instead of collecting at random, however, you may prefer to specialize in one of the categories mentioned above. For example, hundreds of thousands of padlocks were manufactured in the past century. Some extremely interesting ones were turned out by the E. T. Fraim Lock Company, of Lancaster, Pennsylvania, which was established in 1879 and incorporated in 1906. A type of spring shackle, self-locking padlock of steel which this company produced was patented in May, 1897. Some of these had fancy engraved brass drops to cover the keyhole. This company's "New American" line featured padlocks with decorations of stars and bars. In addition to the steel locks, padlocks were made of cast and solid brass and of bronze.

Other well-known padlock manufacturers included among others Yale & Towne, A. E. Deitz, T. W. Langstroth, Staymaker, Barry Company, Eagle Lock Company, and Wm. Wilcox Mfg. Company.

Railroad switch and car door locks were of the padlock type, usually with attached chains. The majority were of gun metal, bronzed. Both round and flat key bodies were made.

This attractive young lady is examining a massive eighteenth-century American prison lock. This object is included in the Yale Lock Collection presented by Eaton Yale & Town, Inc., which made this photograph available.

Padlocks were produced with leaf and others floral designs, geometric patterns, and other types of embossed decoration. One type, known as "Pioneer," featured a hatchet on the front. The "Good Luck" padlock was made in the shape of a horseshoe. Other padlock trade names included "Napoleon," "Rex," "Peer," "Old Oak," "Imperial," "Aluminum," "Guard," "Standard R.F.D." (for mailboxes), "Best," "Ne Plus Ultra," "Eclipse," and "Diamond."

If you are interested in padlocks and have only a small space in which to display them, try collecting miniature padlocks for use on suitcases, dog collars, small boxes, and so on. Some of these were only about three-fourths of an inch high. Costume jewelry in the shape of padlocks and keys also was popular at the turn of this century. Some of these decorative locks were made of gold and sterling silver and sold for $25 to $50 each. Elaborate ones were adorned with pearls and other jewels. They were even smaller than the miniature padlocks designed for utilitarian purposes.

Many firms made bicycle locks, one of the late-nineteenth-century leaders being Staymaker, Barry Company. The simpler sprocket locks were generally oval and could be purchased for about 35 to 40 cents as this century opened. Bicycle padlocks with chains came somewhat higher. Combination locks for bicycles were made later.

Dog collar locks were mostly of the padlock type. An owner could have his animal's name engraved on the lock, but apparently so many dogs were named "Rover" in earlier days that one dog collar lock bore this stock name. They were made primarily in bronze, aluminum, or nickel-plate, though some were of polished brass. In 1909, dog collar padlocks manufactured by Tower & Lyon Company, of New York City, were offered by retail outlets on an assortment board containing a dozen locks. These boards or cards wholesaled for $1.50 to $3.

Some doting owners bought locks of silver or types decked with stones for their pets, which at their deaths were often buried with these collars and locks.

Although they were made in no great variety, a few piano keys and locks should be included in any representative collection of nineteenth-century locks. From the standpoint of eye appeal, the keys here are superior to the locks. Square, triangular, and bitted keys with flat bows are available. The keys generally range from 1½ to 2 inches in length. The locks had either single or double hook bolts.

A few trunk and valise locks will add variety to a collection. The less expensive of these were japanned; some were made in brass. There were spring and tumbler locks. The Eagle Lock Company in 1884 made a trunk lock with a brass drop decorated with an eagle.

In addition, desk, wardrobe, and chest locks will provide plenty of hunting as will combination cupboard and drawer locks.

Miscellaneous locks and keys. Left to right, top: a group of dog collar or charm locks. Second row: two bicycle locks, and a padlock. Third row: handcuffs, leg irons, and a single leg iron with a ball and chain. Fourth row: special bow keys. Bottom: folding keys.

You'll find early keys far more plentiful today than locks. One reason is that so many locks were originally equipped with two keys. Another is that most persons didn't take locks with them when they moved, and house wreckers didn't always salvage all the locks in the houses they demolished. You can make a collection of miscellaneous keys without having to search too far afield.

Undoubtedly the number of simple, tinned malleable iron keys which have been made during the past century will run into the millions. A collection could include simple iron keys, flat steel keys, cylinder lock keys, nickel-plated forged steel keys, keys with unusual bows, brass keys, folding keys, and numerous other types.

Keys with fancy bows are particularly appealing. These were made in a great variety of shapes—oval, rectangular, triangular, square, linked circles, and heart.

Clock keys also are of interest, and you may wish to include one or two bench keys, used by watchmakers, as well as a few watch keys.

(While searching for old keys and locks, don't forget key rings and checks, a tremendous variety of which also have been turned out through the years.)

One can have a great deal of pleasure in collecting various kinds of the aforementioned restraining devices. In addition to early handcuffs and leg irons, these include nippers, which are akin to handcuffs, and "twisters," which are chain devices to secure a prisoner's wrist. Nineteenth-century handcuffs and leg irons will probably bring from $5 to around $25, depending on their age, quality, and condition. A pair of "Tower's Double Lock" leg irons connected by 12 large links of chain was advertised recently at $12. Another pair with a chain 20 inches long was offered at $8.50. Jail keys have been offered of late at prices of from a few dollars to $10 and more.

You can undoubtedly pick up a good many keys for a dollar or two each, but fancy ones may cost you considerably more. To give you a very rough idea of the values of some of the more accessible locks and keys, here are some recently-advertised prices:

Folding key made by Lockwood Mfg. Company, $3.50; heavy solid brass lock used in prohibition days to padlock speakeasies, $5; horseshoe-shaped brass padlock marked "Good Luck," and key, $2.50; early iron lock with brass collar and sliding cover of brass, $3.75; early brass key from Fort Rodman, New Bedford, $12.50; and large brass lock and key dated 1878, $2.75.

Several museums have collections of ancient keys and locks and of early American ones.

17

Brackets

IF YOU INTEND TO DISPLAY ANYTHING ON HANGING SHELVES IN YOUR HOME or office, you should be in the market for brackets. And what's the point of utilizing brackets without character when you can find so many older ones with a personality all their own? These little devices, which do such a big job and at so little expense, have served many purposes in the past—and still do. There are shelf brackets galore, but there also are hand rail brackets, window and door screen brackets, brackets for the lavatory, gas fixture brackets, and lantern brackets, to mention some.

Hundreds of thousands of plain metal shelf brackets have been made through the years, but it is the decorative bracket with which the collector will concern himself; and these, too, were in plentiful supply in the nineteenth century. Of special interest here are the fretwork types with their designs formed by interlacing perforations. The most popular fretwork designs were geometrical, or flower-like, or those formed with scrolls. Some of these were indeed ornamental, and some designers in this field let their imagination run riot. One of the most interesting types of shelf bracket of the late nineteenth century was one in which a bird or animal formed an integral part—that is, was made an actual part of the bracket itself. One of these featured a pair of birds with half-spread wings, a large bird directly beneath the bracket's horizontal, and a smaller one near the bottom of the vertical edge which attached to the wall.

Another unusually attractive bracket was one whose fretwork design consisted of grapes and leaves. Still another was made in interlaced metal circles adorned with rosette-type ornaments.

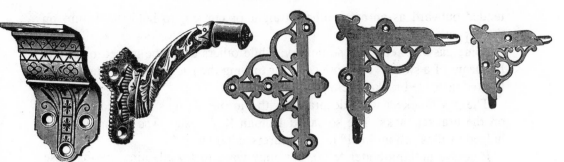

Stair rail, screen door, and window screen brackets.

Shelf brackets were usually made of cast iron, either japanned or bronzed, and of course were manufactured in various sizes, depending upon the supporting job for which they were intended.

Here, again, the most logical places to look for the ornamental brackets of last century and early in this one include old homes and buildings that are being dismantled, and also salvage yards. Within the past year a few such brackets have been advertised for sale at prices of a very few dollars a pair. For example, one dealer offered a pair of lacy brackets measuring 9¼ x 6¾ inches at $2.95. Another advertised a pair of "snowflake" shelf brackets at $8, and a third tendered a pair of 4 x 5-inch lacy brackets at $3. These decorative brackets will enhance the appearance of many types of wall shelves in your home and are far better adapted to shelves holding small antiques than are the starkly plain ones.

Brackets in somewhat similar fretwork designs were made for the corners of window and door screens. They were manufactured in more shapes than was the shelf bracket, which because of the nature of the job for which it was intended consisted primarily of a vertical and a horizontal ledge. Many window and door screen brackets also retained the "L" shape, but some were triangular in form and were intended to serve as decorative centerpieces for the door screens.

Designs featuring wheels, squares, and ovals were popular late last century on screen brackets. If you want to add a nostalgic touch to your own window and door screens, try substituting some of the old brackets, both corner and center pieces, for the hardware that originally came with your screens.

Early brackets for holding lanterns on walls are scarcer than those made later to hold gas fixtures. These, naturally, are entirely different in shape from the shelf and screen brackets. They were attached to the wall by means of a bracket rack, usually a cup-shaped metal device. One end of the gas fixture bracket fitted into an opening in the cup. The remainder of the bracket extended outward as an arm, either straight or curved, to hold the fixture on the opposite end.

Some gas brackets were stationary, while others could be moved or swung by means of a swivel. The hose cock for turning the gas on and off was usually located near the bracket rack.

The gas brackets were decorated with various designs, matched by those on the bracket racks. The so-called Roman Key design was a popular one, judged by illustrations in old manufacturers' catalogues.

If you've nothing better to do, you may want to try adapting one of these interesting old gas brackets to the use of an electric light bulb covered with a small shade. For a most attractive effect, try a shade of art glass. (Be sure to use the services of an electrician for any necessary wiring connections. You don't want to be electrocuted before you complete this book.)

Lantern wall brackets have been used for many years. In fact, this type is still being made for contemporary lighting fixtures. A commonplace model consisted of a metal plate (attached to the wall) with a short arm extending outward to hold the lantern. The arms were made in various shapes—round, square, triangular. Some were in the shape of cyma curves; others tilted upward or downward. Some were designed to hold the lantern by the bottom and others by the top. There also were double-arm brackets attached to the side of the lantern.

If you have an early lantern and plan using it in the décor of a room, look around for one of the old lantern brackets of a type that will accommodate it. Similar brackets can be adapted to hold kerosene lamps. These are excellent for use in decorating cabins, dens, and playrooms.

Gas and lantern brackets may cost you a few dollars each when you find them. Five or six dollars should be a fair price for an iron wall bracket to hold a kerosene lamp, provided it is not a scarce early one.

While looking, you might also watch out for decorated hand rail brackets, some of which were quite elaborate. These also were fabricated of cast iron and in various sizes.

Interesting brackets also were made in the past for supporting open lavatories. Some attached to the wall; others had a leg which extended to the floor. They were often brass- or nickel-plated and had to be quite sturdy because of the weight they supported. One type was made with a curtain piece, which extended downward toward the floor from the lavatory, screening the lavatory bottom and the pipes.

Finally, watch out for brackets used as candle holders (many of these were used above pianos), because these prove to be some of the most decorative of all. Some featured cast replicas of full-length classic figures or of cupids,

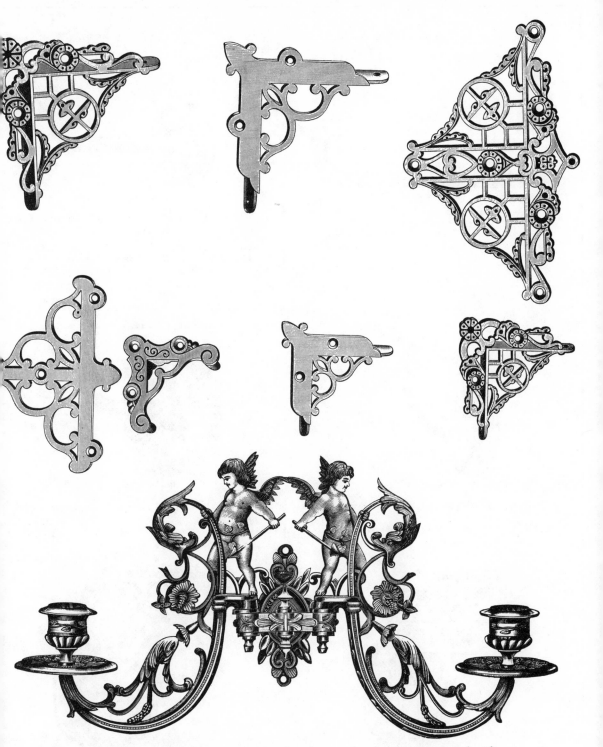

Left to right, top: two screen door corner brackets and a door centerpiece bracket. Second row: screen door centerpiece bracket and three window screen corner brackets. Below: extremely ornate gold-plated candle holder wall brackets.

Hand Rail Brackets.

Half Size of No. 50.

To Screw In.

Per dozen

No. **50,** 6 Inch, Wrought Iron, Japanned, To Screw In, $2 10

Half Size of No. 155 &c.

With 2¼ Inch Base To Screw On.
Wrought Iron.

Numbers		Per dozen
155,	Japanned	$2 70
Y 155,	Bronze Plated, Highly Polished, With Screws	4 50
AB 155,	Antique Copper " " "	4 80

Half Size of No. T 170.

With 2¼ Inch Base To Screw On.

Per dozen

No. **T 170,** Cast Iron, Tuscan Bronzed, Packed with Screws, $1 90

Half Size of No. 160.

With 3¼ Inch Base To Screw On.

Per dozen

No. **160,** Wrought Iron, Cast Base, Japanned $3 00

Half Size of No. T 401.

Per dozen

No. **T 401,** Cast Iron, Tuscan Bronzed, Packed with Screws, $2 10

Half Size of No. T 402 &c.

			Per dozen
No. **T 402,**	Cast Iron, Tuscan Bronzed, Packed with Screws,		$2 50
No. **402,**	" " Berlin " " "		2 80
No. **K 402,**	" " Tokio " " "		4 60

Half dozen in a box. Full cases of Nos. T 401 and T 402 each contain twelve dozen.

A page of hand rail brackets as advertised in a 1901 catalogue, which shows wholesale prices of that time.

and utilized the most ornate scrollwork in their production. Choice ones were gold-plated. These brackets screwed to the wall, some with a single and others with a double arm.

18

Bathroom Accessories

AT FIRST BLUSH, THE BATHROOM MAY NOT SEEM A PARTICULARLY LIKELY place in which to discover collectible items; but give this room more than a cursory glance the next time you have an opportunity to examine an old house.

Actually, "old" is used here in a relative sense. In America, the tub didn't really find a room of its own until about the turn of this century. Bathtubs had been used before that period (though not as frequently as could have been desired), but the familiar bathtub as we now visualize it didn't really take shape until late in the eighteenth century.

When Americans did begin to experiment with the tub form, they devised all sorts of contrivances, including such things as hat tubs, shoe tubs, fancy closet tubs, convertible furniture, and wooden showers that would have been worthy of the mind of a Rube Goldberg. Even the White House didn't take official notice of the tub until 1851—and then in the face of some opposition.

Some years ago, one "G.A.R. Goyle," writing in *Hobbies,* reported that a rich cattle merchant had startled the city of Cincinnati by commissioning a cabinet maker to construct him a mahogany tub 7 feet long and 4 feet wide. When completed, this massive tub weighed 1,750 pounds. A cypress tank was placed in the attic to supply it with water.

Wooden tubs were carted around the country in Conestoga wagons and hung on the sides and walls of frontier cabins. The Saturday-night bather had a crowded time in these, because his feet had to hang over the edge.

The Cleanliness Bureau of New York City has assembled some fascinating photographs of early American tubs and showers. Among them is one depicting a Virginia stool shower. The shower is made of walnut wood with

Looks are deceiving. This is an American-style Victorian tub which doubled as a sofa and a bathtub around 1880-1890. The entire top of the sofa could be removed to reveal a full-length metal tub. Made of scrolled walnut, this one is upholstered in gold brocade and has one curved arm-rest à la Madame Recamier. This tub had to be bailed out and a gutta percha apron was placed around it to protect the carpet from splashes. Some styles were made that were even more ornate than this one. (Photo through courtesy of the Cleanliness Bureau, The Soap and Detergent Association.)

a revolving seat resembling a piano stool. A lever on one side was worked back and forth to pump water up through a hose attached at the back of the shower over the bather's head. Simultaneously, hand action worked a scrub brush up and down the bather's back. The source of the water supply was a pail or basin.

The hat tub was so named because the tub resembled an upturned lady's broad-brimmed hat. Used around the middle of the nineteenth century, it was about the size of the modern galvanized tub. The bather sat on a seat

This is an American Virginia stool shower, dating around 1830-40. The shower is made of walnut with a revolving seat. When worked back and forth, a lever on the right pumped water up through the hose attached at the back of the shower over the bather's head or shoulders. At the same time, the hand action worked a scrub brush up and down the bather's back. The pail served as the source of water. A wooden soap dish is attached to the stool. (Photo through courtesy of the Cleanliness Bureau, The Soap and Detergent Association.)

set into the tub's rim, and splashed the water (which had been poured into the tub) on his person. When not in use, the hat tub could be hung on the wall by a hook. During this period, it is reported, ladies crushed strawberries, which they added to the bath water. This was a forerunner of modern beauty treatments.

About 1880, a closet tub was used in this country. This one could fold up into its own closet or open down into a rather spacious tub. The tub was framed in wood and was supported by ornate wrought iron legs. It had a small drain at one end, which allowed the water to run out into a flat basin. The unit also contained a heater, which provided hot water and resembled a water cooler. When folded into its cabinet, the closet tub could have been mistaken for a Murphy bed.

One of the most fascinating tubs of the late nineteenth century, however, was the Victorian sofa tub, which actually doubled as a living-room sofa and a bathtub. The entire top of the sofa was removable, revealing below a full-length metal tub. The sofa parts were sometimes quite ornate and were upholstered with leather or brocade. The tub itself had to be bailed out, and a gutta percha apron was placed around it to prevent water from splashing on the floor. The habitat of this tub was the parlor or living room.

As a matter of fact, during the early nineteenth century the use of hot baths except on the advice of a physician was questioned. What is more, according to Mr. "Goyle," mentioned earlier, the city of Boston in 1845 passed an ordinance forbidding bathing in a tub except on a doctor's orders.

When the twentieth century arrived, the tub at last found a room of its own. Plumbing and water supplies had been so improved that running water could be piped to any floor. The enameled tub came into its glory, and other elaborate bathroom fixtures were invented, including commodes.

Now you undoubtedly won't want to collect a great many bathtubs—or wooden commodes either—but those museums devoted to the preservation of Americana which overlook the early fancy tubs are missing a good bet: bathrooms of some of the wealthier of our gentry were showplaces. An 1892 catalogue of Rumsey & Sikemeier Manufacturing Company, of St. Louis, depicts some fancy tubs of that period, including the "New York" and "French" styles, with copper linings. These were flat, oblong affairs with slanted backs; they were placed flat on the floor. Others were pictured with four short, fancy legs, and hardwood rims, and were painted or enameled. The rims of wood were really accessories available at a cost of $9.50 extra.

Tubs of this period were made in lengths of from 4 to 6 feet. You could buy an inexpensive iron tub 4½ feet long, complete with hardwood rim, for $27.50, wholesale. If you wanted a more elaborate one, complete with fixtures and a porcelain lining, you could buy one in a 6-foot length for $99.

So-called "pool baths" cost more. These were tubs with lavishly decorated sides and were designed to be set into the floor, many of them projecting only 8 inches above floor level.

Foot and sitz tubs also were popular in the late nineteenth century. The latter was a tub that enabled one to immerse one's thighs and trunk to the

From the nineteenth-century bathroom. Top: Group of embossed silver soap boxes. Second row from left: brass, nickel-plated tumbler holder, nickel-plated soap dish and wall-type soap dish, and a gold-lined soap box. Third row: vaseline holder, cut glass tooth powder box, and French pattern copper bathtub, with a New York pattern copper tub just below. Bottom: lavishly-embossed "Garcia" hopper and tray, "Scepter" hopper, and copper hip tub.

waist. The Rumsey & Sikemeier catalogue pictures one of these with claw-and-ball feet of brass and a front decorated with flowers.

While you'd find a full-sized tub cumbersome anyplace in the home except in the bathroom, you can find uses for the early hip tubs, including conversion to large planters for indoor gardens. Early in this century, small oval bathtubs of copper or other materials were widely used. These had a capacity of about 4 gallons of water and were favorites for Saturday night bathing, particularly when placed in front of a fireplace on cold winter evenings. Originally, these were quite inexpensive, selling for just a few dollars each.

Also during the late nineteenth century there was a fad for so-called "Turkish" baths of one sort or another, their popularity having been fostered by a profusion of manufacturers' advertisements. Some of these consisted primarily of a cabinet or frame covered with a treated cloth. The cabinet had a hole in its top so that the bather's head could be put through it while he or she sat comfortably on a little stool inside. The steam was created by the use of a kerosene-burning lamp or similar contrivance. Such cabinet baths were advertised as cures for various ailments, including the common cold.

The Turkish bath proper was perfected by the Turks themselves and was an extremely elaborate affair, dating back some centuries. The primary bathroom, usually quite large and built in the shape of a cross, featured a fountain that sprayed water (warm water was used during the winter). The bathers entered this large room after undressing in a smaller room and wrapping themselves with towels. Attendants performed on the bodies of the bathers a sort of chiropractic exercise, and then worked them over with a coarse cloth. The bathers subsequently immersed themselves in water and lathered their bodies with soap. After washing, they wrapped the towels around themselves, stretched out on a couch and sipped coffee—Turkish naturally.

It is easy to see, therefore, that the Turkish "Turkish" bath and the American "Turkish" bath of the late nineteenth century had little in common. But you can collect the American "Turkish" bath cabinets if you wish and can find them.

Many smaller bathroom accessories of earlier days can be converted to advantageous use or to display in the modern home. These embrace a diversity of items from towel bars to soap containers.

You probably already have heard that decorated chamber pots are finding some use as planters and that commercial bars in some areas have used them for pretzels and other drink adjuncts. There are chamber pots of glazed pottery and pots of metal. Usually, the former are more attractive. They can be found at prices ranging from around $5 to $25, except for the very early ones. One in the so-called granite ware was offered not long ago housed in

An iron wash stand with decorated doors; and Eastlake sink on legs (primarily for use in the kitchen), and an iron enameled pool bath designed to be set in the floor. All are from the nineteenth century and were offered by Rumsey & Sikemeier Manufacturing Company.

a square container of walnut wood with handles and an upholstered seat for $22.50.

Those made of pottery and ironstone often had lids with decorative finials and were embellished with flowers or other designs. One of white ironstone with a poppy and wheat design and a nut finial on the lid was offered for sale recently at $3.50, which was probably a bargain.

Early towel holders of various types can still be used for their original purpose to add interest to the bathroom or kitchen. Some towel holders were made with swinging bars attached to a plate of lacy iron. Some of the bars were tipped with brass. These should be worth around $10 each today.

A popular type of towel bar at the turn of this century was composed of a nickel- or brass-plated rod with large circular ends held by enameled wood supports that screwed into the wall. The bar itself was held by hooks in the projecting ends of the wood supports. These were inexpensive, wholesaling for only $20 a gross.

Simple late-nineteenth-century towel hangers consisted of a plated steel or wrought bronze rod with a knob end attached to a circular wall plate. These were about 5½ inches long, and the towels were placed folded over the rod.

Wooden towel rollers made of oak could be bought at retail in 1906 for only 11 cents. In the same year, the Cash Buyers Union First National Co-Operative Society, of Chicago, offered, in a thick catalogue, a steel towel rack with three swinging bars for 8 cents.

A walnut continuous post "Jenny Lind" type of towel rack with four legs with bracket feet attached was advertised by an antiques dealer some time ago for $8.50.

Collecting soap containers and cases offers numerous possibilities, because so many different types have been made through the years. Some soap boxes for toting cakes of soap around when on out-of-town visits were fairly expensive. Others were made of gold-lined metal with engraved exterior surfaces and sold for $8 or $10 each half a century or more ago. One side of these boxes was hinged and the other snapped shut with a clasp much in the manner of a change purse. Silver-lined soap containers of this type wholesaled for $2 or $2.50 in 1900. Primary types of exterior decoration included flowers and scrolls.

Soap dishes were made of pottery, porcelain, glass, and metal. The Rochester Stamping Company, of Rochester, New York, offered containers made of heavy brass, nickel-plated, early in the century at prices of $12 to $18 a dozen. The more expensive ones had beaded or embossed edges. The soap was placed on a pierced insert, through which the water drained into the outer shell, which was emptied as needed.

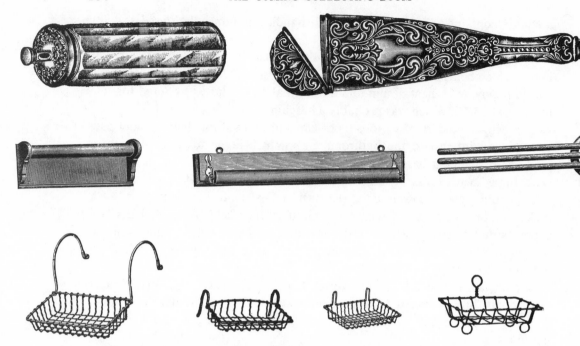

Bathroom adjuncts. Top: a cut glass tooth powder box and an embossed metal toothbrush holder. Second row: two towel rollers and a towel rack. Below: three soap brackets and a soap stand, all of wire.

The W. H. Sweeney Manufacturing Company, of Brooklyn, New York, made less expensive nickel-plated brass soap dishes, which it wholesaled for $4 a dozen in 1906. Other nickel-plated soap containers of a similar type were mounted on the wall by means of a metal bar and wall plate. These wholesaled for about $20 a gross.

Decorated pottery and porcelain soap dishes will make for a more interesting collection than the metal ones. Some of these were produced by well-known nineteenth-century potteries in this country and abroad, and are identified by the name, initials, or mark of the potteries. The better of these are worth several dollars each. Most consisted of an outer container, sometimes covered, with an insert having holes similar to the metal ones described above.

Toothbrush and toothpowder bottles and holders also can provide an interesting collection. The toothpowder bottles were made of glass, often etched, and had plated silver tops. Toothbrush bottles were similar in shape but longer.

Trade catalogues dated early in this century depict toothbrush holders in octagonal-shaped crystal glass. They were about 7 inches high and sold for less than a dollar. Similar glass containers but in different shapes and sizes were made to hold such things as cold cream, vaseline, face powder, and even tobacco.

Of course, metal stands and wall brackets for holding toothbrushes in the bathroom also were produced in great volume, but these are of only minor interest to collectors. The same is true for metal tumbler holders.

Some perfectly fabulous washstands, lavatories, and water basins were manufactured three-quarters of a century ago. Washstands of iron on standards which were enameled or bronzed were lavishly decorated with embossed designs. Of particular interest are the triangular corner washstands. Many corner and square washstands had a cabinet with a door (and sometimes two doors) below the basin. Some cabinets were made of wood, others of metal painted to imitate wood, and there were often decorations in the center of the door panels. One of these, advertised in 1892, bears a likeness of the head of a young girl in the center panel. Some of the stands had marble tops and back splash panels. Favorite woods for the cabinets included walnut, cherry, and oak.

Open lavatories were widely used. Some of these consisted of a basin set in marble with a back splash of Italian or Tennessee marble, a fancy marble front and side aprons, and a countersunk marble floor slab. They were attached to the wall by means of fancy brass brackets. The basin supply pipes and traps were of brass. The countersunk marble floor slab added about $10 to the total cost of the installation.

Some of the more elaborate of these washstands and lavatories cost well over $100, even back in those days, but simple washbasins of iron—either painted or enameled—were available for only few dollars each. Some basins came with fancy iron wall brackets.

In an allied category, kitchen sinks came in square, oval, or rectangular designs and were made of cast iron, crockery, slate, and soapstone. Eastlake designs were available with ornamented legs. Small corner sinks and butler's pantry sinks were made with fretwork wall brackets and splash slabs of marble.

A collection could even be made of interesting basin and bathtub cocks. These were turned out in a wide variety of shapes: many nickel-plated, others silver-plated. Chain stays also were produced in many intriguing shapes.

Beauty is sometimes found where one would least suspect it, and such is the case with a number of nineteenth century earthenware toilet hoppers or closets whose fronts were embellished with classical scenes of maidens, flowers and vines, seashells, and similar depictions. These were intended to impart "class" to the very late nineteenth- and early twentieth-century bathroom. The decorated ones sold at wholesale prices ranging from $17 to about $40 in the late 1800's.

You may or may not want to try one of these for size as a planter—but if you should, you'll have a conversation piece on your hands.

Don't overlook the lattice-work brass brackets, which served to hold sinks, lavatories, and basins to the walls. See Chapter 17.

19

Milady's Boudoir: Accessories

FOR A TRUE FIELD DAY IN COLLECTING FASCINATING SMALL ITEMS NO PLACE will excel the boudoir of 75 or 100 years ago. Numerous boudoir accessories and necessities are already being collected, but areas still remain for the pioneer to explore. This chapter will be limited to a discussion of accessories ranging from puff jars to curling sets, and the following chapter will concern itself with a host of decorative dress accessories and baubles.

Glass puff boxes are still plentiful, and they will make just as attractive an ornament for milady's dressing table today as they did 50 or 75 years ago. They were made in cut glass, pressed glass, and etched crystal, usually with sterling or silver-plated covers highly embossed. Shapes ranged from oval to octagonal. Some boxes in cut glass even had cut glass tops, a few of which had silver-plated rims. Some tops were hinged to the boxes but the majority were not.

These puff boxes, or powder jars, also were made in silver-plated metal, infrequently footed, and of porcelain.

Still more desirable ones were made of types of art glass and of milk-white and satin glass. The C. F. Monroe Company, of Meriden, Connecticut, produced powder boxes in painted opal glassware under its trade name "Wave Crest Ware." These, blown in full-size molds and usually hinged by means of metal collars, will bring fairly high prices today. The same company made similar opaque glass articles under the additional trade names of "Nakara" and "Kelva."

Puff and powder jars will range in price today from a few dollars up to

Boudoir accessories of 1900. Top row: three glass puff jars with embossed silver-plated lids. Second row from left: hair receiver and two quadruple-plated jewel cases. Third row: quadruple-plated glove box and two jewel boxes. Bottom row: silver-plated handkerchief box and two jewel boxes.

No well-equipped boudoir of late last century or early in this one lacked at least certain of these items. At top is a hair crimper with a pearl button and below is a pair of glove stretchers. Left to right, third row, are: two puff boxes and four assorted collar button boxes. Fourth row: two powder puffs with sterling silver tops and silk coverings, and two hairpin boxes. Bottom: a nickel silver and a gold dorine box, a hairpin or trinket box, and a hatpin stand.

$40 or more for quite desirable examples in art glass or fine china. A puff box of pink satin glass with a silver lid is advertised at $25 and one of heavy cut glass for $35. The pressed glass boxes with metal covers may still be found at prices of around $5 and up.

Some of the smaller puff boxes were produced in sterling silver, and some of those made of so-called quadruple-plated silver were gold lined. About the time of World War I, puff jars of glass with sterling silver tops could be bought at prices of from $7.50 to $10. The puff boxes are far more plentiful today than the powder puff themselves, the best of which were made with sterling silver tops or handles.

Most nineteenth-century ladies were fascinated by jewelry made of precious or semi-precious stones, so naturally the jewelry box was virtually a boudoir necessity. These not only housed fine jewelry but often paste stones, which so often imitated costly jewels. Some of the jewelry boxes also were used to hold diamond shoe and garter buckles, the wearing of which was an affection of a number of more affluent ladies.

Fancy embossed boxes of quadruple-silver-plate with tiny feet abounded around 1900. These were fabricated in oval, oblong, and other shapes. The embossed patterns were chiefly floral, but sometimes one encounters such décor as cupids. Lids were occasionally handled.

The most intriguing jewel boxes, however, are the silver-plated ones in novelty shapes, which certainly provided an exercise in ingenuity for their designers. There was one in the shape of a covered well, complete with bucket and a crank handle and with a small bird perched atop the roof of the cover. Another in a truly odd shape bore the figure of a boy on a sled on its top. Still another, with a high curved handle, had a cupid astride the top and a small wheel underneath the front of the compartment, which pulled out to open. Boxes of this type were usually lined with silk.

One will encounter today, among the more inexpensive items in antique shops, jewelry boxes with a white metal base that has been silver-plated and is covered with raised rococo designs. These, too, were generally lined with silk or satin.

So-called trinket boxes doubled as jewelry boxes and were used to hold some of the wide assortment of small trinkets that pleased the ladies of Victorian and post-Victorian days. Some were silver-plated, some gold-plated; and most stood on small feet, frequently in the shape of oval knobs. The 1900 catalogue of Otto Young & Company shows a rectangular one with an embossed border and a pair of crossed rifles and military cap on the top. Another has a United States flag enameled in colors on its lid. Another interesting one was in the shape of a drum with a flag enameled on top.

Miscellaneous bureau boxes were made in silver-plate with plush tops in

QUADRUPLE PLATE SILVERWARE.

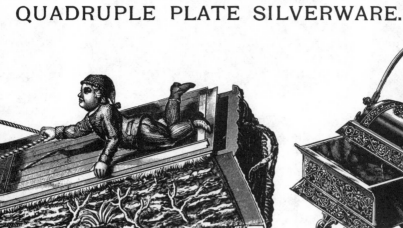

NO. 75. JEWEL BOX.

Silk Lined $10 50

NO. 16 JEWEL BOX.

Roman Border, Satin Lined 9 50

NO. 47.

Satin Lined.....................$6 00
Blue Brocatel, Decorated, Crystal Glass.
Reduced from $10 00

NO. 69.

Well Jewel Satin Lined..........$13 00

NO. 34. JEWEL.

Satin Lined, Fancy Decorated,
White Enameled Figure......$5 50
Reduced from $10 00

NO. 50.

Satin Lined...... ....$8 75
Inches Long, Fancy Gilt Stand, Blue or Pink
Malachite, Crystal, White Enameled Figures.
Reduced from $21 00

NO. 76. JEWEL BOX.

Embossed, Satin Lined, Old Silver.......................$8 50

These intriguing plated jewel boxes were offered for sale in 1892 by B. F. Norris,
Alister & Company, of Chicago.

Boudoir accessories. Top row, two bureau boxes and a hairpin tray. Second row: handkerchief box (with pin box and ring stand below) and a hair crimping and curling set. Bottom row, a toilet set with rose and blue decorated bottles, a toilet bottle, a ring stand, and a bonnet duster.

color and satin linings. These also were designed to hold trinkets, pins, and other small objects.

Cases of this type with embossed scenes around the front and sides are quite intriguing. These ranged from courting scenes to depictions of Colonial homes and gardens.

In an allied category are boxes for hairpins, safety pins, creams and pomades, collars and cuffs, nail paste, and gloves. These were made in plated metal, porcelain, and glass. One round silver-plated safety-pin box of the early 1900's bore a depiction of a safety pin and the words "Baby's Friend" on the top. Hairpin boxes were engraved with such phrases as "I'll Stick to You," "Ladies' Friend," "I'm Here" and "Pin Your Faith to" with a United States flag beneath the last-cited. In addition to hairpin boxes, numerous hairpin trays in metal, pottery, and porcelain—always decorated—were also turned out. Some of these were oval, while others were heart-shaped, clover-shaped, or oblong.

Collar-button boxes were usually oval; glove boxes were oblong. About the time of the first World War, various types of ivory dresser boxes were popular. Most of these, however, can't really compete with the other types for interest. Cream and pomade boxes were usually small and round in shape. The more expensive of these were made of sterling silver. Glass nail-paste boxes with metal tops—sometimes of sterling—were in use early in this century. Collar boxes were sometimes fancifully engraved. One of these made about the turn of the century features a spread eagle perched on a United States shield with the word "Collars" engraved on the top. Glove boxes also were used to hold handkerchiefs but some containers were specifically marked "Handkerchiefs."

Hair receivers were another much-used commodity in the earlier days of this century. Ordinarily, these were of metal, glass, or porcelain; some types were virtually identical in appearance to puff jars and boxes. The glass ones had metal tops; those of porcelain and metal normally had a small opening in the top. Most hair receivers stood 2 or 3 inches high. Wave Crest hair receivers also were made by the C. F. Monroe Company, and judging by the value of these today it is difficult to realize that they once were offered as premiums. Nevertheless, in 1901, *The Youth's Companion* offered a Wave Crest hair receiver 3¼ inches in diameter, in exchange for one subscription and 10 cents extra. Or you could buy it outright for only 85 cents, postpaid! You will pay many times more than that for one today.

Every well-equipped dresser or dressing table of years ago had a dresser tray or a tray set, individual items of which frequently consisted of some of the things being discussed. Perfume and cologne bottles were made as component parts of some dresser sets. The trays themselves were used to hold pins, buttons, and a miscellany of small accessories.

Porcelain trays made by a number of well-known pottery manufacturers in this country and abroad—including several in Limoges, France—are now highly collectible. Limoges porcelain trays will fetch $5 to $15, depending on quality. Dresser trays also were made of plated metal, some of them lavishly embossed, and of glass—primarily milk-white glass. All types can be used in the décor of today's boudoir and will serve utilitarian purposes as well. They came in various shapes and ranged from 2 or 3 inches to nearly a foot in length.

Ring and watch stands (sometimes the ring stands were called "trees") are of considerable decorative value today, and of course these, too, may be used for the purposes for which they were originally intended.

The more commonplace ring stands were of porcelain, but occasionally one of wood is encountered. Many so-called ring trees consisted of a saucer-shaped base from which rose a branched "trunk" just a few inches tall. Rings were hung on the branch-like projections. Sometimes, instead of a branched trunk, a replica of a hand was used so that the rings could be placed on the fingers. Occasionally, too, there were replicas of elk and other antlered animal heads, the rings being placed on the tips of the antlers. A simpler ring stand consisted of a similar saucer-like base or tray from which rose a porcelain vertical bar that tapered a short distance from its top to a circumference larger than a finger. Rings were placed over the narrowed top of this bar.

Late-nineteenth-century ring stands were sometimes made of metal with a round metal ball rising from the tray or stand. Around the ball were placed several small hooks for rings. There was frequently a plush pincushion on top. Other metal trays had rods with hooks attached and a finial at the rod's top.

Watch stands or holders were originally designed to hold pocket watches, which were once made in such profusion. These stands were fashioned in all sorts of shapes, sometimes weird. They were made of brass, plated metal, pottery and porcelain, and wood. Those of the nineteenth century either had hooks at the top to hold the watch or a recess into which the watch was placed.

Some quite elaborate watch holders were produced in the eighteenth century with an open pocket in which the watch was placed so that its face would show at the front. Among the most fascinating were those made in porcelain, some by noted porcelain manufacturers. But other fine ones were made of wood and metals. Expert wood carvers turned out some of the former, then decorated them by painting and gilding. The eighteenth-century watch holders are relatively scarce today, and the good ones come high; so the average collector, without recourse to substantial funds, will have to rest content with the less expensive ones of the nineteenth century.

These were popular in milady's boudoir late last century and early in this one. Top row: decorated hand mirrors. Below: a hat brush and nail buff. Third row, from left: hair brush and three cream or pomade boxes. At the bottom is shown a variety of solid gold, rolled plate, and sterling silver picks and ear spoons, some of these combining the pick and the spoon in a single implement.

A group of interesting hairpin trays in quadruple-plated silverware.

Another boudoir accessory was the glove stretcher. After the glove had been washed, one would fit the glove fingers into it, thus stretching the fingers back into correct shape. The stretchers resembled a miniature pair of tongs or a curling iron, but they were made of highly polished wood—rosewood being a favorite—or of steel with silver handles. Those with sterling handles sold for several dollars each at the end of last century.

Hair curlers and crimpers, which the glove stretchers resembled, were far more widely used. Some crimpers had a pearl button at the end of the short blade, while the other blade ended in a plated handle at the top.

Hair curling and crimping sets consisted of a box-like container; the curling iron or crimper, which could be folded; and sometimes a shoe horn and a button hook. Some curlers had handles of ebony.

Hair curlers and crimpers of the type used at the opening of this century have been largely replaced today by improved devices for beautifying milady's hair and by the beauty shops, that have descended like locusts upon the land, featuring new hair stylings almost every week.

Manicure accessories have been turned out by the hundreds of thousands through the years for the fastidious and even the not-so-fastidious male and female. Some have been sold as individual implements to help assure trim and neat nails and others as components of manicure sets. Contents of the sets have varied through the years. Some contained a nail file, nail buffer or polisher, and a pair of tiny scissors. Others contained a nail file, shoehorn, buttonhook, toothbrush, and perhaps a toothpowder bottle. The last-described set wholesaled for $4 early in this century. In 1900, one type of eight-piece manicure set in a silk-lined leatherette case had a wholesale price of $10.90. It contained a nail file, cuticle knife, scissors, buttonhook, corn knife, nail buffer, and two glass-covered jars—the latter for creams or lotions.

Some manicure accessories, including files, cuticle and corn knives, and buffers, were made with decorated ebony handles. An eight-piece set of this type wholesaled in 1900 for $8 in a plush-lined leatherette case measuring 10½ by 6⅞ inches. Some accessories had dainty ribbons around the handles. Sterling silver handles were popular and not very expensive as this century began. Some three-piece sets with sterling handles and nickel-plated steel blades sold for less than $2. Also highly popular were pearl-handled files and cuticle and corn knives. In 1908, the A. J. Jordan Cutlery Company was wholesaling items of this type at prices ranging from $18 to $40 a dozen. Those with celluloid handles in an ivory finish were cheaper. Still others had handles of bone. Manicure sets in folding leather cases came into rather widespread use early in this century. These sets usually contained three to eight items. Prices of the better sets in folding leather cases had about doubled in price by 1920.

Apparently, hardly anyone is now collecting these manicure accessories; but when collecting starts on a broad scale, watch for prices to ascend rapidly.

"Toilet sets" were quite similar to manicure sets. In fact, some manufacturers used the phrases to describe either sets with manicure accessories or sets with combs, hair and tooth brushes.

Hand mirrors of the late nineteenth century afford an excellent field for collecting, though few have ventured into it thus far. Some mirrors were gold-filled or sterling-silver-filled with backs of finely embossed flowers, cartouches, and geometric designs. In most cases, the decoration extended to the handles. Although the majority of hand mirrors in common use late last century were oval, others appeared in quite odd designs. The reproductions of Grecian, Colonial, and other patterns in mirrors, which appeared on the market in profusion around the time of World War I and shortly thereafter, are not of nearly so much interest as are other types of the late nineteenth century. However, some of the later mirrors with hand-hammered silver designs are worth picking up at reasonable prices; but they were originally not inexpensive, many selling at prices of $35 and $45, which was quite a substantial sum in those days for those handy little implements which told one what one's best friends would sometimes not tell.

Early American mirrors and "looking glasses" of earlier days have been collected for some time. Now it's time for someone to start investigating seriously the attractions of unusual mirrors of the late Victorian period.

Boudoir accessories included various types of brushes, the most commonplace of which, naturally was the hairbrush; but hat and clothes brushes and whisk brooms of earlier days should also be considered.

Dozens of ornate types of women's hairbrushes were produced in the nineteenth and early twentieth centuries, as were numerous types of military brushes. A good many of these had sterling or silver-plated backs and handles with decorations similar to those of hand mirrors of the same period.

Cloth and hat brushes were ordinarily either round or oblong, and among the more interesting of these are those with quadruple-silver-plated backs. The average cloth brush measured about 7 inches in length and the hat brush was perhaps an inch or so shorter. These brushes also came with ebony backs. Whisk brooms with plated decorated handles would be a splendid field to pioneer in. If the brush—usually made of broom corn—is damaged or un-sanitary, the handles alone can be salvaged. Whisk brooms averaged about 9 inches in length early this century.

Whisk-broom handles of silver-plate were made in unusual shapes. Some had hook tops, which often came with pretty ribbons in them. This also was the case with handled hat brushes, sometimes referred to as "bonnet dust-ers." Whisk brooms were sometimes sold with leather or leatherette holders that would encase the brush part when not in use.

Today, Doctors will warn you not to insert anything into your ears for fear of damaging the ear drum—and they're right. But 75 years ago sterling and silver-plated ear spoons were widely used. So were metal tooth picks, which were used over and over again. This may not have been sanitary, but the picks did last a long time. A good many combination ear spoons and picks were made: some of gold with rolled plate mountings. These probably could be considered in the category of jewelry.

Many of the picks and ear spoons had engraved barrels or handles, or raised decorations. Picks, when offered alone, frequently had a round clasp at the end of the barrel. In the last quarter of the nineteenth century, solid gold picks with celluloid handles were sold for less than $2. Simple metal picks could be bought for around 50 cents, and better ones went as high as three or four dollars. Here is another wide open field if you want to be a pioneer, and the best places in which to search are older homes and long-existing estates which are now being auctioned.

A rather vague guide to values of some of the items we have discussed in this chapter is reflected in a few recent advertisements. They have included the following; but be sure not to accept these prices as an indication of actual worth:

Celluloid glove box, 12½ inches long, with a depiction of five cupids on the cover and a fancy brass clasp, $7.50; cranberry glass powder box, brass bound, with enameled flowers on cover and base, $20; small heart-shaped pin dish of Limoges porcelain, $3; Baccarat ring tree with pink swirl deco-ration, $15; porcelain ring tree, $5.50; porcelain hair receiver (Royal Sax-ony), blackberry decorations, $4.50; R. S. Germany porcelain hatpin holder,

$10; carved ivory glove stretcher, $27.50; Nippon porcelain dresser set with powder box, hatpin holder, hairpin box and pin box with slight defect on one box, $8; simple German porcelain dresser tray, $3.50; plated toothpick with handle in shape of owl, $8.50.

Also, Royal Bayreuth handpainted porcelain hair receiver, $6.50; gold toothpick in black enameled case, $10; Nippon porcelain ring tree, $6.75; covered custard-glass powder jar, $8.50; round milk-white glass powder jar with cover, $4.75; Carnival glass "Orange Tree" powder jar, $37.50; Wave Crest powder box, $58; blue satin glass puff box, melon ribbed, $23.50; choice red R. S. Prussia hatpin holder, $32; milk-white glass covered glove box, $8; porcelain covered hairpin box, enameled flowers, $4.50; cut glass powder box, $10.

In view of the rapidity with which prices of many of the newer collectible items have been rising recently, some of the lower prices listed above may no longer apply by the time you read this.

The items discussed in this chapter by no means exhaust the list of collectible boudoir accessories, but they may whet your interest and perhaps even induce you to search around for others.

20

Dress Accessories and Baubles

Bauble. NOW THAT'S A GOOD WORD TO USE IN CHARACTERIZING A LARGE percentage of the items adopted for personal ornamentation by ladies of the late nineteenth century. Baubles made the ladies happy and some manufacturers wealthy.

A large number of baubles actually were in the category of what we sometimes term gewgaws—showy but generally useless finery of little value. On the other hand, some performed yeoman service, and some cost a pretty penny indeed. Nevertheless, ladies whose husbands could ill-afford a plethora of jewelry and adornments of silver and gold found the baubles of which we shall speak here of more than passing interest. These ranged from veil fasteners to hair ornaments, from garter buckles to scarf pins, from belt fasteners to chain picture lockets.

Literally hundreds of thousands of jewelry items were made and worn during the last quarter of the nineteenth century and the early years of the present one; and while jewelry is still being produced in abundance today, most ladies of the late 1960's are not quite so lavish with its use as were their grandmothers. Many of the earlier items of jewelry were made of precious metals or stones, but many also belonged in the category of pinchbeck. This is an alloy of copper and zinc used in imitation of genuine gold. Its name derives, incidentally, from its inventor, one Christopher Pinchbeck, a London clockmaker, who was born in the seventeenth century.

Much of the jewelry you will encounter in second-hand stores and salvage shops today will definitely be of the pinchbeck type; however this does not mean that it should all be ignored. A combination of jewelry set in pinchbeck and other materials with other pieces made of semi-precious stones—as well as a considerable amount utilizing plated or rolled gold and silver—can make a colorful contribution to a collection of baubles and dress accessories. Because these items of jewelry may have been fashioned of inexpensive materials, it certainly does not follow that they all were of poor workmanship or were in poor taste. In fact, excellent craftsmanship characterized a part of the production of just such jewelry, including that made with such semi-precious stones as the carnelian, the garnet, and the amethyst.

Various influences will be evidenced in the jewelry of the type we are discussing and which you are likely to encounter in some abundance today— for example, the classic, the naturalistic, *art nouveau,* and the folk influence. Moreover, it should be remembered that many ladies of years past often wore artificial stones and genuine ones at the same time, while others kept their valuable jewelry in safes or vaults and wore, for most occasions, reproductions of it made with paste. Semi-precious stones considered favorites during the last half of the nineteenth century included, in addition to the three mentioned above, aquamarine, cat's-eye, garnet, carbuncle (garnet cut in a convex rounded form without facets), chrysoprase (a nickel-stained, apple-green chalcedony), and zircon.

A good bit already has been written about Victorian jewelry in general, and we will not delve in detail into it here. If you are interested, you'll find a most informative chapter about it in Violet Wood's book *Victoriana, A Collector's Guide* (G. Bell and Sons, Ltd., London).

It was reported in 1872 that Americans were investing at least $20 million in jewelry annually. A good bit of this was imported, but much of it also was made in this country—notably in Providence, Rhode Island, leading center of this industry. The application of the machine to the production of jewelry reduced its cost and resulted in spiraling increases in consumption during the final quarter of last century. Cost was reduced by the process of using a thin covering of gold in the manufacture of a variety of jewelry items instead of making them of solid gold as had so frequently been the case earlier. It was discovered that the ductility of gold was such that it could be rolled into leaves measuring only 144-thousandth part of an inch, and frequently a pennyworth of gold was worked into plates containing a pound of composition of the copper and zinc mentioned earlier.

With the advent of machinery suitable for the purpose, gold was rolled out into a thin sheet, which was placed upon the composition sheet of copper and zinc. The two were then fused by the application of heat, which melted the gold slightly.

One of the major producers of plated jewelry in this country in the 1870's was Quimby & Company, whose plant was situated at 26 Potter Street, Provi-

Top, left to right: two sash clasps or belt buckles; lady's shopping list; three garter buckles, and a fitted garter. Middle row: vinaigrettes with cut glass bottles
and sterling silver tops. Bottom row: vinaigrette and smelling salts bottles, the
first gold-filled and the others with sterling silver cases. All of these accessories
were popular in the late 1800's.

dence, and whose main office was in Boston, with a branch office in New York City.

Let's examine some of the baubles and dress accessories which should be salvaged and which probably are going to be collectors' items of tomorrow.

Garter, suspender (and even arm band) buckles certainly constitute one colorful category. Garter buckles are metal buckles, nearly always decorated, attached to the cloth garters, frequently made of fine silk elastic webbing. Some buckles were oval; others were square, oblong, triangular, or heart-shaped. Some had imitation amethyst settings or were set with other stones. Some were made of rolled gold, others of sterling silver. Rococo designs predominated, but some were produced with simple beaded borders. They could be purchased at the turn of the century at prices ranging from about a dollar a pair to $30 or more, complete with the garters of course. The ladies' garters were frequently decorated with dainty ribbons in various colors, quite often but not always offering a contrast to the color of the elastic webbing.

Suspender buckles and buckles for arm bands or armlets were similarly made, the mountings often being sterling silver but sometimes gold. The latter were quite expensive, but arm bands could be bought for as little as a dollar with sterling silver mountings.

In a closely-related category are sash and belt buckles and clasps, many made with fancy stone centers and others with enameled scenes. Most of these buckles and clasps were either gold-plated or made of sterling silver in a great variety of shapes. One type had enameled ornaments and an imitation turquoise center; it wholesaled in 1900 at $12 a dozen, gold filled. Some belt buckles of Roman gold plate had elaborate open-work centers; others were adorned with amethysts or imitation rubies. Also, girdles and belts of gold-plate or with a silver finish were popular in the late 1800's. These were set with stones, including carbuncles.

Veil fasteners, which did precisely the job their name implies, also were frequently made of sterling silver. They often took novel shapes, such as birds, butterflies, scarabs, and bugs (ugh!). Others were oblong and served double duty as collar pins. Gold-plated ones on sterling silver sold for a couple of dollars or more each at the turn of this century. They are worth considerably more now. Many were set with imitation stones, and jewel stones adorned some of the more exclusive types.

Veils haven't entirely gone out of fashion today but are used far less frequently than in earlier days, while early veil fasteners are getting scarce.

Quite similar were scarf, lace, shawl, shirtwaist and dress pins, some of which were made in sets. Scarf (or stick) pins were decorative little pins with heads of various shapes mounted on the pin shaft. Some heads were fashioned as horseshoes, crescents, butterflies, beetles, owls, animals, and flowers. Better

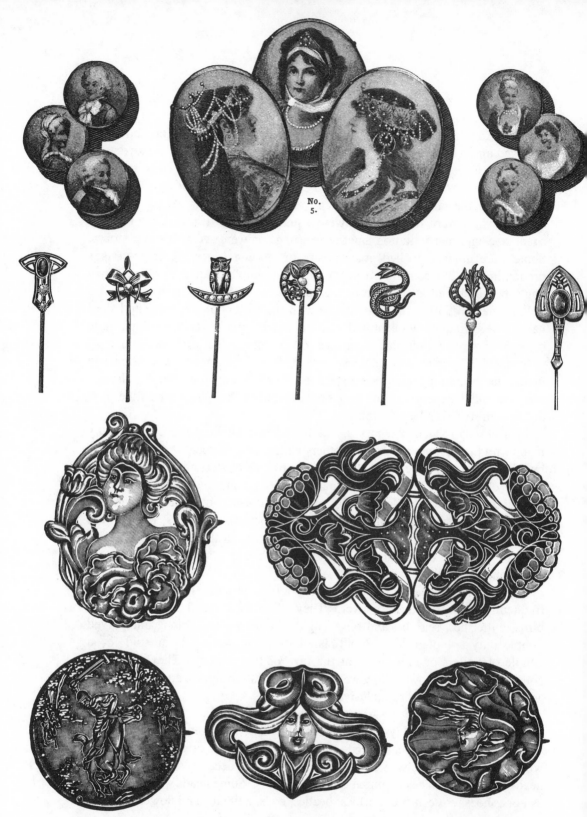

The decorated porcelain belt pins and button sets at the top were advertised as premiums in *The Youth's Companion* for October 23, 1902. They were decorated in colors. A group of gold-filled scarf pins is pictured on the second row. Below are sash and belt buckles of the early 1900's.

types sold for $4 or $5 each early this century, but thousands of less expensive ones were made. There was an attractive type with a cameo head, and one novelty pin was shaped like a rabbit's head, with ruby eyes. Incidentally, it was called "Alice Rabbit." Many fraternal scarf pins also were produced, as of course were numerous other types of fraternal pins and ornaments. Some scarf pins bore imitation diamonds; others contained genuine diamonds. (You aren't likely to find any of the latter in the junk shops.) While most of these were merely described in manufacturers' and wholesalers' catalogues, some, like "Alice Rabbit," were given names. One of the named pins was called "Teddy Bear" and bore a likeness of just that on the head. A rather grotesque pin was topped with a skull and crossbones.

Shawl pins also came in a variety of assorted shapes, an interesting one having been made in the form of leaves on a small twig. Some were set with imitation stones and others with genuine jewels, including pearls. Moonstones were a favorite.

Engraved three-pin blouse sets were popular early in this century. Many were oval, oblong, or square; but others were made in shapes imitating knots, flowers, and numerous other objects. Some blouse sets contained collar and cuff buttons with genuine pearl centers.

Brooches of almost every conceivable type were manufactured as dress clasps or adornments. These, of course, had a pin at the back for passing through the clothing and a catch for securing the pin's point. One can have a field day searching for different shapes of brooches. Some were set with garnets, and in 1900 fetched a neat price for those days — $4 to $20. Solid gold pendant brooches set with real pearls could be worn either as pendants or brooches. Some of these with 40 or 50 small pearls were quite high in price.

Brooches were made in classic and novelty shapes and designs, including crescents, stars, intertwined rings, single rings, rosettes, alligators, turtles, hearts, floral wreaths, birds, butterflies, cameos, anchors, and crosses, to list only a few.

There are some extremely attractive cameo brooches still available. They originally sold for $15 or $20 each. Gold-filled, rolled, and plated brooches were often quite cheap, and some can be picked up today for a dollar or so.

About the first quarter of this century, platinum and solid gold brooches were often worn by ladies of wealth. Some of these sold for more than $2,000, and they, too, are among the things you won't encounter in the junk pile. One good way to date types is to consult jewelry catalogues of earlier years. An array of novelty pins of the type we have been discussing is pictured in an early-twentieth-century catalogue of C. S. Davisson & Company, importers and manufacturers of Philadelphia, at prices ranging from a dime to a dollar each — and those prices included postage!

We don't realize today how deeply indebted we actually are to the lowly pin, which, as we know it, certainly does not date back to antiquity. The thorn may well have been the earliest type of pin; but in the Middle Ages the services now performed by a variety of pins were rendered by strings, ribbons, and various types of skewers, some of the latter made of precious metals and others of bone, ivory, or wood.

Wire-drawing, essential to the manufacture of pins, appears to have been undertaken in this country on some small scale during the latter half of the seventeenth century, and we do know that during the Revolutionary War pins were manufactured in Rhode Island. A Connecticut inventor, Dr. Apollos Hinsley, invented a machine for making pins in the last quarter of the eighteenth century. A much improved machine was devised in 1831 by Dr. J. I. Howe, of New York State, and the manufacture of his machines began the following year. Subsequently, Dr. Howe perfected a rotary machine for producing pins. Pin making was well under way in the United States during the 1840's.

This miscellaneous bit of history is offered gratuitiously, largely to point up the truth of the statement about great oaks growing from little acorns.

We shall return in a moment to other uses of the pin, but let's consider briefly the button, which is neither lowly nor entirely dispensable.

Unusual sleeve buttons can make an intriguing collection. A group of these in rolled plate were offered in an 1887–1888 catalogue of Lapp & Flershem, Chicago. One was made from an 1883 nickel from which the word "cents" had been eliminated. The front of this button pictured the head of the five-cent piece, and the reverse pictured the back. Another button in the same catalogue depicts a young lady with bare breasts, and this, undoubtedly, was considered quite risqué in its day. Still another shows a very faint likeness of Lady Godiva on her horse, and a fourth pictures a running dog, breed quite unidentifiable. These buttons, made of ivory, came in various colors. They wholesaled in those days from $3 to $4 a dozen.

Numerous designs appeared in belt buckles 75 years or so ago. Those in sterling silver were sometimes decorated with amethysts, imitation rubies, and other stones. A catalogue of the early 1900's shows a belt fastener with a buckle in the shape of a swastika, which would not be particularly popular in this country today. Belt fasteners with ornaments attached to silver-plated safety pins were produced. Gold-plated pins also were in evidence and were not particularly expensive, retailing in 1900 for around $2.50.

At about the same time, simple skirt pins in the shape of our present-day safety pins but made of gold and sterling silver were sold in some profusion. Those of 10-carat gold cost $20 or more. Gold-filled wire ones could be purchased for only $3 or so.

Hatpins were virtually a necessity back in the days when the ladies wore broad-brimmed hats and their hair atop their heads; they are still occasionally used, although they are becoming relics of the past. Designers utilized a high degree of imagination in designing hatpins for the ladies of the late nineteenth century just as they did when creating so many other dress accessories. Jeweled hatpins will soon be scarce, but probably thousands of less expensive ones are still around. A collection of hatpins arranged in a group of early hatpin holders can be of exceptional interest.

Gold-plated hatpins of late last century usually featured either imitation or genuine stones, and they could be found in varieties ranging in price from $2.50 to about $30 or more a dozen, wholesale. In the latter price category was one mounted with a bird with outspread wings and set with 33 brilliants and six fancy stones. Some hatpins were in the shape of diadems and crowns, butterflies, bees, flowers, human heads, musical instruments, animal heads, globes, mythological creatures, and even pretzels! Commonplace varieties sold for less than a dollar, and many interesting ones were priced at $1 to $2.50.

Hatpin holders were made of porcelain, pottery, glass, various metals, and other materials. Some in porcelain were produced by famous potteries. Among the more eagerly sought glass ones right now are those of Carnival glass. One of the latter — marked with an "N," indicating it was a Northwood production — was tendered not long ago at a price of $30. It probably sold originally for a good bit less than a dollar. A Bayreuth saucer-type holder was recently advertised for $14.50, one in orange Carnival glass for $7, and one of German bisque for $9. Others may be found now for a dollar or two up.

You will frequently find hatpin holders, and occasionally hatpins, advertised for sale or as wanted in the collector publications. Some time ago a collection of 50 hatpins, all in good condition, was offered for $42. The novelty types of hatpins are usually the earlier ones. These largely gave way to quite sedate types by the first quarter of this century.

Chatelette pins, produced to attach to the lapel or to chatelaines, were made in classic to grotesque shapes and designs. The chatelaine originally was a chain made to attach to the waist and from which to suspend keys. Later it was used to hang a variety of objects from; and these ranged from scissors to decorative ornaments.

Sterling silver chatelaines were sold early in this century with such articles attached as buttonhooks, pencils, scent bottles, or vinaigrettes (aromatic bottles for holding smelling salts, vinegar, or other pungent liquids), small oval mirrors, and memo tablets. Others were available with clasps to which one might attach whatever was desired, including the chatelette pins.

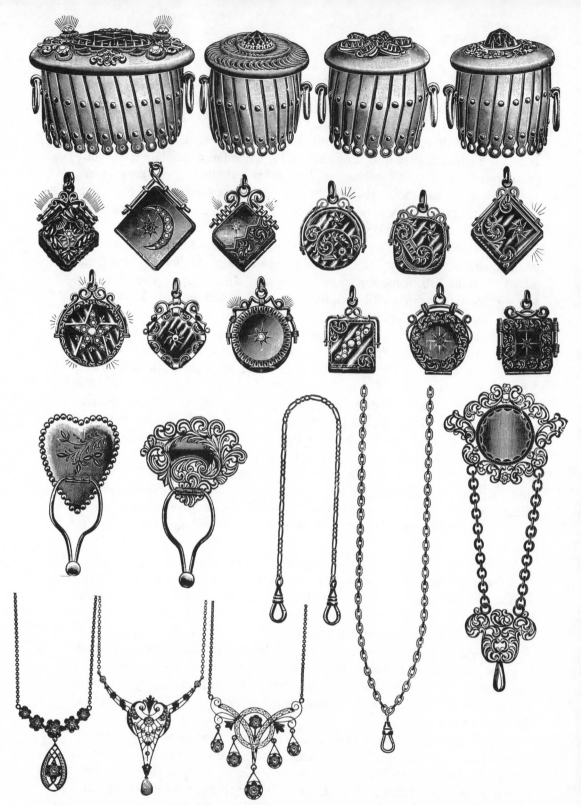

Dress accessories popular at the opening of this century included a number of those shown here. Top row: a group of gold-plated chatelaine bag tops. Second and third rows: a group of gentlemen's gold-front lockets. Fourth row: two handkerchief holders, a muff holder, a purse chain, and a fan or watch holder. Bottom: three solid gold festoons and chains.

The late-nineteenth-century chatelaine was usually suspended from the waistband, and the clasps or hooks had swivel attachments. The hooks, in turn, were attached to metal plates of various shapes, some of them fascinatingly interesting. Chatelaines set with precious stones cost a pretty penny, but silver- and even gold-plated ones with imitation stones were available for only a few dollars. Chatelaines virtually disappeared from use about 35 or 40 years ago.

Decorative chains and picture lockets worn around the neck (the latter sometimes on the lapel) were once treasured dress adjuncts. The lockets, quite tiny and often containing a picture of one's children or husband or some other loved one, were made of gold, silver, and plate.

Double lockets that held two pictures are found in sizes a good bit less than an inch in length and not much more than half an inch wide. Locket covers will be found with both precious and semi-precious stones and with embossed and chased decorations, including pictorial scenes. Some of the single picture lockets measured only half an inch square, but others ranged up to about 1½ inches in diameter or in length. They had a link at the top by which they could be attached to a chain worn around the neck.

Serving much the same decorative purpose as picture lockets, except that they had no interior space for pictures, were charms, — produced literally by the millions and made in approximately the same size as the lockets. Although heart-shaped charms were most popular, numerous other shapes were fashioned; and novelty charms may be found today in considerable profusion. They were made in silver and other precious metals, but plated ones were also turned out by the ton, selling at wholesale for $5 a dozen and less in 1900.

The novelty charms, worn primarily by teen-agers, were devised in the shape of dogs, pigs, horses, fish, barrels, acorns, anvils, compasses, clocks, ice tongs, baseballs, anchors, human hands, pistols and guns, locomotives, wheels, lanterns, vehicles, shoes, pipes, hanging shelves — well, you name it and it probably was made as a charm. Many crucifixes were made, and of course fraternal charms were manufactured in great abundance.

Small dressing-table picture frames, usually of oval or oblong shape, were a feature of many ladies' boudoirs as, a bit earlier, were various kinds of pictures, including landscapes, made of human hair on a background of cloth, frequently satin. Oval frames were utilized for most of these. Jewelry also was made of hair. Hair made into knots and bows and attached to wire frames often decorated the dressing table, and sometimes these were placed on mirrors. These may still be found but are considerably scarcer than the metal lockets and charms.

In much the same category, too, were lavalieres (sometimes spelled La-Vallieres), which were ornamental pendants on small chains worn around the

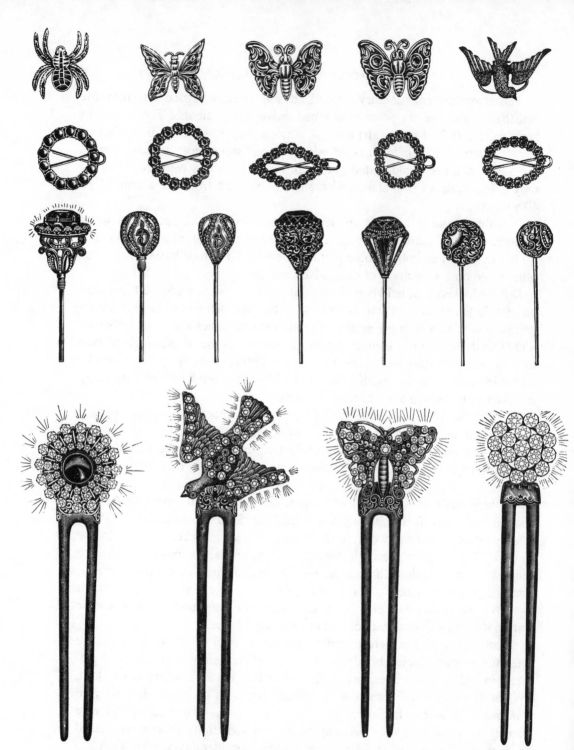

Dress accessories of the late 1800's. Top row: a group of novelties in veil fasteners. Second row: sterling silver hair ornaments. Third row: fancy hatpins with colored stones and brilliants. Bottom row: hairpins with imitation shell prongs and set with brilliants and colored stones.

neck. They were named, incidentally, for the Duchess of La Vallière, who was a mistress of Louis XIV of France. Jeweled pendants were widely worn around 1920 and were sold in better stores at prices starting around $5 and going considerably higher. Sometimes these took the form of festoon neck chains with a series of ornaments attached to chains arranged in festoon fashion. Not many of these were discarded, and you aren't likely to find them in the average antique shop.

Small chains were utilized for other purposes, including that of holding lorgnettes. Lorgnette chains were the fashion early in this century, although comparatively few ladies use these handle-mounted eyeglasses today. Such chains were sometimes set with pearls, turquoises, rubies, opals, diamonds, and imitation jewels. They had a swivel end to which the lorgnette could be securely attached. A 1921 catalogue of Swartchild & Company, of Chicago, offers "The Neverslip Hairpin" for holding eyeglasses. The oblong U-shaped hairpin was securely fastened in the hair, and a small chain was attached to the center of its curve. One end of this chain was then attached to milady's eyeglasses. The hairpin was removed from the hair by pressing a tiny release spring. Pince-nez eyeglasses also were sometimes attached with wire ear loops.

One type of lorgnette chain was worn around the neck and another had a pin end for fastening to the blouse or coat. Eyeglasses also were held in place by silk cords with hook and swivel attached.

Ornaments of an earlier day designed to be worn in the hair provide another challenge to the collector. In the era of the pompadour, which could return any day now (and perhaps it will have by the time you read this, since changes in hair styling are constant), the pompadour comb was fashionable. So were back and side combs, some of which were quite high in size. These combs were often set with stones, especially "brilliants," and many were made of imitation shell or celluloid. Some combs were ornamented on the curved flat surfaces in which the teeth were imbedded, and numerous fanciful shapes were produced.

The ladies of some years ago who wanted to be really well dressed had their choice of some rather striking hairpins and barrettes. The latter are clasps for holding the hair. There were hairpins of rolled plate with such objects as birds, butterflies, and stars set with brilliants or other fancy stones at the top. The prongs themselves were usually of imitation shell. At the turn of the century, this type of hairpin wholesaled at prices ranging from about $12 to $40 a dozen. There were also smaller hairpins of polished rolled plate or sterling silver without the decorative ornaments. Some hairpins and combs were imported from Bohemia; these were quite decorative, some being set with garnets.

The ornamental barrettes with attached prongs to fasten in the hair came

LORGNETTES AND OPERA GLASS HOLDERS.

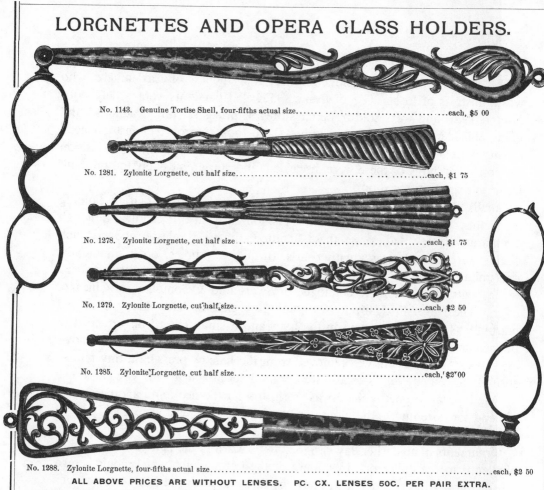

No. 1143.   Genuine Tortise Shell, four-fifths actual size......................................each, $5 00

No. 1281.   Zylonite Lorgnette, cut half size...each, $1 75

No. 1278.   Zylonite Lorgnette, cut half size...each, $1 75

No. 1279.   Zylonite Lorgnette, cut half size..each, $2 50

No. 1285.   Zylonite Lorgnette, cut half size...each, $2 00

No. 1288.   Zylonite Lorgnette, four-fifths actual size..each, $2 50

ALL ABOVE PRICES ARE WITHOUT LENSES.   PC. CX. LENSES 50C. PER PAIR EXTRA.

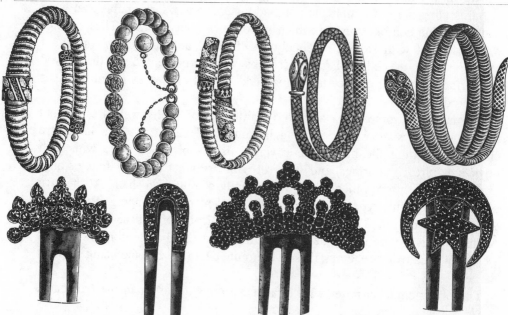

Fancy lorgnettes and opera glass holders were fashionable in the latter part of last century. Note the prices prevailing about 1880. The serpent bracelets are not much more atrocious than some the teen-agers wear today. The back combs on the bottom row are set with stones.

in numerous shapes and also were set with genuine or imitation stones. Some were made of gold and were engraved; others were gold-filled or of sterling silver or plate. Barrettes set with rhinestones were popular in the early 1920's as were rhinestone-set combs. Back combs with Bohemian garnets and prongs of tortoise shell were advertised in 1892 at prices of from $2 to $10 each.

Hair ornaments for ladies date back centuries, and some of their astonishing variety is evidenced in paintings and drawings which have come down from earlier eras. The type of ornaments depended, to some extent, on how the hair was worn — short, long, medium-length, swept up at the back, swept up at the front, made into a bun and so on. In the fourteenth and fifteenth centuries, many fine ladies wore cauls or coverings of silk, the finest of which were set with jewels.

All types of ribbons have adorned the hair at various times through the centuries as have lace towers. The only things there seem to have been more of than hair ornaments were types of hair-dos.

The use of novel hair ornaments was spurred in the nineteenth century by such publications as *Godey's Lady's Book, Peterson's Magazine,* and others, which featured fashions and published colored fashion plates illustrating dress and accessories of their periods.

Some types of hair jewelry suggested by *Godey's* and how they were made are delineated in an informative article, "Hair Work Jewelry," which was published in the April, 1965, issue of *The Spinning Wheel,* under the byline of Lillian Barker Carlisle. Those interested in hair-dos through the ages will find a perfectly delightful article about them in the January, 1951, issue of *Hobbies,* written by D. Tudor Harrell.

In Colonial days, Americans imported their combs from England, although a manufacturing plant that produced combs of horn was in existence in West Newbury, Massachusetts, in 1759. It was operated by Enoch Noyes. In addition, combs were advertised that same year by a manufacturer in Philadelphia. These may have been the earliest comb producers in this country, although a Robert Cook is reported to have made them in Needham, Massachusetts a bit earlier. The first comb-making machine was patented in 1798 by Isaac Tryon, a resident of Connecticut.

Before getting away from the subject of combs: many a male of the 1890's and for some years thereafter used a special mustache comb, and these are collectible. They were usually intended to fold inside a metal case, sometimes of sterling silver and sometimes of plate.

To delve adequately into the field of ear drops and bracelets would require a volume in itself, since they were made in such vast quantities and of so many different materials. Those you are likely to encounter in all except the better antique shops today were probably set with imitation stones, and the bracelets are apt to be plated. Thousands of ear drops were made in the nineteenth century with very small rubies, diamonds, opals, and other stones and were sold at prices which seem extraordinarily low today. Earrings are coming back into style and so, apparently, are pierced ears, a throwback to the aborigines — but who are we to quarrel with the fashion authorities? Ear screws can be fun to collect whether you wear them or not — and you can wear this type, of course, without having a hole drilled in your ear lobes. Small ones made of gold sold for as little as $1.75 a pair in 1907. Even as late as the early 1920's ear screws and drops with French pearls sold in fashionable shops for $3 to $5 a pair, though when you got into the area of finer pearls, the prices rose.

Bracelets of every conceivable design have been produced for centuries, and designers had a gala time with them in the final quarter of the nineteenth and first quarter of the twentieth century.

Particularly popular were solid gold chain bracelets with locks and tiny keys. The padlocks and keys were often available as accessories to the bracelet at an extra cost. Novelty bracelets featured attached hearts: some plain, some with the owner's initials, and some otherwise engraved or embossed. The bracelets made ideal gifts from swains.

Since bracelets are still worn, interesting types of earlier days can serve as intriguing gifts today. Even though most jewelry of value will be found today in the top-quality antiques shops and jewelry establishments, this does not rule out completely the possibility of occasionally making a "find" in a so-called "junk shop." Since not all antiques dealers are experts in jewelry, it might pay you to search carefully through box lots of jewelry and decorative accessories, which often turn up in the shops and at flea markets.

A pair of nineteenth-century 14-carat drop earrings with three gold balls was recently advertised at $15. A pair with inlaid abalone shell was offered at $2. The prices go in both directions from there.

Another decorative and utilitarian accessory was the handkerchief holder. This usually took the form of a metal plate which could be pinned to the blouse. A small metal holder, into which the handkerchief was placed, was attached. Generally, the holder was in the form of a loop, and the plate was of sterling silver, decorated.

Be on the lookout also for so-called ladies' "shopping lists." These were small tablets enclosed within covers of nickel, silver, or plate and were about the same size as calling card cases. Leaves inside the cases were often of celluloid, and the cases themselves usually had a small metal ring at the top so they could be secured to the person. Sometimes mechanical pencils were attached to the cases. External case embellishments were of the rococo style.

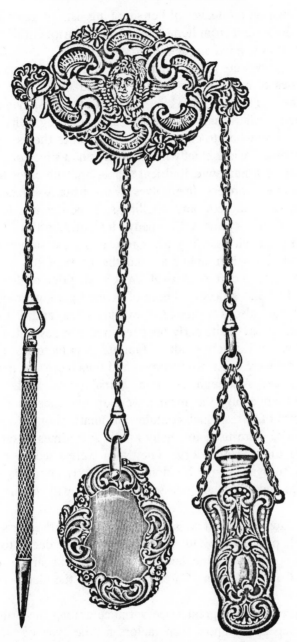

Sterling silver chatelaine pin with vinaigrette, tablet, and pencil.

Milady jotted down on the leaves of her shopping list the items she wanted to purchase when she set out from home on a shopping trip; and if you're absent-minded, you know how good an idea this is.

Chatelaine bag tops were gold-plated and decorated with stones. They were formed of a series of metal leaves with a top and metal rings to which the chain was attached. The tops fitted over the top of the mesh bag or purse.

We mentioned earlier that vinaigrettes and smelling salts bottles were among the articles attached to chatelaines. The bottles themselves, of course, are highly collectible. Made chiefly of glass, they had silver or gilt mounts or cases. Most were of a narrow cylindrical shape, and the cases had hinged or screw tops. Bottle stoppers themselves were usually made of glass.

A fine display of vinaigrette and smelling salts bottles was featured in the 1900 catalogue of Otto Young & Company, depicting bottles of cut glass and some of pressed glass with sterling silver tops and glass stoppers. The metal tops were hinged to a silver collar around the neck of the bottle. Though most are oblong, a few pictured are oval. Wholesale price of those of cut glass ranged from $14 to $24 a dozen. Those of pressed glass were much cheaper.

These little bottles also were made of overlay glass, and of ruby, vaseline, and other colored glass. Quite early ones featured cameos in the case decoration. Some of the bottles were made in famous glass factories, including that at Baccarat; others were mass-produced — and thus there was a wide variance in quality and price. Although the terms "vinaigrettes" and "scent bottles" were used interchangeably, the former were in evidence in the eighteenth century in the form of boxes which contained aromatic sponges.

The scent bottles were used in smelly areas: sometimes in crowded rooms to help alleviate unpleasant odors. They also were used as containers for various types of colognes in the boudoir. A perfectly charming collection of these little bottles and cases can be assembled, but it will require considerable hunting.

The items we have discussed constitute only a part of the dress and boudoir accessories worth preserving. Other items range from decorative miscellaneous buttons to opera caps. Incidentally, an interesting article on the latter entitled "Opera Caps or Earring Cases" appeared in the October, 1956, issue of *The Spinning Wheel*.

Naturally, there will be a great price variance among the articles we have just discussed, depending upon such factors as the type of materials used, scarcity, and condition. However, just for the fun of it, here are a few recently-advertised prices for some of the various categories of these items:

Round porcelain dress pin depicting lovers in a woodland setting, $15; gold belt buckle with engraved slide and floral decor, dated 1918, $6.50; oval dress pin depicting Madonna holding child, $15; large oval dress pin with portrait of Lillian Russell and a facsimile of her signature, $35; mother-of-pearl cameo brooch, $15; carved carnelian brooch with flowers and leaves, and gold and silver mounting, $10; brass locket with embossed flowers and space for single picture, $8.50; Victorian pinchbeck brooch with back designed to hold lock of hair, $58.50; Victorian pinchbeck cameo brooch, $25.75; single-picture locket decorated with 12 coral sets, $26.75; oval hairwork brooch with gold rope and frame, $8.50; hairwork brooch with seed pearls, dated 1856, $12.50.

Also, jet earrings, $2 a pair; pink cameo brooch in gold frame, $8.50; oval locket picture frame with curved glass, $3.50; pierced earrings with carnelian leaf, $12 a pair; hatpin holder in RS Germany china, $5; Lalique scent bottle, $9; cut-glass scent bottle, $14.

Although most of the dress accessories dealt with in this chapter were worn by the ladies, the males also took a fancy to various types of decorative gadgets, and these should not be overlooked.

21

As You Sew . . .

NOT TOO LONG AFTER THE ONSET OF THIS CENTURY THERE USED TO BE A
popular children's game called "Thimble, Thimble, Who's Got the Thimble?"
The answer to such a question now would be that collectors have the thimbles,
and they may soon have all those which have attained collectible stature.

But thimbles are only one of many collectible items related directly to
household sewing operations of years past. Other objects which should be
preserved include early sewing birds, darners, scissors, pin cushions, needle
boxes and cases, glove menders, tape measures, emery balls, sewing sets in
cases, and even some sewing machines.

Home sewing has not yet disappeared as an art, but there was a time when
every female child learned to sew as well as to cook — and not only to be
able to darn a future husband's socks and shirts but to sew and embroider
expertly. Our daughters today devote more attention to other occupations
and far less to the art of sewing, and were we a mother, we'd say "More's the
pity." But not being one, we are content to let the matter lie.

Thimbles once were made of gold, and should you find one today, you're
in luck. You also would be fortunate were you to find one of ivory. But you
do stand a good chance of the little silver thimble boxes decorated with open
work and with hinged tops. Gold-filled, sterling silver, and aluminum thimbles
are still with us in some abundance, but the latter two types are more easily
located than those that are gold filled. At the close of last century, the last-
named were selling from $15 to $30 a dozen. You could buy them in 14-carat
gold at about $6 to $10 each.

Through the years thimbles have been made of a wide variety of materials, including glass, porcelain, bone, rubber, leather, cloisonne, iron, gutta percha, and others. Some have been richly adorned with precious stones and even carved by sailors from whale's teeth. These little protective shields date back to ancient times and are reported to have been used by the early Chinese. European thimbles began coming into widespread use in the seventeenth century.

Nineteenth-century sterling silver thimbles (some of them made by well-known silversmiths) and even those made of aluminum had decorated bands, some with scenes engraved on them. Thimbles were made in circumferences to fit fingers of varying sizes, normally ranging from 5 to 12. As was the case with so many other late-nineteenth-century articles, rococo and floral designs were predominant on the bands, but one also will find cherubs, pastoral scenes, belts with buckles, and buildings.

Advertising and souvenir thimbles abounded early in this century, and this type is still being made. Many were decorated with flowers and scenes. Advertising thimbles usually contain a band bearing the name of the firm that gave them away. Thimble collectors are now on the increase and you may have to scramble to find choice ones.

Thimble boxes, containers, and cases were made of metal, leather, leather imitations, and other materials. Most were lined with silk or plush. Filigree cases are highly desirable as are those made in unusual shapes.

The stores of yesteryear displayed their thimbles in cases or boxes covered on the outside with lithographed paper and lined inside with cloth. These also can be collected but are scarce, since most retailers discarded them after all the thimbles had been sold.

The sewing bird, in case your education has been neglected, is a gadget featuring an ornamented clamp which can be fastened to a sewing table. A bird (or other device) atop the clamp holds the end of the piece of cloth that is being sewed in its beak (or a similar clamp) which is closed shut by a spring. This made the task of stitching easier.

Although sewing birds were most frequently made of iron or brass, some also were contrived of steel, wood, tin, silver, ivory, and even Britannia metal. Some early ones are quite crude, having been made either in a blacksmith shop or in a home by the man of the house handy with tools. Later productions were truly ornamental devices.

Actually the name "sewing bird" seems a misnomer. It's true that many of these cloth clamps were in the shape of birds, but it also is true that scores were not. Some resembled butterflies, animals, cupids, and other objects. However, it might be a trifle awkward to refer to a "sewing butterfly," a "sewing dog," a "sewing cupid," and so on. The shapes and designs changed

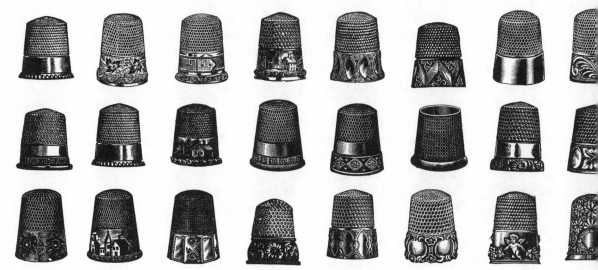

Early-twentieth-century gold and sterling silver thimbles.

through the years. Some were made with attached pin cushions; others had compartments attached for thimbles and thread.

A large number of the sewing birds now available probably will be priced somewhere between $6 and $15, though unusual early ones and the more elaborate ones are worth more. If you want to limit your collecting strictly to the birds — that it, eschewing the animals, cupids, and the like — you would be enlightened to learn just how many types of birds you could find on these devices.

Much enjoyment also may be derived from seeking out early darners, sometimes called "darning eggs" or, in the case of some types, "hand coolers."

Darners were made of wood, ivory, glass, alabaster, marble, quartz, and other hard stones, while later ones were made of plastic. They are egg-shaped and occasionally are attached to stands or handles. Objects of this type made of hard stone or glass are said to have been used by ladies in an earlier era to cool their hands; hence the reference to hand coolers. But they definitely were used for darning — and they still are. In some areas of the country, potatoes were once used for the same purpose. These were somewhat cheaper. Quite attractive are darners made of marble glass (also referred to as "slag glass" or "mosaic glass") and of other types of art glass, and it seems almost a shame to use them for so prosaic a purpose as darning. Occasionally you may find one of these darners covered with cloth.

Among the articles attracting great attention at the Women's Pavillion at the 1876 Centennial Exposition in Philadelphia was an unusual darner in-

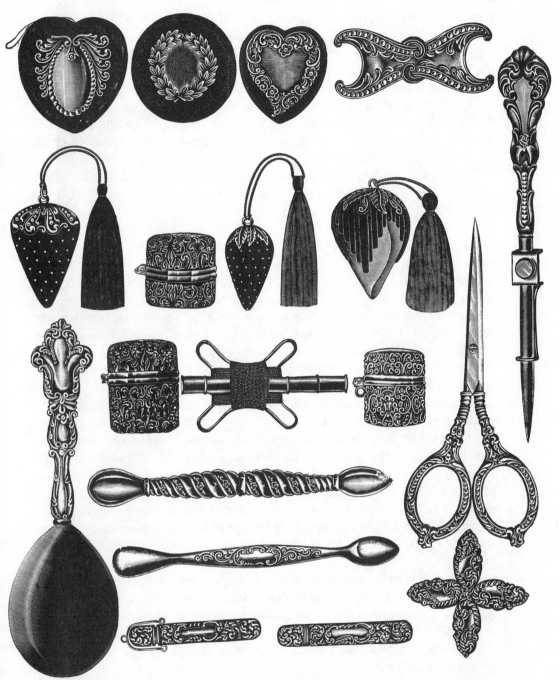

Sterling decorated sewing accessories. Top, left to right: three plush pincushions, a silk winder, and a bodkin with gauge. Second row: three emery balls with tassels and an emery box. Third row: darner with an ebony ball, two thimble boxes, combination silk winder and needle box, and ornate-handled sewing scissors. Below are two glove menders, two needle cases, and a thread reel.

vented by a Mrs. Harley, of Philadelphia. It is described in some detail in
J. S. Ingram's book *The Centennial Exposition, Described and Illustrated,*
which was pubilshed in that same year by Hubbard Bros. Shaped somewhat
like a dwarf gourd, the top was concave so that it could accommodate a
needle, and it could be removed so that a ball of cotton could be inserted in it.
There was a small opening lower down on the darner through which the
thread was pulled. This darner also had a finger-shaped handle for use in
mending gloves, Ingram reported. Not only the top but also the bottom of the
darner was removable and it contained space for the storage of needles.

Darners with sterling silver handles were widely used around the turn of the
century. The darner balls were often of ebony, and the prices of these
ranged from $6 or $7 to more than $10.

There are a number of collectors of pin cushions, and their ranks may well
swell when more persons become aware of just how many charming objects
of this type have been turned out during the past century. Many of the
earlier functions of pins have been usurped today by such things as zippers
and other types of closures, but pins once rendered yeoman service in many
areas. Pins of one type or another have actually been in use for many years,
and for those who would like to know more about their history, Edwin C.
Whittemore wrote a most informative article on the subject, entitled "Pins
and Pincushions," in the March, 1966, issue of *The Spinning Wheel.*

Because of the remarkable variety of shapes in which they were made,
pincushions hold more interest for the average collector than do the pins
themselves. Rather commonplace types may still be found at very low prices,
but the values of the more unusual cushions are advancing and could go far
higher than they are right now. Quite a large number of pincushions were
produced in the shape of animals, birds, and human figures (primarily children). Those made of plush material were also decorated with sterling silver
ornaments, a good many of these in the shape of hearts. Some ornaments were
set with stones, and their prices at the turn of this century ran as high as $15
each.

Other types were fashioned in the shape of flowers or vegetables; such
articles of clothing as hats, caps, shoes; and a variety of inanimate objects,
including for example vehicles or miniature pieces of furniture. These types
are particularly desirable. Mr. Whittemore's article mentioned above includes
illustrations of a pincushion in the shape of a sled and one in the form of a
grindstone that turns.

More prosaic but nevertheless quite utilitarian pincushions were in use in
the 1920's. Many of these featured a velvet pad atop a round base made of
celluloid or other substances. Some pincushions served at the top of small
boxes for jewelry and ornaments.

Not only thimble containers but needle containers or boxes and cases also are collectible. Small oblong cases of sterling silver, nicely decorated, were made 65 or 70 years ago to hold needles. Later, silver cases were issued with compartments for needles, spool, and thimble. Marshall Field & Company sold this type in 1919 for $4.20.

Thousands of sewing and embroidery scissors have been produced through the years, and still available are some of the beautiful ones turned out between the first and final quarters of the nineteenth century. Some of their ingeniously devised silver handles with open work and imaginative shapes are little short of magnificent. Scissors of this type generally ranged from 3½ to 4½ inches in length. Creative designers in all countries turned their talents to scissors. In England, they were made by skilled swordsmiths.

Some scissors were made in the shape of dolphins and fish; others had handles with intertwining silver roses and leaves. Special-purpose scissors included those for making buttonholes . A popular gift for birthdays, anniversaries, and other special occasions in this country was a folding leather case containing three pairs of scissors. Early in this century, these cases were made with silk linings. One fascinating pair of embroidery scissors was in the shape of a stork with a long beak forming the blade and the legs leading to the rounded handles. Novel sewing scissors would make an intriguing collection.

Thousands of sewing sets in cases were manufactured in the earlier years of this century just as they are today. Some sets contained a pair of scissors, thimble, and an emery ball. Others included a darner, spool of thread, and other accessories. Cases were of leather and other materials. One set, housed in a case in the shape of a heart, made an ideal gift for St. Valentine's Day.

Few persons seem to be collecting tape measures in cases, yet these offer a fertile field for the adventurous. These measures were made about 65 or 70 years ago in 3-foot lengths with the measures housed in tiny cases, which were often of embossed sterling silver. Less expensive measures had celluloid covers, some of which were adorned with silver shields.

Some silver cases were etched with interesting scenes or with floral and other types of décor. One such scene shows a house with a fenced yard filled with playing children. On the cover appear the words "A Full Yard." One case dated about 1920 features delicate colors in cloisonne enamel. Some of the later measures contained 50 to 60 inches of tape instead of 36 inches. Not many of these tape measures in cases from earlier days crop up now in the antiques shops, and one wonders what has happened to them.

Another accessory to be on the lookout for is the glove mender, some of which were made of sterling silver. These had tiny balls on each end to fit into the fingers of gloves.

There also were silk winders or thread reels in silver, around which thread or silk could be wound so it would be available for subsequent use. One thread reel was made in the shape of a four-leaf clover; others were oblong in shape with ends having the appearance of being gouged out so that the silk could be wound around them lengthwise and would not slip off.

Of course, there were thousands of emery balls. They were used to sharpen needles. Some had silver handles; others had silver tops with tassels attached. Most commonplace was the pineapple shape. There also were hinged emery boxes of sterling with open-work decorations.

Since bottle collectors seem to be grabbing at every available bottle, they should keep an eye out for sewing-machine-oil bottles, preferably those with lettering in the glass. There are a number of these available, one brand widely used at the opening of this century having been "Excelsior." Most of these bottles are lettered on the glass "Excelsior Sewing Machine Oil, Chicago, Ill." They were made in 2- and 3-ounce sizes. The bottles had panelled sides and originally bore paper labels in one panel identifying the product as "Excelsior Sperm Sewing Machine Oil." The Excelsior Supply Company furnished special labels for those manufacturers and distributors who ordered 100 bottles or more of the oil in a single shipment, however, so that some of these bottles may bear paper labels identifying the seller as other than the Excelsior Supply Company.

And what about the early sewing machines themselves? Individuals and institutions are preserving early phonographs and similar devices, and the early sewing machine deserves preservation too; although in the case of the individual collector, one or two machines will prove sufficient, since space for storage and display is a problem. Museums certainly should salvage the early machines and keep them on view for posterity.

Elias Howe is generally credited with having invented the sewing machine, but one of the first ones actually is said to have been made by a minister-novelist, the Rev. Francis Robert Goulding, in Georgia. Goulding was the author of a series of novels for boys which at one time were about as popular as Stevenson's *Treasure Island*. They included *Marooner's Island; or, Dr. Gordon in Search of His Children* (1869), *The Young Marooners on the Florida Coast, or Robert and Harold* (1852), *Sapelo; or, Child-Life on the Tide-Water* (1870), and others.

Goulding made a sewing machine for his wife in an improvised workshop in the kitchen of his home in Eatonton, Georgia, in 1842. It worked and may well have been the first practical sewing machine in America. But he never patented his machine, and Howe did patent his. In his own journal, the Georgia minister wrote that he had satisfied himself about the machine and that he then set it aside so that he might "attend to other and weightier duties." Others say, however, that Goulding intended to patent his machine and that

Sewing accessories. A group of pre-World War I gold- and silver-plated pincushions is at the extreme left, from top to bottom of the page. To the right of
these on the top row are a "Magic" darning machine, plush sewing box, and a
Pansy hand sewing machine of the late 1800's. Embroidery scissors are shown on
the second row and tape measures on the third (the two at the right having sterling silver cases). On the fourth row are silver thimbles and a sewing basket
lined and decorated with ribbons. On the bottom row, from left, are an emery
bag with sterling handle, sterling floss winder, emery strawberry with sterling
trimmings, and a wax strawberry.

he actually set out in a stagecoach to Washington with it, but that en route the stage overturned and the machine was stolen and never recovered. Another story has it that as Goulding was traveling to Washington by buggy, his machine fell out into the water as he crossed a creek and was never found.

Nevertheless, Elias Howe is regarded, and properly, as the father of the commercial sewing machine industry in the United States and obtained a patent on one in 1846. Sewing machines made in the latter part of last century are still around in some abundance. They were built to last a long time.

Other sewing accessory collectibles include spool racks, work boxes and baskets, sewing cabinets, and bodkins.

Not long ago, a Singer Sewing machine with walnut case, dated 1876, was advertised at $40. The cabinet had six drawers with burl walnut fronts. On the other hand, a nineteenth-century Howe machine with lacy iron legs and walnut cabinet was tendered at only $18, and a small Wilcox sewing machine dating to about 1870 was offered for only $7.50. You should be able to find many machines between these two price extremes, since standard values have not yet been established.

As for prices of some of the other accessories, discussed in this chapter, sewing birds will start at about $7.50 and prices go up from there, depending on age and quality. Other recently-advertised prices include: beaded velvet pin cushion, $2.50; wooden darner, $2; drop-leaf, two-drawer sewing table with center pedestal, $50; Victorian sewing cabinet, two drawers and drop leaves, $37.50; Ladies' Companion sewing kit with one implement lacking, $4.50; and two-tier mahogany sewing box with pin cushion on top, $9.

22

Speaking of Babies . . .

HOW MANY RELICS OF YOUR CHILDHOOD DO YOU STILL HAVE AROUND? IF you're an average individual, you probably have few indeed. Yet there are numerous articles associated with babies of earlier days which can turn collecting into a fascinating search — probably a more fascinating one for the female of the species than the male. These range from ABC plates to toys, from bib holders to spoons, from nursing bottles to combs and brushes.

Let's start with baby rattles. Those of earlier years were made in a perfectly fantastic variety of designs. A collection representing all of the types made in the late nineteenth and early twentieth centuries would fill a sizeable portion of a large room. If you could assemble one of each type made since they first came into use as playthings for children, the average room wouldn't be large enough to hold them.

A few centuries ago there were rattles of gold and silver made in whimsical shapes, but thousands of subsequent ones have been fabricated of far less expensive materials. Those of tin should be of prime interest to collectors, and be sure to latch on to any of years past you may encounter that were made of wood.

The earlier rattles of this type contained tiny pebbles or somtimes even grains of corn, were usually decorated in bright colors, and often were lettered with phrases, or parts of nursery rhymes.

Less than a century ago, combination rattles and whistles, and rattles attached to rings, were popular. A good many were produced with handles or rings of pearl and bells and whistles of sterling silver. Each contained two or three small bells, and they sold at prices ranging from about $1.50 for the simplest to around $5 for the more ornate ones.

Silver baby rattles, an A B C plate, whistles, and teething ring of the late 1800's and early 1900's.

The 1892 catalogue of B. F. Norris, Alister & Company pictures a rattle with a pearl handle and five small bells attached to a silver holder. The wholesale price was $4. The E. I. Horsman Company made a variety of rattles attached to rubber teething rings, and a 1906 catalogue of this company shows a group of this type listed at prices of from $4.50 to $9 a gross. The same company offered a group of rattles with wooden handles and celluloid teething rings in its 1900 catalogue. Some had several small bells and others a single larger bell. Prices started at $4 a gross.

Rattles with ocean pearl rings and sterling silver bells were made in a variety of shapes in the first quarter of this century. Some had sterling handles and mountings. Some bells resembled sleigh bells, other miniature cow and sheep bells, and still others were in the shape of balls. These rattles cost from $2 to $5 each.

Many striking novelty rattles were made 65 or 70 years ago. Some of the them had representations of animals or animal heads — including bears, foxes, and cats — atop their pearl handles. One featured a teddy bear with a bell attached to each of its two front *paws*.

Small silver whistles with embossed designs or other types of decorations also were widely sold about 65 or 70 years ago. These could be bought for $2 or $3 each at the time.

Some years ago parents exercised the art of psychology in coaxing their small children to eat their meals by feeding them in what we now refer to as "ABC" plates, or Alphabet plates. Such plates were made usually of pottery or tin. Pottery ones were decorated with various types of transfer prints, and the majority had borders on which the letters of the alphabet were embossed. Thus, the child was encouraged to learn the alphabet while satisfying also his physical need.

The transfer prints embraced a diversity of scenes with an appeal to youngsters. They included animals and children at play, or sports. One series of plates illustrated maxims from the famous *Poor Richard's Almanac,* written largely by Benjamin Franklin. The transfers were printed in colors, including reds, greens, black, browns, and blues. Many of these plates were hand-colored. While some had the entire alphabet embossed around the borders, others utilized only the first three letters of it, sometimes together with scrolls, flowers, and other decorations.

These plates were produced in large quantities after about 1820 by English potters, among the better known of which were J. & G. Meakin, Leeds Pottery, R. & J. Clews, and Wm. Adams & Company. The plates were imitated by potteries in the United States and abroad toward the latter part of the nineteenth century.

About 1907, variety stores in the United States began importing a "double

Intriguing baby spoons and a couple of alphabet-type plates dated about 1900.

A fine group of children's mugs from the collection of William Flatow, Jr., Stamford, Connecticut.

alphabet" plate. This featured the regular alphabet on the flange and the alphabet for the deaf and dumb in the center and was gaily decorated. This type wholesaled for only 75 cents a dozen! Alphabet plates were made in this country of tin, porcelain, aluminum, and glass.

The early earthenware alphabet plates will sell at prices of from around $5 to $25, and those marked with the name of the pottery which produced them will usually fetch a bit more than unmarked plates.

An earthenware plate depicting Red Riding Hood in color is valued at about $12. A pink lustre ABC plate with a matching cup and saucer is priced $22. A 7-inch plate entitled "Horses for Sale or Hire" is offered at $10.50, and a Franklin maxim plate in green impressed "Adams" is advertised at $10. One dated February 11, 1890, with a design by Palmer Cox, creator of the famous "Brownies," brings a premium — $18.50. It is made of tin.

Some of the later ABC plates of glass have been on the market recently at prices ranging from about $3 to $10. Pewter is said to have been used for some early ones. Early in this century, engraved nickel ABC plates with a silver finish were offered at wholesale prices of from $8 to $20 a gross in 8-inch diameters. In the center of one of these was pictured a horse inside a huge horseshoe, surrounded by a group of animals.

There are many collectors of Toby jugs or mugs, but one could make as interesting a collection of baby mugs, limiting his or her acquisitions to those

A group of the famed Franklin Maxim children's mugs from the collection of Mr. Flatow.

Additional Franklin Maxim mugs from the collection of Mr. Flatow.

made between 1875 and 1920. Thousands of china mugs were turned out adorned with transfer prints and incorporating maxims, Bible verses, and other inscriptions such as "For a Dear Girl."

Some scenes on these mugs illustrate nursery rhymes or fairy-tale incidents, while others have illustrations quite similar to those on the ABC plates. Staffordshire artists in England apparently had a heyday with the maxims of Franklin, *Poor Richard's Almanac* having been printed in England as well as in this country.

Some mugs of very small size were produced, featuring children in everyday settings, and animals and flowers. Souvenir children's mugs were issued to publicize various cities and states and attractions.

Some years ago a magnificent collection of mugs of this type was assembled by Margaret H. Jewell, who later turned over the group, numbering more than 1,200, to the care of the Society for the Preservation of New England Antiquities in Boston. She described and illustrated her collection in an article in *Old-Time New England, The Bulletin of The Society for the Preservation of New England Antiquities, for October, 1934.*

Late last century and early in this one, many baby mugs and handled cups of sterling silver engraved with decorations of a rather chaste nature were produced. Some of these cost $20 or $25 each. This type is still being made, but they are not so intriguing as the earlier decorated china ones.

An outstanding collection of mugs of various periods has been assembled by Mr. William Flatow, Jr., of 380 Rock Rimmon Road, Stamford, Connecticut. He has arranged them in several classifications. One consists of china mugs in canary or yellow-lustre color. These constitute his most valuable category, and their retail prices range from about $40 to $150 each, depending upon their condition. These are illustrated with pictures or sayings, or a combination of both. One, for example, depicts a very wise-looking owl on its exterior and is lettered "An Owl for Thomas."

Another category consists of mugs similarly designed, but not canary-colored, which were given as presents to children by their grandparents, and which bear such phrases as "A Trifle for James." The Flatow collection also embraces an interesting group of Alphabet mugs, each of which illustrates a letter of the alphabet. He also has a few individual mugs which illustrate the entire alphabet. One of his individual Alphabet mugs illustrates the letter "T" by picturing a tiger, a tent, a top, and a target. Others are illustrated in similar manner.

Still another group of mugs in his collection features nursery rhymes or slogans issued by temperance societies. Also included is a representative group of the Franklin Maxim mugs, one of which is lettered:

Baby mugs with nursery rhymes and maxims issued by the Temperance Society.
From the collection of Mr. Flatow.

Children's mugs illustrating letters of the alphabet. From the collection of Mr.
Flatow.

Lost time is never found again.
What we call time enough
Always proves little enough.

Another reads:

Handle your tools without mittens,
Remember the cat in gloves catches no mice.

Still another typical maxim is:

For age and want save what you may;
No morning sun lasts all the day.

Although he already has a fine collection in his possession, Mr. Flatow says he is still trying to learn about children's mugs, which is a characteristic of the dedicated collector.

About the first quarter of this century baby spoons with interestingly decorated handles were produced in some profusion. A typical one has a handle in the shape of a stork. Another features a head of Santa Claus in the caput. Children's flatware sets consisting of a spoon, knife, and fork also were made early in the present century, though not many sets will be found intact today.

Decorated and figural children's napkin rings and holders are a joy to collect. Among those produced were plated holders which featured children, animals, birds, cupids, fruit, and numerous other objects as an integral part of their overall design. Most holders of this type were manufactured by silver-plating companies. Those who wish to study this subject in more detail will find a chapter devoted to them in the author's earlier book *Treasure at Home*.

Bib or napkin holders also are collected. These, of course, were designed to keep baby from losing his bib or tiny napkin. They usually consisted of a chain or a cord from the ends of which clasp holders to secure the bib in place were suspended. The silk cords often had tassels attached, and the clasps were frequently of sterling silver, some set with stones. These were not very expensive, selling at prices of from $1 to $3 about 1900. Later in this century, bib holders with gold or gold-filled clasps were made to sell at prices of $1.50 to $5.

We won't include a discussion of toys in this chapter (these also, are treated in *Treasure at Home*) except to mention that thousands of rubber and celluloid dolls and animal replicas which are worth salvaging have been produced during the past century. Many of these served as pacifiers, and great varieties of them were sold by E. I. Horsman Company, of New York

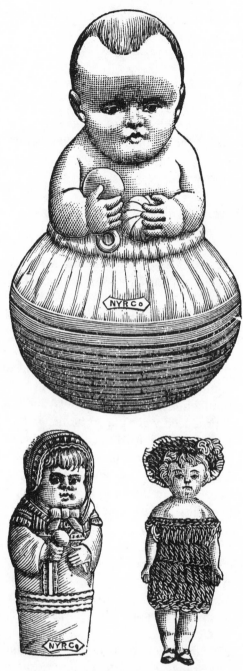

Nineteenth-Century rubber dolls.

Baby's plated napkin ring.

City, among other firms. The "Buster Brown" rubber doll was popular shortly after the turn of the century. Horsman offered one of these 6 inches in length, at wholesale prices of $2 a dozen.

These rubber dolls and animals were hollow inside and many had whistles that sounded when they were squeezed. This type is still being made, of course. Some tiny rubber dolls were dressed in clothes made of worsted, while others were jointed so that limbs and head could be moved. Simple small rubber dolls sold in 1906 for as little as 80 cents a dozen. The New York Rubber Company made some "whistle dolls," which sold at wholesale for 50 cents a dozen.

Other collectible baby mementoes include baby carriages, pins and lockets, comb-and-brush and other toilet sets, tin bathtubs, furniture (including cradles and chairs), lithographed sand buckets, dishes, and nursing bottles. These may suggest still others to you.

23

Toy Vehicles

SOME INTEREST ON THE PART OF COLLECTORS IN TOY VEHICLES OTHER THAN the miniature models seems to be just awakening at present. These vehicles include early velocipedes and tricycles, pedal-motivated autos and hand cars, and doll carriages. Since most of these are of some bulk, one will be faced with a space problem if he attempts to assemble many of them, but museums should preserve them, and there is no reason why the individual should not acquire one or two of them if he or she desires.

Some of these early toy vehicles are a pure delight, and they certainly afforded hours of enjoyment to boys and girls of years past. Numerous companies made them, and they were sold largely through hardware, department, and specialized toy stores. Those produced up to around 1910 will be of most interest.

Early tricycles had a comfortable seat, headrest and arm rests attached to two large rear wheels, and were propelled by foot pedals connected by metal bars to the rear wheels. Steering was provided by means of a long handle attached to a much smaller front wheel. The early velocipedes had a large front wheel and two smaller rear wheels and a saddle-type seat in the center above the wheels. The pedals were attached to the front wheels and steering was by means of handlebars attached to the front wheel. The word "velocipede" also is used to refer to the early bicycles, but as used here, it is intended to describe the child's vehicle of the type just described.

Early tricycles had mud guards or fenders finished in natural wood, and steel tubular frames. The seats were fitted with springs and upholstered with plush material. Wheel sizes varied, the diameter of the rear wheels ranging

238

Late-Nineteenth-Century children's vehicles. Top: a Columbia two-track tricycle and the Horsman tricycle. Below: a four-wheeled propellor and a wooden veloci-pede.

from about 18 to 36 inches. The earliest ones utilized steel tires; rubber tires were used later. In appearance, the tricycle of 1900 resembled some of the vehicles used by invalids except that the latter did not have pedals and, of course, was larger.

Incidentally, those who are interested in collecting early bicycles in general may find an article I have written, which was published in the April, 1965, issue of the magazine *Yankee* (Dublin, New Hampshire) under the title "The Boneshakers Are Back," of some interest.

Juvenile automobile of 1907.

Toy riding-size automobiles made early in this century should be of prime interest. Both one-passenger and two-passenger autos were made. The latter had a front and rear seat and was known as a touring car.

Most of the toy autos were made of galvanized tin, enameled or varnished. The bodies were frequently decorated with stripes and lettering. Some came complete with head lamps, although in other cases the lamps were sold as accessories, as were horns. Steering wheels were similar to those used on contemporary battery-operated automobiles, but the toy ones were propelled by pedals attached by bars to the rear wheels. Many were even equipped with license plates.

In general shape, the toys were patterned after the early model full-sized automobiles. One, named "Red Devil," was modeled after the design of the Cadillac of its day (1909). Some seats were upholstered with tin backs. Rear fenders were featured on swank models.

Falling into the same general classification were hand cars and tandem racers. The hand cars had a long flat seat, usually of wood, mounted on a steel frame to which four wheels were attached: two at front and two in the rear. The vehicle was propelled by steel gears attached to a rear wheel and operated by means of alternately pushing and pulling an upright shaft with a crossbar at the top for the hands—in much the same fashion as the early railroad handcars were operated.

Handcars were frequently pitted against one another in races in the days before whizzing motor vehicles afforded a menace to safety on the streets,

Group of rapidly disappearing toy automobiles, pushcarts, and tricycles of 1909.

As age goes, these children's vehicles are by no means ancient. They were produced about 40 years ago and were offered for sale by Bealknap Hardware and Manufacturing Company, Louisville, Ky., which is still in business. However, they are collectible. Left to right, top: a Ford dump truck, a Packard, and an Austin. Bottom: hook and ladder truck, monoplane, and a fire chief's truck.

and they could be propelled at considerable speed. Some were so sturdily constructed that they could support a weight of a thousand pounds. Some handcars were decorated with transfer designs. The tandem car was designed to accommodate two operators.

These little racing machines bore such names as "Wabash Limited," "Glascock Racer," "Irish Mail Hand Car," and "Glascock's Tandem Racer." In 1909, handcars of this type wholesaled at only $6.50 to $7.50 each. The tandem was priced at $13.

Boys' wagons were favorite Christmas and birthday presents at about the same period, but wagons of quite similar type—only a bit sleeker—are still being produced.

Although doll carriages are not exactly vehicles in the same sense as the contrivances discussed above, they are of interest nevertheless because they were made in so many sizes and designs through the years and had a universal appeal for small girls. They were smaller versions of baby carriages, fashioned primarily of reed or wicker with fancy sides and, quite often, a parasol top. Some doll collectors also collect doll carriages.

Children's go-carts and carriages of the latter part of last century.

Hobby or rocking horses made well over half a century ago.

All hobby horses were not vehicles, but they certainly afforded motion to their young riders, and there were actually some hobby horses mounted on wheels and propelled by pedals. These contrivances for young childlren have been made for years and in amazing variety. They are still being made, and undoubtedly those produced today afford as much joy for their young riders as did those of a century ago.

Wheeled hobby horses substituted a replica of a horse for a tricycle or velocipede seat, but the majority of hobby horses had either a rocker-shaped platform to yield a backward and forward motion or a stationary platform with springs to give the rider both a backward-and-forward and an up-and-down motion. The wooden horses were fine-looking animals in racing posture with tails flowing back with the wind. Many were fully equipped with saddles, bridles, and stirrups.

The early forerunner of the mechanical hobby horse was a stick with a carved replica of a horse's head on one end. There are also in existence some quite early models of the larger rocking or hobby horses, crudely done and undoubtedly carved and fashioned by home artisans. These, like the later commercial models, were painted. Some craftsmen used genuine horse hair for the mane and tail of the wooden model and applied eyes of glass.

An interesting discussion of early hobby or rocking horses will be found in Leslie Daiken's book, *Children's Toys Throughout the Ages,* a new edition of which was published by Spring Books, London, in 1963.

Should you come across a nineteenth-century rocking horse on which the paint has badly peeled or deteriorated, you can use your own judgment as to whether to repaint it. There are some purists who wouldn't think of retouching them.

24

Traps

TRAPS HAVE BEEN USED FOR CENTURIES TO CATCH EVERYTHING FROM BEARS to mice. While there has been some collecting traffic of late in animal traps, little attention has been paid thus far to the intriguing early mouse and fly traps. You can be a pioneer if you are interested in pursuing the latter two types.

An invention for an improved rat trap was described in the *Scientific American* for February 7, 1852. Invented by J. H. Chester, of Cincinnati, Ohio, it was indeed an ingenious device. The rat was enticed to enter the doors of this trap by a tasty morsel of cheese or other food, which was hung over a tilting board. The rat's weight depressed the tilting board, thereby disengaging catch levers from the doors, which promptly fell shut. Alarmed by the sound of the falling doors, the frightened rat began to seek a way of escape and its attention was then attracted by a light issuing from a trap door. At that point (said the inventor) the rat began to ascend an inclined way and by its own muscular power raised another perforated yielding door through which it plunged into a second compartment, which turned out to be its prison. By virtue of these sections, the trap was reset for another unsuspecting rat.

Earlier mousetraps were made of wood and utilized a metal weight. The weight was operated by a release pin, which held it above the wooden compartment. When the mouse started gnawing at the bait inside, a catch was released which resulted in the weight falling on the mouse and crushing it. This was not nearly so refined a way of disposing of a mouse or a rat as was

Mr. Chester's more humane device. Neither, for that matter, are the strong spring traps in use today. Some of the latter don't stop at killing mice; they'd just as soon nip off the tip of one's finger as well.

A type called "Marty's Patent French Traps" was used to catch mice and rats about 1900. First manufactured in France, many were sold in this country. They were made of wire and featured a sort of baffle entrance: The animal could get inside but, once inside, couldn't effect an exit. These traps came in "family" and "hotel and stable" sizes, or what we might refer to today as the "large economy size." The latter measured 27 inches long and had a capacity of 50 rats! In describing it in its 1901 catalogue, Sargent & Co. assured the prospective purchaser: "Notwithstanding the large capacity claimed for these traps, many testimonials prove the several sizes will catch their full capacity night after night as long as the rats hold out."

Quite commonplace at the opening of the century and for some years thereafter were the round traps, some made of wood and some of metal, with several entrances around the circumference. These used steel springs, which were released when the animal poked its head in one of the holes and which choked the critter to death. These were not very humane either—but then, most folk weren't giving much thought to the rat's comfort.

Popular in the 1880's was the "Delusion" mouse trap. An 1884 catalogue of Sargent & Co. described its operation in this poetic fashion:

> *The Mouse goes in to get the bait,*
> *And shuts the door by his own weight,*
> *And then he jumps right through the hole,*
> *And thinks he's out; but, bless his soul,*
> *He's in a cage, somehow or other,*
> *And sets the trap to catch another."*

The principle employed in this sounds as if it were similar to that utilized by Mr. Chester's invention. The "Delusion" was manufactured by Lovell Mfg. Company, Limited, and was first patented on July 18, 1876.

Hotchkiss' Patent No. 20 Improved Rat Killer was a self-setting trap of two sections made of cold rolled steel. When the mouse entered and took the bait, a steel loop, released by a coiled spring, caught the animal on the back of the neck and killed it.

There were dozens of very simple mouse traps made of wood and metal or completely of metal and utilizing a coiled spring and metal loop in use early in this century. One well-known brand name was "E-Z Ketch Trap," manufactured by E-Z Mfg. Company. Some of these had printed directions

Left to right, top: Mascotte "delusion" type rat trap; a tin choker, and a complicated rat trap mechanism patented by John I. Yedder in 1852 as originally pictured in *Scientific American*. Below these to the left are an improved rat trap patented by J. H. Chester in 1852 and operated by means of levers and trap doors, and a bee smoker. Third row: The "Marty" and the "Holdfast" wire rat traps. Fourth row: two Newhouse animal traps; and bottom, mole, muskrat, and fox traps.

for setting them pasted on the top flat side. This was helpful to the accident-prone.

Various kinds of fly traps and catchers were used in Victorian and subsequent days. A good many were made of wire mesh. They were baited with honey or other lures. The flies gained entry through a baffle cone of wire in the base, which tapered toward the top, and had a very small opening for entrance. The fly could get inside without difficulty but was rarely able to make it out again. One type had a tin top which could be lifted to take out the dead flies. Another was shaped like a balloon with a metal base.

Somewhat similar traps were made of glass in decanter shape with the bait placed in a small rim around the inside. These usually had a stopper which could be removed from the top to take out the flies.

Fly killers or swatters with wire or rubber broom ends have been made in more or less the same shape for a good many years, but some of the early ones are worthy of preservation, as "primitives."

The majority of animal traps available to today's collector date from the early nineteenth century, and those in use prior to 1850 are becoming rather scarce. They have been used for both large and small game. In past years thousands of boys living in rural areas made their own simple rabbit traps which they baited with a carrot or a similar delicacy of which these animals were fond.

Strong spring traps are used for larger game such as bears, wolves, and foxes. A well-known make of nineteenth-century bear trap was the Newhouse, of which several different models were offered.

Traps of this type may bring fairly good prices. A dealer offers a Newhouse No. 5 for $27.50 and a Newhouse No. 6 for $75. A primitive iron bear trap with a heavy chain is advertised at $23.50, an early hand-forged one for $15, and a grizzly bear trap for $48.

An Oneida Victor 19-inch mountain-lion trap with a chain 48 inches in length was recently offered for only $5, which sounds as if it were a bargain. An early hand-forged beaver trap was tendered at $7.50. A crude hand-forged device with a double spring used for trapping wolves recently was available for $16.50.

Various types of other animal traps are available at prices of around $5 up. They can make an interesting display when arranged along one wall of a cabin, a log home, or in one's den or study. And an early mole trap or two might be included.

Slightly akin to the trap is the bee smoker, consisting of an inverted bellows attached to a tin container, usually with a tin handle attached. Rags burning inside the container were fanned to smoke with the aid of the bellows.

They were made with various sizes of metal containers, which were called "stoves." You can remove the cap from the container and convert the bee smoker into a most interesting flower holder.

As for values of fly and mouse traps, they may range from around a dollar to $10 or $15 for scarce types. An individual advertised for sale not long ago a glass fly trap dated 1914 for $7. It was, he averred, "just the thing if you are interested in trapping live flies!" Wire rat traps of the Marty type should bring $3 to $5 or so. The earlier glass fly traps should be worth more.

25

School Days

QUITE EARLY SCHOOL BOOKS OF CERTAIN TYPES, SUCH AS THE BLUE-BACKED spellers and the McGuffey readers have been collected now for a good many years (although most persons seem to have an exaggerated idea of the value of most of these), but not many other items associated with the school of seven or eight decades ago have moved yet into the arena of collectibles. We hereby predict they soon will. Chances are that some of the articles we will talk about here may be found where they were stashed away years ago—in your attic or some other long-neglected storage area of your home.

What about those 5 x 7-inch slates? Have you ever used one? They were used by both pupils and teachers as this century opened, and they had been used for years before. Standard sizes usually ranged up to 9 x 13 inches, and not many were made smaller than 4 x 6 inches. The slates were enclosed in wooden frames.

Before the so-called noiseless slate was marketed, the pupil who set his mind to it could make splendid screeching sounds by writing on a slate with chalk—much, we hasten to add, to the annoyance of the teacher and the snickering delight of his fellow-students.

In addition to the single-face slates, there were hinged slates with two writing surfaces and book slates of several slate leaves. (There also was a slate used in counting houses—a hinged affair with four writing surfaces.)

Quite simple old-style 4 x 6-inch slates could be purchased at wholesale in case lots early in this century for as little as 45 cents a dozen, but the "Emack Improved Noiseless Slate" was a good bit higher—$2.40 a dozen for the 5 x 7-inch size.

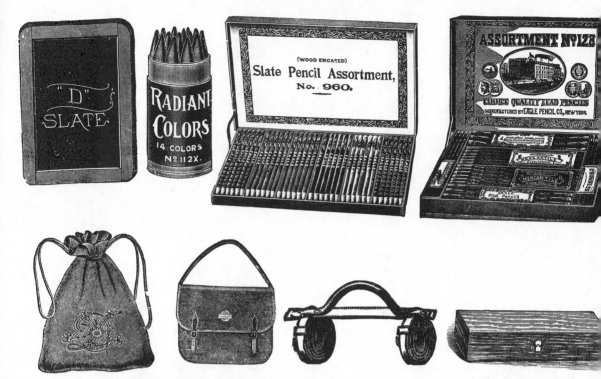

Left to right, top: school slate, box of early crayons, slate pencil assortment, and lead pencil assortment in display cases. Bottom: Two school bags, a book-carrying strap, and a pencil-ruler box.

In an allied category were the early blackboard erasers with wooden handles and wool felt wiping surfaces or stitched all-felt ones. In general design, they were not radically different from those in use today. Blackboards themselves, of course, offer very little in the way of collecting possibilities, although a roll blackboard was made. This rolled up like a map and was offered in 1908 in sizes ranging from 2 x 3 feet to 4 x 5 feet at wholesale prices of $1 to $3.50 each.

Some of the early world globes used in the teaching of geography are of much interest. For one thing, they will show you just how much the geography of the world has changed during the past hundred years. The small globes usually had heavy wire stands attached or were mounted on small iron legs, but the larger ones often sat on full-length metal stands. Six-inch diameter globes on metal ring stands cost only $4.50 a dozen in 1908, but an 18-inch full-mounted one cost $30.

Early-twentieth-century book straps and book carriers were made of leather or a combination of leather and wood. The straps had buckle fasteners. There

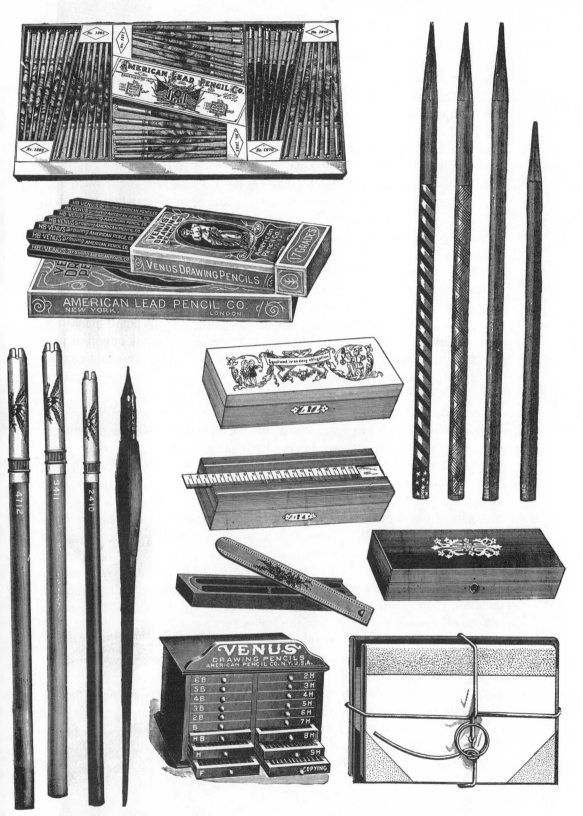

Top left, early-twentieth-century pen holder assortment. To the right, German slate pencils. Below, a box of lead pencils, three school boxes for pencils, rulers, crayons and so on, a Venus pencil display cabinet, a "Simplex Knot" book holder, and, at left, three straight-japanned-handled pen holders with double tips, and an "Anti-Cramp" pen holder.

was a combination carry-all, which consisted of a strap attached to a narrow base of soft wood and included a wooden pencil box and a ruler. The books were strapped between the wooden base and the pencil box. Telescopic book carriers consisted of a leather strap with a steel japanned frame, which could be extended from 8½ to 15 inches in length to accommodate extra-large books or two stacks of books, side by side. Shawl straps could be fastened over the shoulder. Similar to the book straps were skate straps.

Although some school bags used early in this century resembled those in use today, there are a number of early collectible decorated ones made of denim, linen, and other fabrics. Some of these had designs embroidered in colored silk on their exteriors. The cloth bags were closed with draw strings which served as the carrying handles. Another type of denim bag was square in shape with a handle, resembling a modern briefcase in shape. Some of these had pockets. Double shoulder school bags were popular, because they could either be carried by hand or slung across the shoulder. They, too, were made of cloth, and some were lined with muslin. They usually had a carrying chain attached to metal handles around the bag, though some were made with leather strap handles. Briefcase-type school bags, similar to today's, were made of canvas with leather trimmings and, often, of oilcloth.

Early slate pencils are worth collecting, but even more collectible are the early pencil boxes. A large number of the pencil boxes of 75 years ago were imported from Germany and Japan. Both hinged and sliding covers were made, and many boxes were gaily decorated in colors. Those for very young children had nursery scenes and rhymes on their tops. The majority were equipped with locks and accompanying keys. One type was made with a ruler inlaid in its top. Inside were two or three compartments. A standard size for the pencil boxes was 2½ inches in width and 8½ inches in length with a few slightly larger and a few slightly smaller.

More elaborate boxes had silver or imitation silver mountings, and others had nickled corners and centerpieces. Some were decorated with decalcomania pictures. There was one type of box with both an upper and a lower section with compartments for pencils and the like in each.

Pencils in the early part of this century were packed in fancy containers, usually boxes of cardboard, sometimes of wood. Many containers were decorated with interesting labels. The American Pencil Company packed half-gross lots of round and hexagonal pencils in hexagonal, dome-topped boxes. The top lifted off so the pencils could be removed. This company also offered a "Pyramid Assortment," displayed in a pyramid-shaped box. The "Shield Assortment" was packed in a shield-shaped box decorated with 13 stars on a blue background. Still another assortment was packed in a lyre-shaped container.

School mementoes of 1908. Left to right, top row: A Brownie ruler and a combination book carrier and pencil box. Second row: Lunch baskets of fancy straw and willow. Third row: shoulder school bags of cloth, lined with muslin, linen or silk. Fourth row: pencil tablets with pictorial covers and a pencil assortment in display case. Fourth row: book carrier and straps. Bottom: English cork pen holder and a handled book strap.

Eagle Pencil Company manufactured "Teddy Bear" lead pencils, each with a gilt top protector in the shape of a teddy bear. The container featured an illustration of a large teddy bear on the front.

School crayons also were often packed in fancy boxes, as were penholders. Since most retailers discarded the containers when the pencils were sold, these early containers are quite scarce but are worth picking up whenever you come across them.

A pencil collection should prove a stimulating pursuit for the young collector. One objective could be to see how many brands one could find. There were literally hundreds of trade names, among them: "Knickerbocker," "Forum," "Clover," "Eclectic," "Faultless," "Medal," "Scribbler," "Sphinx," "Army & Navy," "Union," "On the Square," "Rex," "Studio," "Progress," "Diagraph," "Laurel," "Pilot," "Herald," "Alabaster," "Rob Roy," "Seminole," "Golf," "Good Luck," "Alpina," "Tennis," "Express," "Chameleon," "Polka-Dot," "Florette," "Zebra," and many others.

School drawing books are worth salvaging—some for their contents, others for their lithographed covers. The same applies to school tablets. Some lithographed covers of tablets of earlier years are quite fascinating. Their illustrations included elephants, pelicans, horses, clowns, children, early automobiles, frogs, Indians, and a host of patriotic and sentimental scenes. The "Don Quixote Writing Tablet" bore a depiction of a fine windmill on its front cover. The "Wedgwood" had a Wedgwood ceramic design. A Chinese design with a dragon featured the "Imperial China Silk" tablet, and the "Sweethearts" tablet bore a drawing of a male and a female angel holding hands!

Note and composition books featured similar lithographed covers, many in colors.

Decorated rulers would afford an interesting collection. One brand of these, the "Brownie" ruler, was decorated with a series of the famous Brownies created by the illustrator Palmer Cox.

These school accessories will undoubtedly suggest others to you. Since you're at the end of this chapter, why don't you take a trip up into the attic and poke around?

26

Waterers, Pails, Oilcans, and Fillers

HAVE YOU BEEN CASTING ABOUT FOR SOMETHING NEW IN THE WAY OF flower containers? You won't know the possibilities you've missed until you start looking around for early lithographed or painted watering cans, children's decorated sand pails or buckets, and old oilcans and oil fillers. Those not already decorated or whose decorations have worn off cry out to be handled creatively by your artistic hand. The charmingly-decorated sand buckets were once a drug on the market—but no more. Youngsters used them on their trips to the beach or in the sand pile at their home.

Oilers were made for many purposes, in many sizes, and of different materials: including tin, brass, copper, steel, and nickel-plate. Although handles, for example, were formed in a diversity of shapes, the oilers all had one common feature: the spout; but these varied considerably in length and shape. Machine oilers might have spouts ranging from 2 to 9 inches long, whereas a railroad oiler's spout might range from 10 to 18 inches in length.

Among the different varieties of oilers were: engineers oilers, which were often produced in sets containing five or six oilers of different sizes and capacities and with spouts of varying lengths; similar railroad oilers, which were quite sturdy affairs made of steel to withstand frequent use (the steel was sometimes copper-plated); tiny oilers for bicycles; and small ones for mowing machines, sewing machines, and various other household purposes.

The best oilcans were copper-plated inside to prevent rusting and to keep the oil from becoming gritty. Some spouts were tapered in a straight line while others hooked over at the tip to reach difficult places. Oilers used on ships

257

Nos. 20, 20½, 21, Lamps

Nos. 22, 23, 220, 230, Lamps

Mill Siphon Oilers

Engineers' and Steamboat Sets

Bent Spout Oilers

EXTRA HEAVY "COPPERIZED" SPRINGBOTTOM MOWING MACHINE OILER No 600

Automobile Can
When not in use the Spout is inverted and conce[aled] inside the can

Straight Spout

No. 19, &c. Engineers' Fillers

Mowing Machine Oilers

A variety of oilers and fillers of the late nineteenth century.

were made with trays equipped with receptacles to keep them from tipping over with the motion of the ship.

Although some tiny oilcans were made for use of clockmakers and repairers, most of these artisans used small oil cups, made of glass or a combination of boxwood and glass.

Comparatively few oilers were lettered with the name of the manufacturer on their surfaces, so if you have any artistic talents, you might want to try exercising them in decorating the cans. Then unscrew the spouts and use the can for small arrangements of flowers. If the oiler has a fairly short spout, you can leave this attached and use it as a bud "vase."

Similar to the oilers were the fillers, which had a nozzle-shaped spout attached to the front instead of the top and which always had a carrying handle for ease in pouring or filling.

From left to right, top: lithographed pails, tallow pot, textile mill oiling can, and straight-nozzle oiler. Second row: mowing machine oilers, auto pump oilers, engineer's drip oiler, straight-nozzle oiler, and two oilers for farm machines. Bottom: two engineer's fillers and a bicycle oiler.

Some early watering cans were lithographed in colors. They are not now plentiful, but you can occasionally find one. If the lithographed scenes haven't worn too badly, you may prefer to leave them as they are and press them into service in flower arrangements. Otherwise, you may wish to decorate them also.

Toward the latter part of last century many watering pots were made of galvanized steel with two handles and a long spout. Fabricated in various sizes, they had capacities of from 4 to 12 quarts. Though not particularly fascinating in their natural gray finish, they can be decorated attractively in colors.

The children's tin sand buckets mentioned earlier usually came complete

Decorated sand bucket and plain watering can.

with a miniature shovel and were sold by the variety stores and the five-and-ten-cent establishments. Although first produced much earlier, buckets of this type were still being sold after the first World War, and the more intriguing of them were gaily decorated in colors with scenes which often featured children at play. They held sand splendidly but water would leak through the loose seams—so watch it if you intend to use them for plants that need frequent watering.

Other items of heavy tinware from earlier days also were decorated with lithographed scenes or large pictorial labels which covered a major portion of the exterior surface and which often included the manufacturer's name. Milk kettles and large milk cans offer one example. The latter are now being re-decorated and converted into use as lamps and umbrella stands.

Similar heavy tin articles for which you may wish to watch out and some of which can be used as planters include dairy pails, milk coolers, cream cans, dinner buckets, lunch boxes, and well buckets.

About 40 years ago, Belknap Hardware and Manufacturing Company produced a line of "Old Kentucky Home" milk cans, featuring on the exterior a large woodcut-type illustration of a Southern mansion.

27

Thermometers and Barometers

BAROMETERS AND THERMOMETERS MIGHT BE CALLED KISSING COUSINS. THE barometer, invented by an Italian physicist, is used to determine the pressure of the atmosphere and is of considerable aid in various kinds of scientific work. In its simplest form, the mercury barometer is a glass tube closed at the top, open at the bottom, and partially filled with mercury; it extends down into a vessel that also holds mercury. Should you desire to know more about the technical construction and operation of barometers, please feel free to look this up in some good reference book, since it will not be included here.

The thermometer consists basically of a tube containing mercury (or alcohol), and it records the temperature. We need not be concerned here with the technicalities of its operation—though here again this fact need not deter you from searching for material about it in the musty reference files of your library. We say this with apologies to all modern librarians who somehow or another seem to have banished mustiness along with dullness from the confines within which they labor and shine.

What we are interested in here are ornamented or decorated barometers and thermometers or those fashioned in unusual shapes, the production of which in America did not begin much before the middle of the nineteenth century. Even then, there were not many really fancy barometers made in this country, so that those which are found today should be treasured. Even those early American-made barometers which are purely utilitarian in design and shape ought to be preserved.

When it comes to household thermometers, it's a different story. These

262

were made with all types of fancy decorations and designs which should titillate even the stodgiest individual. While the earlier thermometers were designed solely for utilitarian purposes (so you could determine whether it was as hot or as cold as it seemed), the later ones reflected a sort of *joie de vivre* and lent themselves admirably to decoration as well as to usefulness. Thus, one would find them not only in the kitchen or the living room but in the parlor too.

The best sources of information about the numerous shapes and decorations are probably nineteenth-century trade catalogues, and from the illustrations in these, one discovers that it is really the "housing," the case or the stand, that is intriguing; or, more rarely, the recording glass or dial.

Thus, folk now are beginning to seek out the figural thermometer, just as quite a few years ago they started salvaging figural bottles and flasks. Late-nineteenth- and early-twentieth-century catalogues depict thermometers with stands or bases decorated with or actually in the shapes of dogs, elephants, dragons, and other figures. Sometimes figures are perched atop the thermometer. These, made of pottery or metal, have represented literary celebrities from John Milton to William Shakespeare and also have included historical personages, animals, and birds.

Some bases and tops were made of decorated metal, and decorated metal cases also abounded. These featured flower forms, scrolls, and other assorted

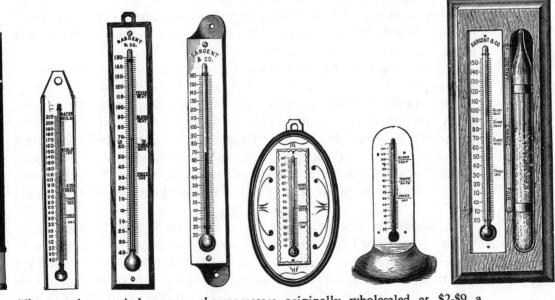

These early-twentieth-century thermometers originally wholesaled at $2-$9 a dozen.

curlicues. A 1906 trade catalogue depicts a thermometer with a frame of quadruple-silver-plate 5¼ inches high. A metal dog, which appears to be a German Shepherd, crouches on the base. Quite often the cases or stands were made by a manufacturer who bought the thermometers themselves in quantity from plants specializing in thermometer manufacture so he could put them in an attractive or at least an interesting setting.

Perhaps the majority of figural thermometers have been kept through many years by the families of the original purchasers. At any rate, they certainly are not offered in profusion by antique dealers. The same situation prevails with regard to early barometers of any type. Of special interest—if you can find them—are barometers with porcelain dials and broken pediment or eagle tops.

Some early barometers were housed in cases with clocks, and some nineteenth-century thermometers had mirror tops, usually quite small. Should you find either, the former will cost you a great deal more than the latter.

A large four-page pictorial leaflet issued by Aug. Neubeck & Company, of New York City, apparently in the late 1800's, depicts a large group of mercury and aneroid barometers, hygrometers and humidity indicators, and thermometers and hydrometers in varied shapes.

Aside from the figural and highly-ornamented thermometers, inexpensive types once given away or sold quite cheaply for advertising and good-will purposes and lettered with advertising can be collected. Thousands of simple thermometers were made with a metal ring at the top so they could be hung on a wall, but others had handles, made of metal or wood, so they could be toted about from room to room. Still others simply had small holes in their tops so they could be placed over a nail.

Although not many barometers and thermometers have recently been advertised for sale, here are a few recently-asked values for various types:

Thermometer mounted on stand in shape of heavy brass turkey claw, $4.75; advertising thermometer, 11½ inches tall, $10; round barometer in walnut frame, about 4½ inches in diameter, $9; wall barometer in walnut case with leaf-and-scroll carving, 18 inches long, $35; wall barometer in walnut case with sculptured horse's head and horseshoe on top, 19 inches long, $37; and English barometer in oak case, 36 inches long and 10 inches wide, $45.

Antique dealers who have been concentrating on Americana might be interested in prowling about a bit in old homes to see if they can locate any of these early barometers and thermometers with which the owners are willing to part. The values of the better ones ought to advance before long, not only because they are fairly scarce but also because collectors are likely to start asking for them soon.

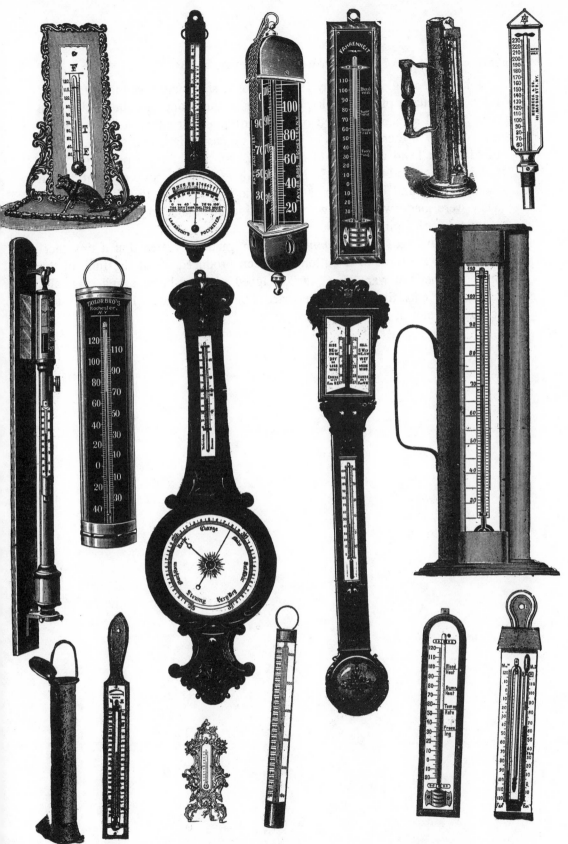

Thermometers, barometers, and hydrometers of the late nineteenth century, including a couple of silver-plated ones. Most are quite inexpensive.

An Otto Young & Company 1900 catalogue shows a thermometer mounted on a stand made of quadruple-plate silver in the shape of a huge claw and with a metal chicken mounted on a bow ribbon at the top. It was priced at $3. A group of thermometers in japanned tin cases of various shapes are pictured in the 1884 catalogue of Sargent & Co. at wholesale prices of $5.50 to $8 a dozen, and the 1901 Sargent catalogue offers a group of combination thermometers and barometers at wholesale prices of $6 to $7.50 a dozen. They were made with both wood bases and japanned tin cases with hooks at the top for hanging.

Some years ago, *The Spinning Wheel* magazine revealed that a tiny thermometer in the form of a button had been produced about the time of the Spanish-American war. They were designed as lapel buttons and originally sold for 50 cents, the magazine reported. One of these would be a choice item for the collector of thermometers.

28

Special-Purpose Table Silverware

SILVER AND TABLEWARE HAVE LONG BEEN COLLECTED, AND THE RANKS OF the specialized field of souvenir spoon collectors swell almost daily. Collecting early American silverware can be fun—and it can be costly. It also can be profitable if you know what you're about. Let us give consideration here to the possibilities of collecting special-purpose silver and silver-plated tableware, for here is an area in which sheer fascination abounds, largely because of the intriguing, and often lovely, shapes and forms in which these implements were made. In effect, we find here the same sort of appeal offered by the collecting of souvenir spoons except on a much broader scale. In this category we will lump special-purpose knives, forks, spoons, and food servers.

One may, if she wishes, specialize in the knives, or the forks, or the spoons, or the servers. It was in these areas that the silversmiths and the tableware manufacturers of the nineteenth century exercised their full creative ingenuity; and if you'd like to have a pleasant day feasting your eyes upon an array of these delightful creations, study the pages of old catalogues of silversmiths or of wholesalers or distributors of silver and silver-plated tablewares.

Let's take a look first at special-purpose knives. Did you know that "one-armed knives" were made for handicapped persons? These consisted of a combination knife and fork in a single implement, which made it much easier for a one-armed individual to cut and eat his food without the necessity of constantly changing from knife to fork. This utensil was a handled knife blade sharply curved at the end and with tines fashioned at the lower extremity. Thus, a one-armed person could cut his food with the blade, then pick it up

One-armed man's combination knife and fork, 1906.

on the tines at the end of the blade. The A. L. Jordan Cutlery Company offered these with ivory handles early in this century at wholesale prices of
$75 a dozen. It also had them available at lower prices with celluloid or ebony
handles.

However, we will not be concerned primarily in this chapter with unique
implements but rather with special-purpose types commonly used in the homes
of most families of some means and types of which, incidentally, are still being produced today.

Fruit knives offer examples of special-purpose tableware made in various
shapes and numerous interesting designs. As was the case with most other
tableware, the handles of these were of various materials, including silver
and silver-plate, pearl, horn, ebony, and others; and were often extravagantly
engraved or otherwise decorated.

Orange knives in some examples were made with serrated or saw edges
for cutting the oranges; others merely had a slightly curved sharp cutting
edge, or a straight keen edge.

Butter knives, of course, appeared in far more shapes and designs, including a wide array of conventional patterns and quite a few unconventional
ones. Those with lavishly decorated handles and blades are of prime interest:
many had decorations of fruits and flowers which extended from their handles right on down along the upper edge of their blades. Designs of roses and
violets are frequently encountered. A good many butter knives with twists
between handle and blade were made. Pattern names of these included "Berk-
shire Twist," "Columbia Twist," "Vesta Twist," and "Lotus Twist."

Numerous types of smaller individual butter spreaders are available, and,
of course, there are all sorts of butter picks, some with a single prong or pick
at the end, others with two. The majority of blade surfaces were rather broad
but you also occasionally will find narrow blades with a pick-like prong at
the end. Ends of some butter knives were rounded, others slightly curved or
pointed.

John Round & Son, Ltd., of Sheffield, England, made an almost aston-

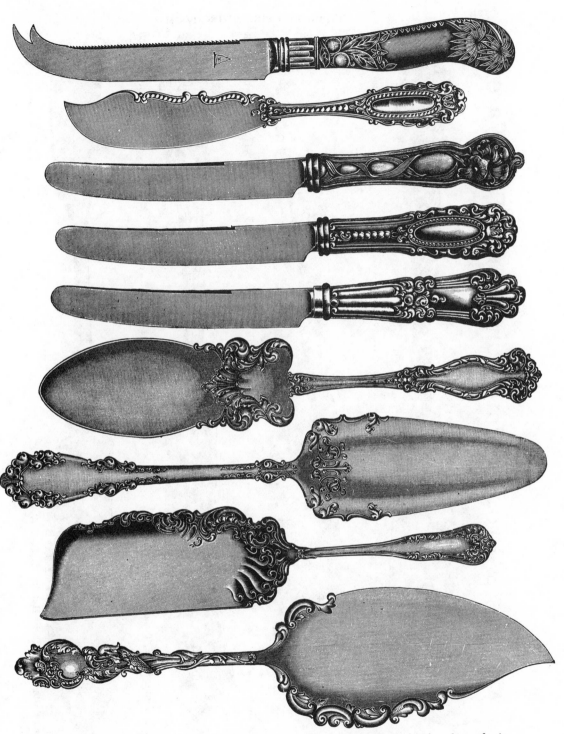

Special-purpose knives. Top to bottom: orange knife, butter knife, three fruit knives, two jelly knives, crumb knife, and fish knife.

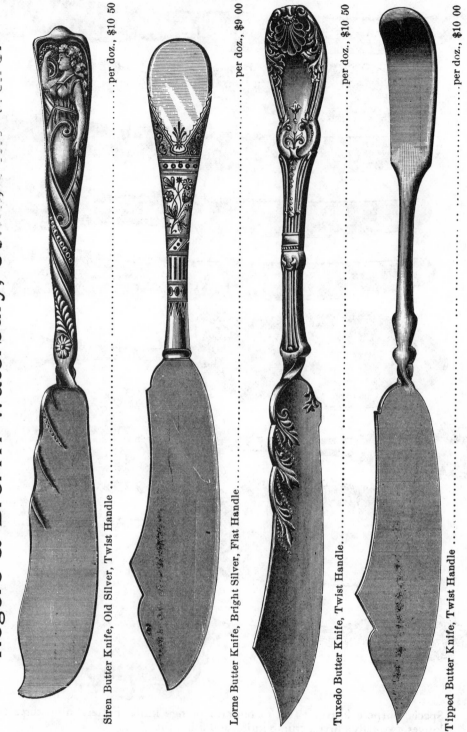

*Rogers & Bro. A1 Waterbury, Conn., Flat Ware.

Siren Butter Knife, Old Silver, Twist Handle ....per doz., $10 50

Lorne Butter Knife, Bright Silver, Flat Handle ....per doz., $9 00

Tuxedo Butter Knife, Twist Handle ....per doz., $10 50

Tipped Butter Knife, Twist Handle ....per doz., $10 00

A group of Rogers & Bro. butter knives of 1892 with the wholesale prices then current.

ishing variety of butter knives which were electroplated on nickel silver with ivory, pearl, and plated handles and the entire blade surface decorated. Some blades bore depictions of scenes, such as maidens with water or wine vessels atop their heads. The blade of one of this company's butter knives shows a milkmaid engaged in her evening (or perhaps it was her early-morning) chore. She is seated on a milking stool beside a cow that looks quite contented indeed. Cows in other settings are often depicted on the butter knives. Other types of blade decorations include cornucopias, geometric designs, and all types of flowers and trailing vines.

The only adequate way to visualize the beauty of some of these knives (as well as that of the other items of flatware we will discuss) is to inspect them personally or to look carefully at some of the illustrations reproduced in this chapter.

Incidentally, the John Round firm illustrates in one of its nineteenth-century catalogues in my possession a large group of somewhat similarly decorated fish carvers and fish eating knives, and one could conceivably form a truly magnificent collection of such knives alone, given the time, patience, and the necessary financial outlay.

These fish carvers were offered in silk and velvet lined cases. Scenes pictured on their expansive blades included fishermen in various poses, shocks of corn, fish leaping from the water, fish swimming among seaweed, Neptune in a setting of scrolls, flowers and vines, and a variety of geometric designs. One carver is decorated with a thick rope whose ends are formed of chubby fish. Another features two lissome mermaids with a sea dragon.

The fish-carving sets consisted of a large-handled blade and a broad fork. The fish-eating knives, smaller than the carvers of course, were similarly decorated. In addition to its handsome carvers electroplated on nickel, John Round made a cheaper line electroplated on steel.

Embellished pie and cake knives offer many opportunities for collecting. Some pie knives were made in the general shape of oversized spoons so that the slice of pie could be lifted easily on the broad, oval-shaped blade. Cake knives were made with serrated blades; servers with broad flat blades were made to be used interchangeably for serving pie or cake.

Carving knives have been made in literally dozens of shapes and sizes and with handles of steel, stag horn, zylonite, ivory, celluloid, ebony and other woods, and silver. The same variety applies to steak knives.

Other special-purpose knives of much appeal for the collector include cheese, jelly, lemon, bread, oyster, banana, and paring knives. Should you desire to wander farther afield, you can collect early hunting and skinning knives.

If you're interested in special knives, you probably also will want to con-

FISH CARVERS—ELECTRO-PLATED ON NICKEL SILVER.
In Silk and Velvet Lined Cases.

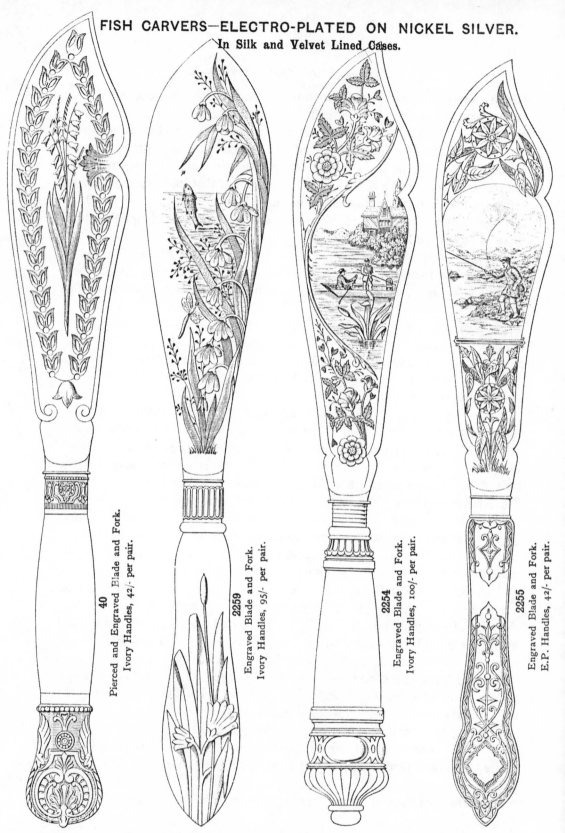

40
Pierced and Engraved Blade and Fork.
Ivory Handles, 42/- per pair.

2259
Engraved Blade and Fork.
Ivory Handles, 95/- per pair.

2254
Engraved Blade and Fork.
Ivory Handles, 100/- per pair.

2255
Engraved Blade and Fork.
E.P. Handles, 42/- per pair.

These extraordinary fish carvers were offered by John Round & Son late last century.

sider novelty knife rests and perhaps even knife boxes. The rests were made of silver, silver-plate, porcelain, glass (pressed and cut), wood, and white metal. A 1914 trade catalogue pictures a group of fine cut-glass knife rests at prices of from 60 cents to $4.25 each—and that's enough to make your mouth water. The conventional rests were frequently made in the shape of miniature dumbells. Glass ones were cut on the ends and often along the center portion also. It is the novelty shapes, however, which are the more fascinating. Metal rests were fashioned in the shapes of pairs of dogs, baby chicks, swans, squirrels, and other animals and birds. Normally, the small metal bar upon which one's knife was placed to rest was attached to the shoulders or backs of the animals. A pair of quadruple-plated squirrels, however, were fashioned sitting on a small metal fence with the bar rest across the fence. And the swans hold the bar in their beaks.

Special-purpose spoons were made for even more uses than were knives. Souvenir spoons are discussed in my earlier book *Treasure at Home* and in other works, which are listed in the suggestions for further reading at the end of this book. This broad category should also include Christmas, birthday and special month, and state spoons. Some manufacturers of silverware issued "month" spoons in 12 different designs, one for each month, so they could be given as birthday gifts. One company engraved a verse in the bowls. One of these for December reads:

> *If cold December gave*
> *   you birth,*
> *The month of snow and ice*
> *   and mirth,*
> *Place on your hand a·*
> *   turquoise blue,*
> *Success will bless you*
> *   if you do.*

That's not likely to go down to posterity, but it gives you the general idea of the stuff the hacks turned out in earlier days for such purposes.

Many of the Christmas spoons, like so many souvenir spoons, were charming. Both handles and bowls were usually decorated. One Christmas spoon has a likeness of Santa Claus on its handle and a Christmas Eve hearth scene in the bowl with stockings hung on each side of the fireplace. The Santa Claus handle was quite popular in the late nineteenth century. Another popular Christmas spoon was labeled "Little Bo Peep" and had a full-length likeness of the nursery rhyme lass of that name on the handle and the words "Merry Christmas" engraved in the bowl.

Special-purpose spoons. Top, left to right: berry, bon bon, orange, and horse-radish spoons. Center: sugar sifter and bon bon spoon. Bottom left, individual salt spoon. At bottom right are four after-dinner coffee spoons with the patterns from top to bottom: Pine Cone, Moccasin, Wheat, and Sunflower.

Decorated fruit spoons can be a joy to seek, particularly since there is always the possibility of finding those with figures sculptured at the ends of the handles. These included a group of classic figures clad in the costumes of their times. The bowls were made in various shapes, but were most frequently oval or round. Some bowls were decorated with fruits, others with rococo designs, flowers and even scenes.

Orange spoons usually had a pointed tip—sometimes quite pointed. Those with decorated bowls are special interest.

Broad-bowled berry spoons were sometimes almost gaudily decorated, and bowls usually were oval or circular, although some were rectangular. Those with engraved bowls and embossed handles afford a multitude of designs. Some with sterling silver handles had gold bowls. Most of those in sterling were quite large as compared with the conventional teaspoon and were heavier.

Of particular interest in the spoon family are sugar shells, which are in a category similar to butter knives when it comes to variety. A late-nineteenth- and early-twentieth-century product was the quadruple-plate combination sugar bowl and spoon holder. The bowl was equipped with brackets around the outside to hold spoons—usually eight. These bowls normally came with a removable top and a pedestal base.

In the same family was the sugar sifter spoon with its perforated bowl which permitted sifting the sugar over cereals and fruit. The great majority of shells and sifters had oval bowls though some of these, too, were rectangular. Of course, sugar tongs also should be included in a collection of special-purpose tableware.

Another special type of spoon was the cheese scoop with its unusually sturdy handle to withstand pressure. Salt spoons, along with salt dips and shakers, have long been collected. Although most individual salt spoons had small round bowls, one was made with a bowl resembling a miniature shovel scoop, and a good many with gold bowls were produced.

Long-handled lemonade spoons are of interest, and you may still find some with heart-shaped bowls and a tiny knob at the extremity of the handle.

Olive spoons had perforated bowls with the punctures in such shapes as teardrops, crosses, ovals, and stars. Some handles terminated in a pointed spear: If you couldn't land the olive in the bowl, you could capture it with the lance. Bon bon spoons also often had perforated bowls, but the most fascinating of these spoons are those with bowls formed by filigree-type scrolls and arabesques. Bowls sometimes were scoop-shaped.

Of interest, too, are blade-bowled horseradish spoons; mustard spoons with their tiny bowls; almond or nut spoons with filigree-type bowls (these were sometimes used as ice and pea spoons); broad-bowled preserve and jelly

Sterling silver "fancy" after-dinner coffee spoons, including the souvenir-type month and state spoons.

Special-purpose forks. Extreme left, cake fork and beside it, ice cream fork. Top, left to right: sardine, fish, and lettuce forks. Bottom, individual salad and pickle forks.

spoons; various types of salad spoons; ice-cream and ice-cream-soda spoons with fairly sharp-edged bowls and long, slender handles; and bar spoons with twists in their handles. Also in the spoon family are perforated julep strainers and brandy burners.

Some of the most charming fruit spoons imaginable were produced by John Round & Son, Ltd., with bowls of decorative leaves and flowers and embossed fruits, and some with finials in the shape of humans on their handles. This firm also made a mustache spoon with a ledge for the mustache to rest upon.

Just as there are collectors of figural bottles, there are collectors of figural spoons, including the souvenir spoons, literally hundreds of thousands of which have been made during the past century. Handles were designed to represent a tremendous variety of objects. A glance through a series of catalogues issued between 1875 and 1910 shows spoons with handles in the shape of Indians, clad and unclad maidens, sheaves of wheat, all types of flowers, acorns, eagles, lions, saints, harps, leaves, historical, mythological and literary figures, fruits, vehicles, cupids, horses, cows, and other objects both animate and inanimate.

Somewhat less frequently one finds bowls decorated with outdoors objects and scenes, particularly in the case of baby spoons with their illustrations based on nursery rhymes.

In the category of special-purpose forks, there is the ice cream fork, sometimes called an ice cream "spoon," the bowl of which usually ends in three tines. Cake forks normally feature three long tines also.

Olive forks will have either two or three sharp tines. They are similar in general appearance to pickle forks (which customarily have three tines) and also to oyster forks, although the last-named have shorter handles. Occasionally, pickle forks with two tines are found. One of these, with its handle twisted in the center in much the same way that bar spoon handles are twisted, is pictured in a late-nineteenth-century catalogue.

Sardine forks are rather wicked-looking implements with seven or eight tines stemming from a broad base at the end of the handle. The tines are quite short as contrasted with the unusually long and slender ones of the far more delicately designed fruit and berry forks. Overall length of the latter will average about 5 inches, and the tines frequently are 1¾ or 2 inches in length.

Four-tined cold meat forks were made in several sizes and numerous designs. Some early illustrations show cold meat forks with straight tines and others with two tines curved in one direction and the other two curved in the opposite direction. One type was made with perforations above the tines,

Special-purpose servers. Left to right at top: salt shovel, butter pick, pie server or ice cream slicer, cucumber server, and jelly server. Below left: oyster server. Right: two food pushers.

STERLING SILVER WARE.

Pomona, Sugar Shell, Oxidized, Gold-lined, Engraved Bowl.... .... each, $5 75

No. 23.   Cream Ladle, Twist Handle, Engraved Gilt Bowl.............................. ....each, $6 50

No. 190.   Sugar Shell, Extra Heavy, Gold-lined Bowl........... ....each, $5 00

Louis XV. Sugar Shell, Gold-lined Bowl........ ....each, $4 50

No. 122.   Jack Rose Sugar Shell, Engraved Handle and Engraved Gold-lined Bowl........... ....each, $4 50

No. 35.   Sugar Shell, Engraved Handle and Engraved Gold-lined Bowl ....each, $4 25

Sterling silver sugar shells of late nineteenth century. Prices shown were wholesale then.

which were adorned with gilt. Some of these forks were intended to be used interchangeably as cake forks.

Salad forks with exceptionally fancy tines were manufactured in great abundance in the latter part of last century. Handles were frequently almost torturously elaborate, featuring twisted flowers and leaves and vines. Carving forks also were produced in almost endless variety with handles of wood, metals, ivory, bone, pearl, and other substances.

Many specialized food servers are available for the collector, as are some other types of quite specialized implements such as marrow and lobster scoops, sugar crushers, sardine tongs, lobster cracks, and brandy burners (similar to the brandy spoon mentioned above).

Food pushers usually were featured by a long but narrow flat blade attached to the end of a handle and came in a variety of sizes. The tomato server, which probably should be considered in the spoon category, had a flat, perforated, and usually round surface attached to a handle, permitting the juice of tomatoes to strain through the perforations. The cucumber server was similar in appearance and design.

Pie and cake servers (for the most part used interchangeably) are really in the knife family. They have long, flat blades attached to relatively short handles. Blades are rounded at the ends. There also are some delightfully decorated tart servers around. The blade-like surface was triangular or heart-shaped as a rule though sometimes oval. Grape shears bear a kinship in design and appearance to embroidery scissors.

And you won't want to overlook such food and beverage accessories as tea balls and strainers, all types of ladles and cream dips, caddy spoons, and nutcracks.

These lists by no means cover all of the collectible and often fascinating special-purpose table implements. Should you come across items you can't identify, try consulting old catalogues of silversmiths or silverware manufacturers.

29

Wire That Wove History

WHAT WOULD YOU CONSIDER THE MOST UNLIKELY OF ALL UNLIKELY ITEMS TO seek out and preserve? Should you answer barbed wire, you'd probably be with the majority. And yet, barbed wire is beginning to be collected, and a boom could be in the making.

Stop for a moment and consider whether, after all, it is so unlikely an object for preservation. Turn on your television set. Are you focused on a "Western"? If so, it may revolve around barbed wire. For this is the wire that played a colorful and extremely significant role in the settlement and subsequent history of the Western United States. Its use led to bloody entanglements between farmers and cowmen, and such incidents provide the plots for dozens of "Western" motion pictures made during recent years.

The so-called "Law of the Open Range" generated feuds, hassles, debates, and shootings from the time barbed wire began to be used in the final quarter of the nineteenth century until cowmen finally reversed their earlier stand and saw it as a boon and not a deterrent to their own operations.

Early in the history of the West, farmers fenced in order to protect their crops from assault by unruly cattle which roamed the great open spaces of a part of our nation then largely uninhabited, and some of it even unexplored. Only by doing so could they safeguard their means of livelihood, and plain, smooth wire wasn't adequate for the task.

The art of making wire is by no means a recent one. It dates back almost to the dawn of civilization when it was used to fashion small ornaments. But barbed wire was a nineteenth-century innovation. You may think it strange that anyone should write an entire book about barbed wire, but Henry D. McCallum and his wife, Frances T. McCallum, have done just that, and as

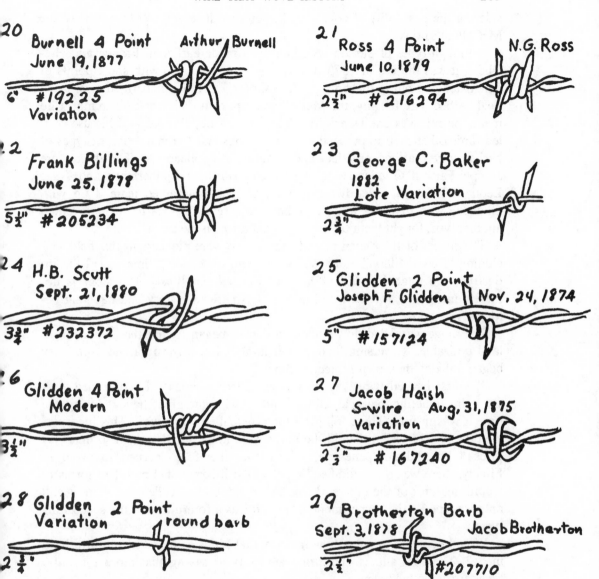

20 Burnell 4 Point   Arthur Burnell
June 19, 1877
6" #19225
Variation

21 Ross 4 Point   N.G. Ross
June 10, 1879
2⅓" #216294

22 Frank Billings
June 25, 1878
5½" #205234

23 George C. Baker
1882
Lote Variation
2¾"

24 H.B. Scutt
Sept. 21, 1880
3¾" #232372

25 Glidden 2 Point
Joseph F. Glidden   Nov. 24, 1874
5"   #157124

26 Glidden 4 Point
Modern
3¼"

27 Jacob Haish
S-wire   Aug. 31, 1875
Variation
2⅓"   #167240

28 Glidden 2 Point
Variation   round barb
2¾"

29 Brotherton Barb
Sept. 3, 1878   Jacob Brotherton
2⅛"   #207710

A few of the many collectible types of barbed wire. (Illustration courtesy of H. M. Cook, Whitney, Texas.)

for interest, it is pure fascination. Their book is titled *The Wire that Fenced the West* (copyright 1965 by the University of Oklahoma Press, Norman). In it they relate the story of the invention, perfection, and use of barbed wire and tell of many of the conflicts that resulted from its use. If, when you finish this chapter, you should find yourself interested in wire and perhaps even considering the possibility of collecting it, you owe it to yourself first to read the McCallum's book.

Although types of barbed wire had been made earlier in France and elsewhere, it was the use in 1873 of a wooden rail equipped with short points of wire extending out in sharp projections that "triggered" the perfection of practical barbed wire fencing, the McCallums report in their book. The man who made the rail was one Henry M. Rose, of DeKalb, Illinois, and his use of it led three other men to proceed with inventions and the marketing of types of barbed wire that had practical and widespread applications. The three were Joseph Farwell Glidden, a farmer; Jacob Haish, a lumberman; and Isaac Leonard Ellwood, a hardware merchant. The last-named teamed up with Glidden, who invented a type of barbed wire, while Haish, who invented another type, fought them bitterly for years through the courts.

The stories of these men and of others who were pioneers in this field (including "Bet-a-Million" John W. Gates, who once, for a time, ruled the industry), are related in *The Wire that Fenced the West*. The story is not merely intriguing; it is part and parcel of American history and has long belonged in a book.

The range wars died down when cattlemen began to find the ownership of land desirable. Reversing their earlier antagonism toward barbed wire, they began utilizing their own protective fencing.

The first barbed wire was of a type called "vicious": It controlled livestock by inflicting physical injury, and it wrought great havoc during the time it was in use. There followed the type called "obvious": This incorporated the idea of visibility, and the barbs were made small enough so that they pricked but did not penetrate. The cattle, therefore, learned to avoid it. Finally, there was the "modified" type, which incorporated modified forms of helpful features of the others. From the standpoint of collectors, there is still another type — the "experimental," which was a forerunner of the succeeding types.

Would you care to guess how many actual kinds of barbed wire have been made? The McCallums quote one authority as saying that more than 400 types are actually known.

Mr. McCallum, incidentally, owns one of the finest collections of what we now so frequently hear referred to as "bob" wire in the world. The book which he and his wife wrote is of especial value to collectors, because it contains a chapter on identification in which a set of original bynames is used to identify 36 prominent types. These also are illustrated.

Another collector of and dealer in early barbed wire, H. M. Cook, of Whitney, Texas, told this writer facetiously that a prerequisite of collecting barbed wire is to fall out of a tree or be kicked in the head by a mule! But he then

BARBED FENCE WIRE

FOX, TWO POINT

Per Roll.

Galvanized, Hog. Barbs 3 inches apart, 14 gauge wire, 15 gauge barbs, about 22 feet to the pound _____

80 rods to the spool. Weight per spool, 60 pounds gross. 55 pounds net.

FOUR POINT

Galvanized, per lb.

Hog. Barbs 3 inches apart, about 12 feet to the pound _____
Cattle. " 6 " " " 15 " " " " _____

GLIDDEN PATTERN. TWO POINT

Galvanized, per lb.

Hog. Barbs 3 inches apart, about 14 feet to the pound _____
Cattle. " 5 " " " 16 " " " " _____

BAKER PATTERN. TWO POINT.

FLATTENED BARB. MADE FROM No. 12½ FINE GRADE, SMOOTH STEEL WIRE. THE BARBS ARE No. 14 WIRE FLATTENED. THE BARBS FIT TIGHTLY. THE CABLES ARE TWISTED VERY CLOSE TO SECURE THE GREATEST POSSIBLE STRENGTH.

Galvanized, per lb.

Hog. Barbs 3 inches apart, about 16 feet to the pound _____
Cattle. " 3 " " " 18 " " " " _____

Rolls contain from 90 to 110 pounds.

POSTS, STAPLES, AND WIRE REQUIRED FOR 1 MILE OF BARBED WIRE FENCING

Posts placed apart, feet	8	10	12	16½	20	25	30	33
Number of posts	600	528	410	320	264	211	176	160
Pounds of staples	8¼	6¾	5½	4	3⅓	2⅔	2¼	2
Pounds of common barbed wire, single strand (Approximate.)	352	352	352	352	352	352	352	352

POUNDS OF COMMON BARBED WIRE REQUIRED FOR DIFFERENT SIZE FIELDS (APPROXIMATE.)

Number of acres	640	320	160	80	40	20	1
Number of miles	4	3	2	1½	1	¾	(60 Rods)
Pounds of common barbed wire, single strand (Approximate.)	1408	1056	704	528	352	264	66

DISTANCE FROM GROUND FOR MORE THAN ONE STRAND OF BARBED WIRE FENCING

Two strands, 22 and 44 inches. Three strands, 16, 30 and 48 inches. Four strands, 12, 24, 36 and 48 inches. Five strands, 8, 15, 24, 36 and 48 inches.

Page of a Belknap Hardware and Manufacturing Company catalogue at the turn of the century, showing types of barbed wire now being collected and listing materials needed for erecting a mile of wire.

summed up the attitude of others truly interested in this field by remarking: "It's a big field and wide-open — colossal, gigantic, stupendous, and fascinating beyond expression."

"Collecting wire," he said, "is a pursuit for those with a pioneering vision. It isn't to be confused with collecting art or coins or antiques. Yet, there are already thousands of collectors. I'd say more than 150,000. Associations of these collectors have been formed."

Mr. Cook's collection includes samples of what he considers the rarest of all barbed wire — Meriweather's Snake, patented in 1853, or 15 years before the next patent was obtained on a wire known as the Kelly Thorny Fence.

Collectors usually cut their wire into lengths of 18 inches. The recent price range for types that are not extremely scarce has been from $1 to $2 a length, or "stick," but some types will bring $5 and more a stick. Types avidly sought include these:

Meriweather's Snake; Reynolds' Hanging Knot; Snail wire; Merrill Twirl; Kelly's Thorny Fence; Spur Rowel; Knickerbocker; Stover Clip; Pooler Jones; Jaynes and Hill; Kittleston's Half-Hitch; Haish's "S" wire; Glidden's square wire; Kennedy Barbs, Three-Point; Basque Company Hand Made, and Concertina Steel wire.

"I find wire," Mr. Cook told the author, "by driving along old roads. Old fences along these roads in the West are largely destroyed now, and the wire is on the ground. The posts have long since rotted. Most antiques shops and trading posts in Texas and other parts of the West now have this wire for sale.

"The role of barbed wire in the old West was really comparable to the role of the Colt .45," Mr. Cook says. "And it's still against the law to cut wire fencing in Texas. Probably the majority of ranchers in Texas today collect barbed wire. Youngsters and retired people also collect it. Not long ago I encountered two elderly women traveling in a Cadillac. They were out collecting barbed wire.

"One of them said to me, 'We're just two old nags from a horse family.'"

Mr. Cook is known to acquaintances and friends as "Barb Wire Cook." Born in Texas in 1891, he spent his early manhood first as a trapper and later as a rancher. He became interested in collecting wire some years ago when he remembered unusual types he had seen in earlier days. So he began cutting off pieces and taking them back to his camp with him. Persons who stopped by saw the wire and asked questions about it. Mr. Cook began giving them samples, and word about numerous types of wire spread. It wasn't long before he found that he could sell it; and since that time, that's what he has been doing.

The bulk of patents on barbed wire were obtained between 1868 and 1884. Many "moonshiners" made numerous types of barbed wire to protect their illicit properties.

In more recent years, of course, barbed wire has been utilized in warfare. It was used extensively in World War I and has been used in Viet Nam.

The McCallums point out that all types of "armoured fencing devices" made prior to 1873 and which used some form of metal for "armour" were divided into two groups: "those granted patent in the United States or in Europe as variations of defensive barriers; and those recorded in some form of written document — official or otherwise — but, for one reason or another, never patented."

Naturally, if you intend to collect barbed wire, you don't go around snipping fences. Obtain permission first from the owner, and replace the small piece of wire you snip off after permission has been granted.

Collectors display their samples in various ways. One way is to mount the sticks on boards and then mount the boards along a wall. The sticks should be identified, for identification is a part of the fun of collecting. There are a few dealers in this wire who distribute price lists illustrated with sketches of what they have for sale.

Barbed wire also is sometimes illustrated by types in early hardware and farm equipment manufacturers' catalogues.

Don't become so fascinated by barbed wire that you overlook other types of wire and articles made of wire which either are starting to be collected or soon will be. These include, by all means, pictorial window screen cloth, mentioned earlier in this book. In the latter part of last century, the New Jersey Wire Cloth Company made a wire cloth window screen with an attractive landscape. It was produced in widths of from 12 to 48 inches and was put up in rolls containing 100 square feet. Figured wire for window screens also was made in a variety of designs.

Elaborately designed window screen corners are collectible. So should be steel wire bale ties, of which several types were made. These were used for tying up such things as bales of cotton and, sometimes, hay. Patent wire fence hooks should be looked for along with the early barbed wire strands. One type was made which, when screwed into trees, slid on fence wires when the trees swayed with the wind so it wouldn't cause damage to the trees. A special wire fence hook brace was made to be utilized in attaching the hooks to trees and fence posts. In appearance, it resembles a brace and bit set.

Why not also start collecting fancy wire fence samples? You'd be surprised at just how many types have been produced through the years. Ornamental fence posts of wrought iron or cast iron may often be utilized to handsome

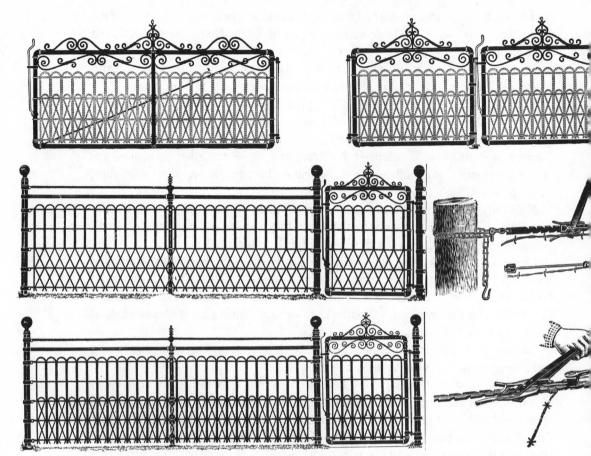

Examples of late-nineteenth-century ornamental fence gates and fencing together with two wire-stretching devices: an Ellwood Lever with a rod, which is a straight line stretcher, above; and a double ratchet steel flat bar stretcher, below.

advantage at the entranceway to your home. Some of these are still standing before once-proud residences which long since have decayed. Salvage yards will occasionally yield them, too.

If you're interested, there is a Texas Barbed Wire Collectors Association, which publishes a monthly newsletter called *The Barb-arian*. Its objectives are to collect data about the manufacture of barbed wire and to preserve and display the early wire.

Many persons who collect wire also collect early fencing tools.

30

Lamps, Shades and Globes

FOR THE PAST SEVERAL YEARS NINETEENTH- AND TWENTIETH-CENTURY ART glass has been experiencing a boom. Prices have moved upward on the better pieces with a speed that has delighted dealers and horrified incipient collectors.

The sky has been the limit for Peachblow vases, Burmese pitchers, Agata bowls, Aurene compotes, and a great variety of other articles produced by such firms as the Mt. Washington Glass Company, England's Thomas Webb & Sons, the New England Glass Company, Boston and Sandwich Glass Company, L. C. Tiffany's Corona Furnaces, the Steuben Glass Works, Hobbs, Brockunier and Company, and other producers who devised glass in the Art Nouveau tradition with such names, in addition to those above, as Amberina, Rubena Verde, Vasa Murrhina, Kew Blas, Pomona, Quezal, and Mother-of-Pearl Satin.

Yet, so anxious have collectors been to garner in vases, bowls, compotes, creamers and sugar bowls, plates, pitchers, tumblers, ewers, candlesticks, and cologne bottles that they have largely overlooked, until recently, one of the most commonplace of all articles made in art glass— the gas and the electric lamp shade.

Fine art glass ewers, tall vases, and the like have been selling at prices of $200, $300, and $500. Yet, many shades made of the same type of glass have sat around almost unnoticed with going prices of a relatively few dollars. Few practitioners of art-glass collecting have called attention to their desirability and to the feasibility of including them in any collection of art glass. Among those few who have, however, is Eric E. Ericson, of Denver, Colorado — collector, historian, and authority on the wares of the late Frederick Carder —

Collectible light shades and globes from earlier in this century.

who, in his *A Guide to Colored Steuben Glass, 1903–1933, Book Two* (available from the author, Stagecoach Stop, 1901 Kipling Street, Denver 15), says:

"The public has finally become aware of the fact that in vase form, identical techniques utilizing the identical glass type are ten times the price of a shade. Only the physical difference of the 'extra' hole is noted, and then only when the object is handled."

That's it. Display the shade in a cabinet or on an open shelf, and the "extra" hole is noted only when one picks it up. Not only that, but one can use these beautiful shades in one's home for lighting décor — and to handsome advantage.

And even though some collectors now are realizing the desirability of shades, they still represent the best bargain available in art glass form today.

Thousands upon thousands of shades were produced for gas and electric fixtures by the very firms whose other art glass articles are so avidly sought, among them the works operated by Carder, Tiffany, and Victor Durand. To assemble a large collection of so-called cabinet pieces from those companies would require the outlay of a small fortune, but one can acquire a splendid

A group of so-called leaded glass and painted glass lamps. These enjoyed popularity earlier in this century, fell into disfavor, and now again are beginning to be snapped up at good prices. Tiffany made lamp shades resembling these but of much better quality. Some of those shown here were designed for use with either gas or electricity. The two larger ones had lights in the base as well as at the tops. Prices originally ranged from about $12.50 to $20.

Highly collectible light shades in art glass. Gold threaded shade is shown in center. (From author's collection.)

collection of their gas and electric shades for a fraction of that cost. Name-marked shades, however, are likely to cost one considerably more even now than those which bear no factory identification.

There are thousands of unsigned art glass shades available. Some dealers who do not specialize in art glass may let these slip from their grasp at unreasonably low prices: No dealer can be an expert in all phases of antiques.

The Steuben Glass Works, incidentally, was the nation's largest producer of light shades at one time. Mr. Ericson ventures an educated guess that this company may have turned out an aggregate of about 48,000 of them. Being breakable commodities, a good many shades undoubtedly have perished, but plenty are still around. These include shades made by Tiffany and by Victor Durand, of the Durand Art Glass Company, although the latter apparently signed no shades, according to Mr. Ericson. Shades similar to those turned out by the above also were made by the Quezal Art Glass & Decorating Company, of Brooklyn, New York, between 1916 and 1918. These are usually marked "Quezal." There is no reason whatsoever not to buy an unsigned light shade if the quality is good and the price is right.

Another mass producer of light shades early in this century was the Phoenix Glass Company, of Monaca, Pennsylvania, whose output included cut and etched shades, many of them interestingly decorated. In his book *American Cut and Engraved Glass* (Thomas Nelson & Sons,, New York), Albert Christian Revi pictures a diversified group of the Phoenix Company's shades.

Carder's Aurene and Tiffany's Favrile shades, of course, are extremely desirable, but so are numerous other fine types, including a good many whose exterior surfaces are threaded. Some made of shaded glass will probably be selling in a year of two at well above their current prices. Glass shades with painted decorations, while of less interest and value generally than those whose decorations were achieved by cutting, etching, and other methods, need not be eschewed. There are some particularly attractive ones of this type awaiting collectors. They must be judged on the quality of their art work. Still available in some quantity are shades of iridescent glass, including Carnival glass. An exceptionally fine collection of these was assembled by Charles K. Bassett, a retired engineer and manufacturer, of Buffalo, New York. A group of Mr. Bassett's shades was illustrated on the cover of *Hobbies* magazine for July, 1961, and Mr. Bassett himself did an excellent article on the subject for the June, 1964, issue of the same magazine.

Thousands of the iridescent blown glass shades were produced earlier in this century, made to fit the standard sizes of brackets which were used on most lighting fixtures in the first quarter of the 1900's. When signed by the manufacturer, the shades usually bear his name, initials, or trademark on the inside rim of the base, though a few are marked elsewhere. The marks are frequently engraved, and a great many have been worn to the point where they may be quite difficult to detect or to read. Many collectible shades are marked "Lustre Art," and were made by one Conrad Vahlsing at Elmhurst, Long Island; and many which are not marked at all were made abroad and imported into the United States. Undoubtedly, too, a good many unsigned ones were the productions of small American glass factories.

In the July, 1961, *Hobbies,* Mr. Bassett was quoted by an interviewer for

Art glass light shades. Amberina shade on extreme right. (From author's collection.)

96603   **Each 23.20**
Table Lamp; shade with rich amber; green glass panels; handsome bronze finished standard; height 22½ inches; diameter of shade 18 inches; two lights; regulation socket; chain pull.

96601   **Each 23.20**
Table Lamp; height 22½ inches; diameter of shade 19 inches; rich amber glass panels; shade with blue border; antique finished standard; two lights; regulation socket; chain pull.

96639   **Each 33.00**
Table Lamp; height 23½ inches; diameter of shade 18 inches; artistic hand decorated landscape in natural colors; bronze finished standard with verde green finish; two lights; regulation socket; chain pull.

96627   **Each**
Table Lamp; height 22½ inches; diam shade 16 inches; rich amber glass panel with blue bordered panel; Jacobean finished standard; two lights; regulation s chain pull.

96629   **Each 31.00**
Table Lamp; height 25 inches; diameter of shade 20 inches; beautiful sunset color panel with blue bordered glass shade; Jacobean bronze finished standard; two lights; regulation socket; chain pull.

96637   **Each 31.50**
Table Lamp; height 26 inches; diameter of shade 20 inches; amber top panels bordered with green; shade and standard finished in old gold; two lights; regulation socket; chain pull.

96604   **Each 23.20**
Table Lamp; height 24 inches; diameter of shade 16 inches; handsome amber top shade; bordered with blue panel; antique brass finished shade and standard; two lights; regulation socket; chain pull.

96631   **Each 33**
Table Lamp; height 26 inches; diameter shade 21 inches; rich amber green panel gl shade with blue border; antique brass finish standard; two lights; regulation socket; cha pull.

96638   **Each 41.00**
Table Lamp; height 24 inches; diameter of shade 18 inches; shaded with panels of rich amber glass; standard and shade finished in statuary bronze; two lights; regulation socket; chain pull.

96635   **Each 41.00**
Table Lamp; height 26 inches; diameter of shade 19 inches; shade of rich amber glass panel; standard finished in green bronze; two lights; regulation socket; chain pull.

96636   **Each 3**
Table Lamp; height 26 inches; diameter of shade inches; rich amber top panel shade is paneled in hands amber glass with sunset border; standard finished antique brass; two lights; regulation socket; chain pu

Marshall Field & Co., Chicago featured these decorated and leaded glass-type shade lamps in its 1919 catalogue. These were not cheap even nearly half a century ago.

the magazine as saying that Frederick Carder had told him that many of Steuben's standard patterns were "formed by spinning a fine thread of glass around the inflated ball of glass from which the shade was eventually developed. It was then rolled on the marver to flatten and incorporate these threads — then reheated and the surface hooked with a device like a button hook into a selected pattern. A five-lobe feather-shaped pattern and variations of it were favorites."

Various types of art shades are illustrated in early-twentieth-century manufacturers' and distributors' catalogues. When pictured by the latter, the manufacturers are not usually identified.

Lamp globes also may be collected. By "globe," we refer to larger globe-shaped shades as opposed to the small vase-shaped ones. Many of these were hand painted. They require considerably more space for display than the smaller shades, however. Some unusually attractive ones were made in Satin glass, most frequently diamond quilted. These are being reproduced.

Right now, too, some collectors are going after leaded shades, the most sought-after type of which was made by Tiffany. You certainly wouldn't want more than one or two of the huge leaded shades, which hung below large ceiling fixtures, but thousands of smaller ones were manufactured early in this century to fit over smaller table lamps.

Metal-base lamps with either round or octagonal leaded glass shades were produced in this country by the carload between 1915 and 1930. Marble or "slag-type" glass panes were most frequently used and were fastened together with metal strips that extended down the panes and then around the base of the shade, usually fashioned into a design. Bases were made of bronze metal, brass, and white metal. Catalogues frequently referred to the shades as made of "cathedral" glass or termed them "metal overlay" shades.

In the 1920's lamps of this type, complete with shade, sold at prices ranging from about $10 to $25. Some of these lamps were made with solid round or oval glass shades decorated by hand instead of the leaded glass panes. For some reason, these leaded glass lamps are now attracting a large number of collectors. Their prices started off in 1962 or 1963 at $25 to $30 for lamp and shade of average size with larger ones bringing a little more. Now, shops are asking $45 to $100 for them. Shades with a pane of glass missing are sometimes encountered at prices a good bit lower. There are establishments that will duplicate missing panes.

Somewhat similar lamps with two smaller leaded glass shades attached to opposite ends of a metal arm also were produced during the 1920's. The majority of glass panes were made in an amber-brown or a nile green color.

In great demand for the past several years have been large leaded glass chandeliers made for the Coca-Cola Company by Tiffany. These were de-

Highly desirable Tiffany chandelier shade originally made around the turn of the century to advertise Coca-Cola, primarily in the drug stores. (Photo Courtesy of the Coca-Cola Company.)

signed primarily as advertising pieces and were used largely in drug stores around the turn of the century. Around the outside of the shades was the lettering "Coca-Cola."

Wilbur G. Kurtz, Jr., of The Coca-Cola Company's Advertising & Sales Promotion Department, began collecting these shades himself a little more than two decades ago, when prices ranged from about $20 to $40 a unit. But during recent years both the demand for them and their prices have skyrocketed, and some have changed hands for sums of $800 to more than $1,000.

These chandeliers were particularly popular in the Eastern part of the United States, and that is where collectors currently are searching for them most actively.

In 1961, arrangements were made to have this chandelier reproduced, but using plastic. These reproductions, too, became popular almost overnight. The company doesn't promote their sale, but the word has spread, and the demand has been substantial. The reproductions were sold in 1966 at $50 per unit.

Signed Quezal shades have been selling recently at prices of from $18 to $35. A signed Steuben Verre de Soie shade was offered at $40 and a Steuben Ivrene at $21. An Aurene shade will often bring $40 or more. The asking price of a pair of Burmese gas shades in $300. Large leaded glass hanging lamp shades will fetch $75 up — frequently way up.

On the other hand, many unsigned shades will be found, through diligent searching, at a price of $10, or a little less. This is particularly true of simple painted shades and simple shades with some type of acidized exterior surfaces. As the art glass shades disappear, however, prices of the currently inexpensive types are likely to start moving upward.

Old lamp bases on which the vase-form shades may be used are still fairly abundant. In addition, reproduction bases are being marketed at prices of about $5 up. These are made of solid cast brass. The shades are held in place by adjustable screws. Shades mounted on bases of this type, which come complete with a standard socket, make excellent television or boudoir lamps.

Old homes which are in process of being dismantled will frequently yield fine glass shades still attached to their original fixtures. You may be able to make a deal with the contractor for such jobs to take the shades off his hands at a reasonable price.

31

The Child of Avarice

THERE IS AN ADAGE WHICH GOES: "GAMBLING IS THE CHILD OF AVARICE BUT the parent of prodigality."

Man has gambled since time immemorial, but mechanical gambling devices such as slot machines don't go back nearly so far. The "one-armed bandits" of yesterday (and today) are destined to become collectors' items of tomorrow. We are willing to predict that early vending machines also will work their way somehow into more collections.

Of course, there are dozens of types of gambling accessories which can be collected, but the big push ahead is likely to be on mechanical gambling devices rather than on such things as dice, cards, and lottery tickets. Early lever-operated games of chance — and there was a wide variety of these — can provide the basis for a collection which, accompanied by some serious study, may provide an interesting insight into human nature and the fascinating lure of taking a chance. Let us add quickly at this point that we make no pitch for gambling here. In most areas it's illegal, and a good case may be made out for its immorality. But the apparatus used in gambling is, after all — unfortunately or not — a reflection of one aspect of the times in which it was made and used and it should not, therefore, be completely lost to posterity. Had someone preserved the pillar of salt into which Lot's wife was turned, it would be quite an attraction today. It would even point a moral.

Still around in large quantities, though getting scarcer every year, are late-nineteenth- and early-twentieth-century slot machines of various types, which were operated by coins. The best-known type is the "one-armed bandit," so-called because it was operated by a single lever or arm. Some of these paid the winner in merchandise, some in tickets or checks good for merchandise, and some in cash. Thousands of modern, streamlined versions of the last-named are still in use today in plush and not-so-plush gambling establishments and private clubs around the country. In Las Vegas and Reno, for example, their operation is perfectly legal; in other areas in the United States it is illegal.

The type most familiar half a century ago and, in fact, almost right up to the present, featured moving circular bands upon which fruit and other objects were pictured. One inserted a coin, pulled the lever, and the bands began spinning. If, when they stopped, objects of all the same kind were lined up across the front row or viewing window of the machine, or if they were lined up in a specified way, the operator was a winner. Fruits, such as oranges, lemons, apples, and so on were often used as illustrations on the bands. In the early twentieth-century devices, the winner was paid in coins ejected through a slot. The odds were well stacked against the player, but the possibility of winning made addicts out of many otherwise good husbands and providers.

Dozens of different varieties of this same basic machine have been produced and used through the years right up to today, but the earlier, table-top types will appeal most to collectors with limited space and funds.

In the closing years of last century, numerous other types of mechanically-operated games of chance were in use. Some were activated by pulling a lever, others by pushing a button. Some types were used on counters in such business establishments as food and drink vending firms or cigar and tobacco shops. A few of these offered the gambler a chance at winning merchandise. Again, more often than not, he lost. One type paid off in checks good against the purchase of merchandise.

There were types of machines (and there still are) which automatically threw dice cubes; and winning combinations, which were specified, paid off, either in cash or merchandise.

Later came the gambling machines which featured "games of skill." Many of these were electrically operated. You'll find this type around in abundance today, but its forerunners date back to the turn of the century. One type was an upright machine with curved slots corresponding to card faces, such as Ace, King, Queen, or Jack. The player attempted to land little balls in the proper slots. The price was five balls for a penny, and the player flipped the balls around a track in an effort to make them land in the slots which would give him a winning poker hand. One of these machines was offered for sale not long ago at $26.50. It was about the size of a gum-vending machine.

Other early machines were filled with various kinds of merchandise. You dropped a penny or a nickel in the slot and took your chance on the type of merchandise that would be automatically vended to you through a delivery cubicle. It usually was worth less than the money you paid, but once in a rare while you received something that was worth more than the coin you deposited.

Forerunners of the present-day food and drink vending machines also will be collected. This is particularly true of early-twentieth-century gum machines, of which numerous types were manufactured. Gum ball machines may now be found at $10 to $50.

In the latter part of the 1800's a coin-operated machine was made that vended perfume. It was often seen in penny arcades and at fairs and carnivals. The player deposited a coin, then held a handkerchief under an opening on the

This early gambling machine was known as "New Century Musical Puck." The player put a nickel in a slot at the top, then pulled down on a slide at the side, which set the spinning mechanism at the top in motion. A small music box, which fitted into the opening at the bottom, played while the machine was being operated. (From the collection of Paul Wilmot, 3520 Gordon Road, Elkhart, Indiana.)

outside of the machine, and perfume was dropped upon it. It was operated by a hand-wound clock mechanism. You had a choice of brand names of perfume. One type of such machine was made by the New England Perfume Machine Company in Boston. A device of this type with an 1897 patent date was advertised for sale a few months ago at $22.50

Other types of machines vended photographic views, peanuts, matches, and numerous other items. These were all early prototypes of sleek, handsome machines in use today which vend everything from coffee to sandwiches.

Depending on their size, condition, and intricacy of mechanism, the early vending machines will now be found at prices ranging from $10 or $15 to several hundred dollars.

There were literally dozens of types of penny arcade machines which gave you, in exchange for a penny or a nickel, a series of views of everything from championship boxing matches to ladies posed in various states of undress. Some even "vended" accompanying sound to you through a tube which fitted into your ear. Early music "vending" machines are also beginning to be collected and compose a large category of their own.

The machines were made of wood, metals, and even papier-mâché. With diligent searching, you probably can assemble a varied collection of small counter-top machines, but the big ones will require considerable space for display and a large outlay of cash if you acquire more than a few.

Here's a good field for the research-minded individual, because insofar as the history of gambling devices and vending machines is concerned, the surface has barely been scratched.

A most intriguing collection of early gambling and vending devices has been assembled by Mr. Paul C. Wilmot, of 3520 Gordon Road, Elkhart, Indiana. Typical of the interesting machines he has acquired is one called "New Century Musical Puck." This is a machine with slots at the top and a music box in a lower compartment. One inserted a nickel or nickels in the slots, then pulled a side lever to operate the machine. While the device was in operation, the music box played a tune. If you lost your money, you at least got music.

Another item in his collection is a dice machine called "Square Deal." This allowed the flip of five dice and the "lock-out" of the dice one wanted to keep. The dice were then flipped again (in three shakes or clips) to score the highest points. "Square Deal" was patented in February, 1891.

He also has a contrivance called "Bicycle Wheel." This device accepted a nickel and was used as a trade stimulator for the purchase of cigars. With the deposit of a nickel, the device always vended at least one cigar and sometimes two or more, the number being indicated on a pointer.

Still another item in his possession is a small early-type bicycle with num-

Machines from the collection of Paul Wilmot, Elkhart, Indiana. In front is the "Square Deal" dice machine. At the left rear is "The Bicycle Wheel," used as a trade stimulator for cigars. At right rear is a small old-fashioned bicycle designed to be used by two persons for gambling. Operation of these machines is described in the text.

bers on its front and rear wheels. Each wheel actually had a series of numbers. The wheels were spun and the person who had the highest numbers after the wheels stopped spinning was the winner. The machine itself made no physical payoff, but the losing bettor paid the winner. The two-wheel machines were made between 1885 and 1890.

Mr. Wilmot also possesses the original wooden-case "Yellow Kid" gum dispenser, which research indicates was one of the earliest if not the earliest gum machine. It was named after a well-known early cartoon character. This machine was later housed in a metal cabinet. Pulver Gum Company originated this device.

32

Wicker Furniture

WICKER FURNITURE WENT OUT OF STYLE BEFORE THE SO-CALLED "GONE with the Wind" lamp came back into style, but right now it appears to be snuggling its way again into the hearts of homemakers in many sections of the country.

This is only mildly disturbing, because, after all, wicker chairs, settees, and davenport-sofas can be mighty cool in the summer; and in the winter, the padded cushions provide at least a modicum of warmth.

No one seems to know exactly why this type of furniture (and wicker has come to be accepted now as a generic term for furniture made of such materials as reed, willow, rattan, and other fibers) is once again being embraced, but throughout history we have returned time and again to styles and whims of the past. At any rate, wicker furniture sales appear on their way up, and choice pieces are now bringing rather fancy prices. This type of furniture was popular in the United States during the latter part of last century and continued in demand until well into the present one. However, prior to World War II, literally hundreds of thousands of reed chairs, rattan tables, and willow sofas found themselves in the discard. Many pieces were carted into attics so they wouldn't be seen; others were hauled off by the junkman. It's the junkman who saved them who is going to get rich.

Furniture and general merchandise catalogues issued between 1900 and into the 1920's abound with illustrations of wicker furniture. Catalogues of the Larkin Company published between 1920 and 1925 carry pages of illustrations of spacious armchairs at prices of $10 to $25; settees at $25 or so, parlor tables at $9 to $15, and bird cages with stands at around $30.

303

Reed and rattan furniture of the first quarter of this century.

Much of the reed furniture was offered as suites, usually consisting of an armchair, a rocker, and either a settee or a davenport-sofa. Chairs were particularly roomy. They often had removable seat cushions and partially upholstered backs, utilizing cretonne in blues, greens, browns, and other colors. The upholstered backs were padded with cotton. The padded seats frequently had springs to make them more comfortable.

Reed parlor tables were round or oblong. Small round tables were made with tops and a shelf of closely woven reed with wooden centers. Oblong tables often had flat wooden tops with a woven reed shelf below. The legs were woven of half-round reed. Chairs most frequently had sides of either closely or loosely woven reed. There were even reed smoking stands and sewing tables, and of course there were numerous reed work baskets. The reed itself was finished in a light color or green or brown, sometimes called "Baronial Brown."

Willow furniture included day beds, rockers, settees, ferneries, jardinieres, tea wagons, and other pieces. In 1922, Larkin offered an interesting willow tea wagon with a removable top tray, a shelf and two wooden wheels with rubber tires for a cash price of $22.50 or free with a $45 purchase of its products.

Footed reed or similar fiber ferneries could be had at prices of $7.50 to $10. There also were willow hanging baskets and window baskets for plants and flowers.

Much reed fiber furniture was especially designed for use on the porch or veranda. In addition to chairs and settees, this also included reed swings and small tables which could be used as plant stands.

A good many reed and willow chairs had skirts of closely woven fiber across the front with the bottom of the skirt slightly arched. Sofas and settees normally had similar skirts.

The furniture was a good bit sturdier than it actually looked, although, after a few years of use, the chairs would creak a trifle when one sat in them. Chairs and tables were well braced. Many of the chairs had wide arms that entended out in a semi-roll.

In 1926, Spear & Company, of Pittsburgh, was offering fancy reed fiber suites consisting of a straight chair, a rocker, and a davenport for $77.45. The furniture had spring-filled loose cushions, and the reed came finished in Baronial Brown or Jade Green. The upholstery added a touch of color to the porch or living room.

Rattan rockers, divans, couches, and odd pieces were popular in this country at the turn of the century. Many of these rockers had wide, fancy backs entirely of rattan without upholstering. Some rockers had wooden seats but most seats also were of rattan. One unusual piece was a reception chair

Fiber-rush and reed furniture dating about last of nineteenth century. Chair at bottom has Mission-type frame and reed back and seat.

Reed rockers and nursery chair of the late nineteenth century.

with an arching fan back and a single arm. It was finished with white shellac. Some rattan chairs had large oval backs which resembled the barrel chairs of today.

In its 1905–1906 catalogue, the Cash Buyers Union First National Co-operative Society, of Chicago, offered a three-piece reed suite for only $19.75.

There also were fancy wicker parlor stools with upholstered tops for use inside the house or on the porch or lawn. Some had velvet carpet tops.

Reed lamps came in numerous sizes and shapes. There were upright lamps about 5½ feet tall and table lamps ranging from about 22 to 24 inches in height. Some reed shades had flowered cretonne linings. These weren't necessarily cheap. Marshall Field & Company's 1919–1920 catalogue offered the table lamps at prices of from $13.50 to $39 and the tall standing lamps at from $40 to $58.

Hundreds of types of woven reed baby carriages were turned out in tremendous volume throughout the first quarter of this century. There were fancy "Pullman Sleeper Coaches" with attached parasols and upholstered interiors. Many were perfectly charming in appearance. Some could be purchased with upholstered interiors optional.

Other fiber carriages were made with adjustable tops, and some with small windows in their tops or hoods. There also were "Park Carts" without tops and semi-collapsible "Go-Carts" and "Sulkies." The Sulkies were pulled along with handles (as were the reed Strollers) and came with only two wheels instead of four.

It's a big jump from the junkyard to the antiques shop, but that's the jump wicker, rattan, and similar fiber furniture is beginning to make. Wicker stands will now cost you $15 to $35; tea wagons, $35 to $65; chairs and settees, $35 to $65; sewing or work tables $35 to $65. And the interest seems to be picking up at such a rapid rate that values may be even higher by the time you read this.

Although a good bit of wicker furniture was produced in this country from imported fibers in earlier years, much of it was made in the Orient, as a large amount of it still is. Much of that which came from China was fashioned with great care and was superior to a lot of the mass-produced pieces turned out in this country. Though the bulk of rattan and similar pieces were utilized earlier in this century during the summer months and in summer vacation resorts and summer cottages, it can be utilized throughout the year in some cases in which an atmosphere of informality is desired.

Suggested for Further Reading

(NOTE: *Some of the magazine issues recommended below may still be available from the publishers; others may not. However, back issues of magazine may often be located in public libraries; they frequently are advertised for sale in various collector periodicals; and some dealers in back issue magazines may have them.*)

BELLS

HATCH, ERIC. *Little Book of Bells.* New York City: Duell, Sloan & Pearce, Inc.

MEYER, A. C. *Travel Search for Bells.* Chicago: Lightner Publishing Corporation.

MORRISON, GOUVENEUR. *Bells: Their History and Romance.* Santa Barbara, California: J. F. Rowny Press.

NISBETT, CLARA. *"Horse Bells from Abroad."* Article in *The Spinning Wheel,* May, 1966.

SPRINGER, LOIS E. *"Cow Bells."* Article in *Hobbies,* October, 1958.

GAMES

BELL, ROBERT C. *Board and Table Games from Many Civilizations.* New York City: Oxford University Press.

COLE, ANN KILBORN. *How to Collect the "New Antiques."* New York City: David McKay Company, Inc.

HERTZ, LOUIS H. *The Handbook of Old American Toys.* Wethersfield, Connecticut: Mark Haber & Company.

309

HUNT, SARAH E. *Games and Sports the World Around.* New York City: Ronald Press Company.

MURRAY, HAROLD J. *History of Board-Games Other than Chess.* New York City: Oxford University Press.

WOOD, CLEMENT, and GLORIA GODDARD. (Eds.). *Complete Book of Games.* Garden City, N. Y.: Doubleday & Company.

THE GENERAL STORE

CARTER, JANE. *"Cigar Cutters."* Article in *The Spinning Wheel,* January, 1960.

FREEMAN, LARRY. *Country Store.* Watkins Glen, N. Y.: Century House.

OUR FOREFATHERS' OFFICES

BLIVEN, BRUCE, JR. *The Wonderful Writing Machine.* New York City: Random House.

SCOTT, AMORET and CHRISTOPHER. *Collecting Bygones.* New York City: David McKay Company, Inc.

THE KITCHEN

ANONYMOUS. *"Antiquity of the Corkscrew."* Article in *The Spinning Wheel,* January, 1962.

BURRIS, RON. *An Illustrated Guide for Collecting Fruit Jars with Price Guide.* Visalia, California (2941 Campus Drive): The Author.

COLE, ANN KILBORN. *Antiques.* New York City: Collier Books.

———— *How to Collect the New Antiques.* New York City: David McKay Company, Inc.

DREPPERD, CARL W. and MARJORIE MATTHEWS SMITH. *Handbook of Tomorrow's Antiques.* New York City: Thomas Y. Crowell Company.

LANTZ, LOUISE K. *"Kitchen Gifts from Kris Kringle."* Article in *The Spinning Wheel,* December, 1965.

———— *"Kitchen Tinware."* Article in *The Spinning Wheel,* October, 1964.

———— *"Old Mashers and Beaters."* Article in *The Spinning Wheel,* December, 1964.

WATKINS, MALCOLM. *"The Early American Domestic Machine."* Article in *Antiques,* February, 1940.

SERVING TRAYS, BASKETS, AND BOWLS

COMSTOCK, HELEN. (Ed.). *The Concise Encyclopedia of American Antiques.* New York City: Hawthorne Books, Inc.

DEVOE, SHIRLEY SPAULDING. *"Loveridge and Company Tea Trays."* Article in *The Antiques Journal,* April, 1966.

GOULD, MARY EARLE. *Antique Tin & Tole Ware.* Rutland, Vermont: Charles E. Tuttle Company, Publisher.

HOKE, ELIZABETH S. *Painted Tray and Free Hand Bronzing.* Washington, D.C.: Paul A. Ruddell.

POWERS, BEATRICE F. and OLIVE FLOYD. *Early American Decorated Tinware.* New York City: Hastings House, Publishers, Inc.

SHULL, THELMA. *Victorian Antiques.* Rutland, Vermont: Charles E. Tuttle Company, Publisher.

WINCHESTER, ALICE. *How to Know American Antiques.* New York City: The New American Library.

CLOCKS

DREPPERD, CARL W. *American Clocks and Clock Makers.* Newton Centre, Massachusetts: Charles T. Branford Company.

JENKINS, DOROTHY. *A Fortune in the Junk Pile.* New York City: Crown Publishers.

LLOYD, H. ALAN. *Collector's Dictionary of Clocks.* Cranbury, New Jersey: A. S. Barnes and Company, Inc.

PALMER, BROOKS. *Book of American Clocks.* New York City: The MacMillan Company.

SHULL, THELMA. *Victorian Antiques.* Rutland, Vermont: Charles E. Tuttle Company, Publisher.

SLAUGHTER, L. W. *"On Time."* A monthly department appearing in *Hobbies.*

HARDWARE

ARONSON, JOSEPH. *The Encyclopedia of Furniture* (third edition). New York City: Crown Publishers.

BROENDEL, ETHEL. *"Three Hundred Years of Drawer Handles."* Article in *The Spinning Wheel,* August, 1960.

GREELEY, HORACE, et. al. *The Great Industries of the United States.* Hartford, Connecticut: Burr & Hyde. (1872).

JENKINS, DOROTHY. *"Furniture Hardware."* Article in *Woman's Day,* September, 1965.

SCHIFFER, HERBERT. *Early Pennsylvania Hardware.* Whitford, Pennsylvania: Whitford Press.

SYMONDS, R. W. and B. B. WHINERAY. *Victorian Furniture.* London, England: Country Life Limited.

KEYS AND LOCKS

BUEHR, WALTER. *The Story of Locks.* New York City: Charles Scribner's Sons.

COMSTOCK, HELEN. (Ed.). *Encyclopedia of American Antiques.* New York City: Hawthorne Books, Inc.

KAUFFMAN, HENRY J. *Early American Ironware, Cast and Wrought.* Rutland, Vermont: Charles E. Tuttle Company, Publisher.

MCCLELLAN, CLAIRE T. *"Of Locks and Keys."* Article in *The Spinning Wheel,* June, 1966.

MCCLINTON, KATHARINE MORRISON. *The Complete Book of Small Antiques Collecting.* New York City: Coward-McCann.

BATHROOM ACCESSORIES

ANONYMOUS. *"Biography of the Bath."* Mimeographed article prepared by The Cleanliness Bureau, New York City.

ASHE, GEOFFREY. *The Tale of the Tub.* London, England: Newman Neame Limited.

MILADY'S BOUDOIR

FLOWER, MILTON E. *"Watch Holders."* Article in *Antiques,* June, 1966.

JENKINS, DOROTHY. *A Fortune in the Junk Pile.* New York City: Crown Publishers.

LICHTEN, FRANCES. *Decorative Art of Victoria's Era.* New York City: Charles Scribner's Sons.

WOOD, VIOLET. *Victoriana, A Collector's Guide.* London, England: G. Bell & Sons.

DRESS ACCESSORIES AND BAUBLES

BAERWALD, MARCUS, and TOM MAHONEY. *The Story of Jewelry.* New York City: Abelard-Schuman, Ltd.

CLARK, HAZEL BAKER. *"Our Colonial Comb Industry."* Article in *Old-Time New England* (The Bulletin of The Society for the Preservation of New England Antiquities), Fall, 1950.

COGHILL, MARY B. *"Costume Accessories of the 1840's."* Article in *The Spinning Wheel,* March, 1955.

DARLING, ADA. *Antique Jewelry.* Watkins Glen, New York: Century House.

FLOWER, MARGARET. *Victorian Jewellry.* New York: A. S. Barnes and Company.

GREEN, MRS. H. G. *"The Contents of Milady's Pocketbook."* Article in *The Antiques Journal,* October, 1965.

WHITING, MRS. J. D. *"Charms and Amulets."* Article in *Hobbies,* October, 1965.

SEWING ACCESSORIES

ANONYMOUS. *"Pincushions as Collectibles."* Article in *The Spinning Wheel,* November, 1955.

DREPPERD, CARL W. and MARJORIE MATTHEWS SMITH. *Handbook of Tomorrow's Antiques.* New York City: Thomas Y. Crowell Company.

McCLELLAN, CLAIRE T. *"Thimbles as Collectors' Items."* Article in *The Spinning Wheel,* December, 1950.

McCLINTON, KATHARINE MORRISON. *The Complete Book of Small Antiques Collecting.* New York City: Coward-McCann, Inc.

SICKELS, ELIZABETH GALBRAITH. *"New York Thimble Makers from Huntington, Long Island."* Two-part article in *The Antiques Journal,* September and October, 1964.

BABY COLLECTIBLES

ANONYMOUS. *"Whitall & Tatum Nursers."* Article in *The Spinning Wheel,* May, 1965.

McCLINTON, KATHARINE MORRISON. *The Complete Book of Small Antiques Collecting.* New York City: Coward-McCann, Inc.

PARRY, ELSIE A. *"The American Infant Goes A-Riding."* Article in *Old-Time New England* (The Bulletin of The Society for the Preservation of New England Antiquities), July, 1937.

TOY VEHICLES

DAIKEN, LESLIE. *Children's Toys Throughout the Ages.* London, England:
Spring Books.

DREPPERD, CARL W., and MARJORIE MATTHEWS SMITH. *Handbook of Tomorrow's Antiques.* New York City: Thomas Y. Crowell Company.

TRAPS

McCRACKEN, HAROLD, and HARRY VAN CLEVE. *Trapping.* Cranbury, New
Jersey: A. S. Barnes and Company, Inc.

REINFELD, FRED. *Trappers of the West.* New York City: Dell Publishing
Company.

THERMOMETERS AND BAROMETERS

FREUND, H. H. *"Barometers."* Article in *The Spinning Wheel,* July-August,
1965.

HOWARD, SUSAN B. *"Figural Thermometers."* Article in *The Spinning Wheel,*
January, 1965.

HUGHES, G. BERNARD. *The Antique Collector's Pocket Book.* New York City:
Hawthorne Books, Inc.

MIDDLETON, W. E. KNOWLES. *History of the Barometer.* Baltimore: Johns
Hopkins Press.

TABLEWARE

ANONYMOUS. *"Fifteen Famous Actresses."* Article in *The Spinning Wheel,*
October, 1964.

——— *"Poor Man's Tiffany."* Article in *Hobbies,* July, 1961.

BEAUMONT, J. *Early American Plated Silver.* Watkins Glen, New York: Century House.

FELGER, DONNA. *"Advertising Spoons."* Article in *Western Collector,* September, 1966.

(GUNNERSON, PEARL V.). *"Spoons from the Collection of Pearl V. Gunnerson."* Article in *Western Collector,* October, 1964.

HARDT, ANTON. *Further Adventuring in Spoons.* Published by the Author:
335 Bleeker Street, New York City.

——— *Souvenir Spoons of the 90's.* Published by the Author. (See information in listing directly above.)

OWEN, PAT. *"The A. Michelson Christmas Spoons."* Article in *Hobbies,* December, 1963.

SCHMIDT, GERTRUDE. *"Choice Spoons."* Article in *The Spinning Wheel,* July-August, 1966.

STICKELL, DOROTHY ALBAUGH. *"Spoons Are as Old as Soup."* Article in *The American Antiques Journal,* May, 1949.

BARBED WIRE

GLOVER, JACK. *Bobbed Wire.* Sunset, Texas: Privately printed.

MCCLURE, C. BOONE. *History of the Manufacture of Barbed Wire.* Canyon, Texas: Panhandle-Plains Historical Society.

TURNER, T. *Barbed Wire Hand Book.* Waco, Texas: Privately printed.

GAMBLING

CHAFETZ, HENRY. *A History of Gambling in the United States.* New York City: Bonanza Books.

DAVID, F. N. *Games, Gods and Gambling.* New York City: Hafner Publishing Company.

FIGGIS, ERIC. *Gambling: Challenge to Chance.* Hackensack, New Jersey: Wehman Bros.

Index